3 9153 00939900 9

DISCARD

P9-DFF-527

A HISTORY OF
MODERN MALAYA

HISTORY OF MODERN
SOUTH-EAST ASIA SERIES

Editor: K. G. Tregonning

Books in the Series

A History of Modern Malaya
K. G. Tregonning

A History of Modern Thailand
Walter F. Vella

A History of the Modern Philippines
H. de La Costa, S. J.

A History of Modern Indonesia
Robert van Neil

A HISTORY OF MODERN MALAYA

K. G. TREGONNING
Raffles Professor of History,
University of Singapore

DAVID McKAY COMPANY, INC.
NEW YORK

First published in Singapore 1964

© K. G. Tregonning, 1964

Library of Congress Catalog Card Number, 67-12911
Printed and bound in Japan for
David McKay Company, Inc.,
by DAI NIPPON PRINTING CO., LTD., TOKYO

CONTENTS

To Judy

PREFACE

In this book an attempt is made to tell the history of modern Malaya in general terms. I have confined my attention to the peninsula itself, taking it as my frame of reference, and considering the activities of the many peoples in it as my interest. My aim is to give due weight, within this Malayan framework, to every element that has gone to create the modern State of today, always endeavouring to look at these many elements of society from within Malaya. Many of my predecessors have stood away, and in a manner of speaking, have viewed Malaya from the office of the colonial powers, or from the deck of a foreign ship. I would have you stand with me on the beach, watching him arrive. For the historian of Malaya, that is the only true position.

The nucleus out of which this book has grown were my lectures to the Honours School of the Department of History at the then University of Malaya in Singapore (now the University of Singapore). All my students, while listening to me with one ear, were busy at the same time with their own piece of Malayan research. Together we explored the past.

I have used their detailed monographs (as published in the *Journal, South-East Asian History*), to a small extent. The major part of this work is based on my own research and on published material, a short list of which is noted in the bibliography.

A vast amount of research remains to be done on Malayan history. I hope that this essay will provide a framework or a guide to the many who will attempt it, and to the many others, Malayans in particular, who wish to understand how the present came to be, in order that they can plan hopefully for the future.

It is planned that this work will be the first of a series which will deal with the modern history of each country of South-East Asia.

K. G. Tregonning

1. THE NON ISLAMIC BACKGROUND

Modern Malaya begins early in the fifteenth century, with the foundation of Malacca and the acceptance of Islam. It is impossible, however, to begin our narrative without looking briefly at those formative centuries that preceded the Malacca Sultanate. Although modern Malaya was born then, it had previously been influenced by many factors, and a great deal that had happened was of importance to the peninsula at that time, and it is still of some relevance today.

The country itself had been shaped by many factors at work during eons of time. Physically it is a long, thin peninsula jutting out from the mainland of Asia into equatorial waters, a country of jungle with a ridge of mountain that runs down the centre, and which is closer to the west side than the east. Thus the eastward flowing rivers, nourished by a hundred inches or more of rain each year, are bigger and longer than those to the west. It is a country with little flat land, except in the north and near the coast; everywhere else hills and spurs isolate each river system from its neighbour. To the west lies a long island, Sumatra, similar to Malaya in many respects and easily reached across a narrow Strait. To the east there is the China Sea, leading northwards to the flat lands of Cochin China and China itself.[1] All this is relevant to our story, for the geography of the Malayan peninsula has affected its peoples throughout history.

Some of its peoples, by A.D. 1400, had lived in the peninsula for many generations, having sheltered in the caves of Malaya, as elsewhere in South-East Asia, throughout the last Ice Age. Some of the pre-Ice Age animals survived with them. One in particular deserves separate mention, the extraordinary tapir. This animal, jet black for half its length, and clear white the other, is of

[1] It would appear that all this area was connected in prehistoric times, in the days of the Java Man (500,000 B.C.). The melting of the last Ice Cap, and the rising of the waters that resulted, probably resulted in their present separation by shallow seas.

immense antiquity, one of the oldest mammalian forms living; yet it has never evolved, never changed. Its bones, found today in England, and undistinguishable from those of the living tapir, are in layers of soil laid down in the Miocene period. By the time of the Pleistocene period, when elephants and rhinoceroses played in the Thames valley, the tapir was extinct; yet in Malaya it has survived the millenia unaltered. As Sir George Maxwell has said, "Long before the days of the hipparion, the three toed ancestor of the horse, the tapir existed in its present form; and while the three toed horse evolved through countless generations, species after species passing away to be replaced by a form more nearly approaching the one toed ideal, the tapir has remained unchanged."[2]

While this mammal and some other strange and beautiful animals roamed in the otherwise almost empty jungle, a few thousand people trickled into the peninsula, some to move on to Java and beyond, others to stay.[3] Those who remained on the peninsula, living in obscure coastal corners or huddling in the caves of the central mountain range near to rivers, passed through three distinct Stone Age periods. These correspond very closely to the beginnings of man's culture elsewhere. Signs of a rough, clumsy Paleolithic period, earlier than the last Ice Age, have been found by the Perak River, while in a number of caves has been found a subsequent and much more advanced Mesolithic culture, with finely polished stone implements, and evidence of the use of fire.

Both these two cultures necessitated a nomadic life in search of game, and as each day of man's existence was taken up with this struggle for food (as with the Hottentot or Eskimo today), there was no time left for anything else. It was a cultural dead end. A Neolithic, or New Stone Age culture, where nomadic hunting was replaced slowly by settled fishing or agricultural

---

[2] Sir G. Maxwell, *In Malay Forests* (London, 1957), pp. 96–97.

[3] The migratory movement of the aboriginal-Malay is exceptionally widespread. Traces of him can be found over nearly all of South-East Asia, as well as Polynesia, out in the Pacific, and Madagascar, on the other side of the Indian Ocean, almost to Africa.

villages, came later, as the third of these stages.[4]

In most parts of the world where Stone Age cultures have been examined, the break-through into settled civilization has been claimed to have been always the result of hunting being replaced by agriculture. It has been reasoned by Egyptologists and others that once a hunter has discovered the secret of growing a crop, and has finally settled by his field, his wife in particular had time on her hands.[5] With her new found leisure, she learnt to make pottery, to weave, to tame and domesticate animals such as the hen, the dog and the goat, and not to kill them. Slowly an agricultural village would take shape, a leader would stand forth to organize defence and to control irrigation, specialists would emerge, and a civilization would be born. Such is the classic picture; but is this altogether applicable to the tropics?

It does not appear as if wet rice growing, the basic crop in South-East Asia, the crop which would have produced stability and the break-through into a civilization, was practised to any extent in Malaya until comparatively recent times. The flat land did not exist, and the skill was not known. There was never a need for irrigation control (the underlying motive for an agricultural leader elsewhere), and although dry rice growing, a semi-nomadic skill practised on the slopes of valleys, was and still is undertaken by the aborigines, this never has led to a settled village. It is difficult to believe that agriculture, that is the growing of padi, was the factor that brought a settled civilization to the peninsula, or to South-East Asia in general. It may be that for its origins we should look more closely at the other basis of the South-East Asian way of life: the fishing village. This, it seems, pre-dates any agricultural village, and it may be that these coastal and river fishing villages were the first permanent settlements, and that here were first evolved the arts

---

[4] For a detailed account of this, see M. Tweedie, *The Stone Age In Malaya* (JMBRAS vol. 28, pt. 1, 1955).

[5] C. Darwin, in his *The Descent of Man* (London 1871), was the first to propound agriculture as the essential requisite for civilization. The theory was accepted and enlarged by, for example, J. H. Breasted in his *Ancient Times: A History of the Early World* (Boston, 1911), and V. Gordon Childe, *The Prehistory of European Society* (London, 1958).

of pottery making, animal rearing, weaving, and rudiments of government. Looking at the jungle of Malaya even today, this does seem possible.

There are three main groups of primitive[6] peoples in Malaya today, three distinct races who have wandered in from the north, and it is easy to say that each one brought in, or represents, one of the three Stone Age cultures; easy, but on the information available, not permissible. Even though it is over fifty years since Skeat and Blagden wrote of "the supreme importance to Governments in the tropics of intimately studying and carefully considering the peculiarities of the alien and less civilized races committed to their care", little anthropological or pre-historical archaeological work has been done in the Malay Peninsula, and at this stage of our knowledge little can be said with certainty about these early peoples.[7]

Today there are still 10,000 Negritos, small, almost dwarf like people, negroid in appearance, who live unobtrusively in small groups deep in the jungle by the remote headwaters of the Pahang, Trengganu, and Kelantan rivers, and in the far interior of Kedah and Perak. They live today unchanged, except probably that they have retreated inwards from the coastal regions, for they shun contact. They still lead a nomadic, terrified life, the confining jungle restricting their vision and reflecting their ignorant fears and their narrow mental outlook. They are a living reminder of the antiquity of this land.[8]

A second, more numerous, more advanced group are the 60,000 Senoi, relatively fair and wavy haired individuals, who may be of the same stock as the Melanesians, and some Australian

---

[6] This is an objectionable word to anthropologists, who contend that even the most 'primitive' people are not primitive at all and that they live a life complex in many ways. By 'primitive' I mean people whose political structure is simple in comparison with that of a national state; and people who are illiterate, whose way of life scarcely transcends a daily demand and satisfaction for food, and where specialists operate singly, if at all.

[7] F. W. W. Skeat and C. O. Blagden, *Pagan Races of the Malay Peninsula*, 2 vols. (London, 1906), vol. 1, p.x.

[8] For some account of them see I. H. N. Evans, *The Negritoes of Malaya* (Cambridge, 1937).

aborigines. These Senoi group themselves together into larger units than the Negritos, with several layers of authority in their sub-tribes. They move in a small defined area, moving from clearing to clearing in a semi-nomadic way.[9] The third group, the 30,000 aboriginal-Malays, or proto-Malays, in most cases are completely settled. There is still an aboriginal-Malay settlement over the water opposite the main harbour of Singapore, for example. Although many of the fishermen now possess transistor radios their way of life reflects an age-old balance with nature that goes back, surely, to the Stone Age, as do other settlements on the Johore, Selangor and Pahang rivers.

It is thought that as they are still settled on the coast, or near the mouths of various rivers, they must have come later to the peninsula than the Senoi or Negritos. Their government, too, was more complex; and in this respect it is interesting to note that of the three, they were the only people who established settled fishing villages, but they did not grow wet rice.

Their political organization was headed by a *Batin,* the executive and administrative head of a collection of settlements, either around a bay, on a strait, or along a river. Under the *Batin* was the *Jinang,* or *Mentri,* who acted for him when he could not administer his executive commands. Another officer to whom authority over more than one village was delegated was the *Penglima.* The administrative officer of a single kampong was the *Penghulu.*

This organization, or variations of it, still survived over south Malaya, wherever the aboriginal-Malay lived, as recently as fifty years ago, when Skeat and Blagden wrote their *Pagan Races of the Malay Peninsula.* Despite all the developments brought from other lands, some of this system still remains. The *Mentri Besar* is an officer of the modern Malay State, the *Penglima* is by no means forgotten, while the *Penghulu* has remained throughout the millenia as the key figure in local rural administration, the essential elemental core or operative unit. Here, better than

[9] The figures given here are from P. D. R. Williams-Hunt, *An Introduction to the Malayan Aborigines* (Kuala Lumpur, 1952). See also, for a most interesting account of the Temiar of Kelantan, J. Slimming, *Temiar Jungle* (London, 1958).

anywhere else can be seen the quiet, indigenous strength and adaptability of the Malay. These indigenous elements should not be forgotten; on the contrary, there should be a far more detailed investigation of them than has hitherto been attempted.[10]

The aboriginal-Malay movement into the peninsula may have been a trickle from the north-east for over a thousand years. It began perhaps as early as 1500 B.C. It was still continuing when between 300 B.C. and A.D. 100 the last of these Malay type movements brought metal (and many words of Mon-Khmer origin), to the fishing villages down the east coast of the peninsula. The drums, daggers, swords and helmets that have been found of this period are of bronze, and the metal culture they represent has been named the *Dongson*, after the site in Annam where material remains of the culture were first found.

These people may have brought, along with metal, the art of growing wet rice, to supplement the sago already cultivated, but, as Winstedt has pointed out, this movement of Indo-Malays, speaking perhaps a Mon-Khmer language, was the last of the Malaysian migrations into the Malay Peninsula from the north-east.[11] The aboriginal-Malay was to develop into the Malay between A.D. 200–1400 by further admixtures not from the north-east (where the Malaysian peoples were squashed by the great States that emerged there), but of peoples of a very similar stock from the south, in Java and Sumatra in particular, where they had advanced considerably in culture. It may well have been on the flat fertile lands of Java that wet rice growing first was discovered, and it came to the peninsula not from the north but from the south. If this could be established, it would be the most basic contribution that Java ever made to the culture of Malaya, and an early example of the influence of Indonesia that was to be exerted on the peninsula from this time until the present.

---

[10] An historical study of the powers and functions of the *Penghulu*, for example, is long overdue. It would be of great immediate benefit to the directors of the modern State.

[11] R. Winstedt, *The Malays: a Cultural History* (London, 1953), p. 10.

2

Throughout the history of the Malay Peninsula and indeed of South-East Asia in general, the major developments that have occurred have been brought about by indigenous reaction to overseas contacts. The first such contact that needs to be considered (after the arrival of the aboriginal-Malay himself), was the coming of the Indian. Indian culture flowed over South-East Asia for a thousand years, to such an extent that many think that if you remove everything Indian in origin from the Malay you will find a naked savage, and that Malaya is merely part of a Greater India. This is not so; nor is the peninsula a little China. It is a part of South-East Asia. Yet without doubt, by the time of the beginning of the Malacca Sultanate (circa A.D. 1400), a great many aspects of Indian culture, mixed with and adapted by indigenous elements, had been assimilated by the peninsula.[12]

Indians began coming to the Malay Peninsula at least several centuries before the beginning of the Christian era.[13] They came primarily because they were sailing to the rich, cultured civilization of China. They sold peppers and cottons there, and bought silks, porcelain and precious objects. Morever, they discovered that the most precious object of all, gold, could be secured also in the Malay Peninsula. The country then became not an obstruction to be sailed around or walked across, but a land attractive for itself, particularly the east coast.

It is easy to forget that for thousands of years the east coast was the most important part of Malaya, and that before the

---

[12] It should not be forgotten that this cultural exchange was two-way. South-East Asian traders reached India at much the same time, and there has been always a give and take in culture. Remember also that most of this 'Indian' influence came in all likelihood from Java and Cambodia. But for the strong indigenous element, see, for example R. O. Winstedt, *Karamat: Sacred Places and Persons in Malaya* (JMBRAS vol. 2, 1924), and G. G. Hough, *A Pre-Islamic element in the Malay Grave* (JMBRAS vol. 18, pt. 2, 1940) for the indigenous element even in death.

[13] For a condensed account of this period in Malayan History see K. G. Tregonning, *World History for Malayans* (London, 1957). It is dealt with in detail by P. Wheatley, *The Golden Khersonese* (U. M. P., 1961).

foundation of Malacca all the early accounts of the Malay Peninsula stress constantly the east coast rivers.[14] Even up to the foundation of Singapore in the nineteenth century, most of the peninsula's scanty population was along the banks of these great rivers, the Pahang, the Kelantan and the Trengganu, which flow into the China Sea. Before the coming of the Indian the rivers had provided the basis for the simple life led then, the flat land perhaps for wet or dry rice, or more especially sago, the coconuts, *rembutans, durians,* and bananas overhead, while the river itself yielded fish, prawns and crabs in abundance. Now with the arrival of the Indian there came not only an economic diversification, with gold and tin being mined in the headwaters and easily transported downstream, and with the marketing and trading of various goods by middle men, but also a political elaboration, the simple river control being developed and made more complex by the sophisticated visitors.

A few of them had come from such ports on the Bay of Bengal as Amaravati, at the mouth of the Kistna River; or Tamralipta, near the modern Calcutta; or Kanchipuram, near modern Madras. Just as today these ports have well established commercial links with Malaya, so 1500 years ago their ancient counterparts waited for the monsoon and then sent their ships to the peninsula. The trade was naturally very much smaller, for there was no great flood of Indian migration, but rather the slow establishment of small groups dotted here and there while similar groups of South-East Asians settled in South India. However, as time went on and they stayed in the peninsula and elsewhere in South-East Asia, their culture and their blood blended and merged with indigenous elements to produce an amalgam, something not Indian but Indianised, of which the political expression was a number of states and Empires.

Modern research has shown that during the 1500 years or so of Indian or Indianised influence on the Malay Peninsula, at least thirty states were formed and flourished. Almost all of them were on the east coast; and almost all of them are best described not by Indian sources, although the inspiration for

[14] For their early history see Anker Rentse, *An Historical Note on the North-eastern Malay States* (JMBRAS vol. 20, 1947).

their origin comes from there, but by Chinese accounts. The Chinese had been coming to South-East Asia as early as the Indian. He too was a trader, and although he lacked those things of the spirit and the religious outlook of the Indian and so never gained a spiritual hold over his customers, being more interested in their pockets than in their hearts, nevertheless his experiences were recorded for the Emperor, and it is to Chinese dynastic histories that we turn for much of our early knowledge of this area.

These describe, for example, the state of *Tun Sun,* situated in the northern part of the peninsula. Even as early as the third century A.D. there were over 500 Indian merchants and many priests living there very happily, for as the Chinese commented "the people of Tun-Sun practise their doctrine and give them their daughters in marriage; consequently many of the Brahmins do not go away."[15] No doubt many an "Indian", so called, was the son of an Indian father (a trader sent out by his father from Cambodia perhaps, or possibly a Javanese port, to open a branch where trade looked promising, or a Brahmin looking for a quiet life), and a Malay mother (or even vice versa, a Malay returning from India with a Tamil wife) ; for it was in this way that Indian culture spread.

Another state on the east coast, although of not the same importance as *Tun Sun,* was *Ch'ih-Tu,* (or Red Land—*Tanah Merah* in Malay, still a common name for the numerous red bluffs of Malaya). This may have been situated up the Kelantan or Trengganu River, near Kuala Brang perhaps, where four rivers from the interior meet. Here Buddha was worshipped, and the Chinese accounts frequently mention the gold from the interior, and the gold goblets and gold thread of the capital. It was this gold and the tin that brought both Indian and Chinese traders, (the Chinese mention scores of them in the main city), although the strong northeast monsoon made it very difficult

---

15 See the translation of a Chinese account in P. Wheatley, *The Malay Peninsula as known to the Chinese of the Third Century A.D.* (JMBRAS vol. 28, pt. 1, 1955) ; also his *Chinese Sources for the Historical Geography of Malaya before AD 1500.* (Malayan Journal of Tropical Geography, vol. 9, 1956).

to sail other than south, and then only dangerously, for several months of the year.

This difficulty of arriving and leaving during the monsoon may have been overcome by *Chii-Li,* which was at Kuantan, the capital of modern Pahang, for there is much evidence to suggest that one overland route right across the peninsula, went up a tributary of the Pahang river and then there was a walk of a few miles to the westward flowing Muar river.[16] Thus, when the monsoon was too strong for the Indians to sail round to Kuantan, or the pirate packs were too vicious, or Sri Vijayan control too effective, they went up the Muar River and down the other side; again in search of gold, and tin, and in hopes of selling their cotton.

Perhaps the most important of these east coast states was *Langkasuka.* Earlier chroniclers would have placed *Langkasuka* in Kedah, but modern research has proved this incorrect. There are so many descriptions in Chinese sources of this wealthy state, all of which place it in the east, north of the present frontier of Malaya, that it cannot now be disputed. It lasted possibly for over a thousand years, at times extending its control to the west. The unexcavated ruins of South Thailand probably conceal the capital city, and it would be a worthwhile task for Malayan archaeologists to investigate them. If the early accounts are correct, with their descriptions of gold rings and cups, golden ornaments, statues of Buddha, incense containers and so on, there will be much to discover, probably far more than has been unearthed so far in Kedah.

Kedah possessed none of the gold or the tin that attracted traders to the east coast, but the ruins of its settlement, by the banks of the small stream that tumbles down the precipitous slopes of Kedah Peak are the most extensive archaeological remains in Malaya.[17] Although much research is still needed to

---

[16] For this see P. Wheatley, *An Early Chinese Reference to Part of Malaya* (Malayan Journal of Tropical Geography, vol. 5, 1955); see also his *Belated Comments on Sir Roland Braddell's Studies of Ancient Times in the Malay Peninsula* (JMBRAS vol. 28, pt. 1, 1955).

[17] These ruins were first examined in detail by H. Quaritch-Wales, shortly before the Japanese Invasion, and described by him in JMBRAS, vols.

explain these ruins, it may be that they represent a religious centre, where sailors, grateful for having crossed the Bay of Bengal, and guided over the last of it by the towering landfall of Kedah Peak, came ashore in the sheltered Merbok River, and paid tribute to the gods before venturing further south. It is difficult to believe that any important settlement, other than an active fishing village supporting a religious centre, could be sustained in this swampy, tinless and goldless area hard by a mountain, unless it was another trans-peninsula terminus.

Kedah was once held to be *Kalah,* the west coast port made famous by Arab writers between the ninth and fourteenth centuries. From these Arab sources we hear of a palisaded city noted for its tin trade, where Indian Brahmins and merchants maintained a paramount position, and where vessels from Sumatra and Java met the ocean going craft from China, India and Arabia. Recent research, however, maintains this settlement to be where the modern Klang is today, in the heart of the tin area of Selangor; but the changing coastline has removed all vestiges of this ancient port.[18]

It should be realized that Indian influence does not mean necessarily influence directly from India, for the Indian impulse that merged with indigenous elements to produce these states in the Malay Peninsula was effective in other parts of South East Asia also, and it is largely from the Indianised states in Sumatra, Java and Cambodia, and not directly from India itself, that Indianised culture spread over the peninsula.[19]

Two elements are discernible in this. The Indian trader may claim precedence, in that possibly he came first in time, but the

---

21, 1940 and 22, 1946. Post-war expeditions, initiated by K. G. Tregonning in 1955 and continued particularly by H. Lamb, have revealed more temple sites up the mountain slopes, and elsewhere in South Kedah. See A. Lamb, *Chandi Bukit Batu Pahat* (Singapore, 1960) and his articles in the Federation Museums Journal, vols. 5, 6, 1960–1961.

[18] For a most detailed examination of this see S. Q. Fatimi, *In Quest of Kalah* (Journal, South-East Asian History, vol. 1, no. 2. September 1960).

[19] Both J. L. Moens, *Srivajaya, Yava and Kataha* (JMBRAS, vol. 17, pt. 1, 1939), and R. J. Wilkinson, *Early Influences in Malaysia,* (JMBRAS, vol. 13, pt. 2, 1934) make this point very clear.

more important element in this spread of Indianised culture appears to have been the Brahmin, the priest. The economic structure, the trading techniques and the commerce of the Malay Peninsula were affected by this influence only slightly. The great developments occurred (as will be outlined shortly) in matters of the mind, in government, language and spiritual things, all pointing to the paramount importance of the Brahmin (or Buddhist) priest, and to the relative unimportance of the trader. The acceptance of the more spiritual or less tangible aspects of this culture indicate an insufficiency, possible even a collapse, of the previous intellectual basis of life. It reflects a need for something more fulfilling than anything previously possessed; a mental or spiritual satisfaction, it should be noted, not merely an economic one. We see this again when we come to consider the acceptance of Islam.

However, it seems difficult not to believe that it was the economic motive which first lured Indians eastward, and that the other South-East Asian states were founded in much the same manner as those in Malaya, by Indians on their way to China, and seeking either convenient stopping places where they could wait for the monsoon, or where they could secure food and water before continuing, or goods suitable for sale in China such as tin and spices. They may well have brought the simple faith of Buddha with them, but it was not until the petty ruler sought the assistance, or accepted the arrival, of a Brahmin Hindu, that he was able to exploit the ritualistic and magical aspects of an exclusive religious aristocracy, to transform himself into a god.[20]

One of the earliest of these Indianised States that influenced the east coast of Malaya was Funan, situated on the flat lands of Indo-China. Here a great state arose in the early centuries of the Christian era, of which only the ruins of its cities now remain. Solidly based on a thriving agriculture, it yet turned to the sea for expansion. It was one of the earliest to demonstrate that he who commands the sea commands South-East Asia. Funan became so powerful that the surrounding lands were forced to pay submission to it, and much of the gold of the east

[20] The most detailed description of pre-Islamic South-East Asia is in D.G.E. Hall, *A History of South-East Asia* (London, 1956).

coast of Malaya went in submission across the waters that joined it to Funan.

It would seem that Funan for several centuries controlled these river-states, but they had no sooner secured their independence with the break-up of Funan than they fell again under the control of another Indianised state, the mighty empire of Cambodia. Cambodia, with its magnificent capital of Angkor, was largely a land empire, but the north-east of the Malay Peninsula at least came within its control, and the tribute gold continued as before. For perhaps hundreds of years the small river states were under the influence, if not the control, of the mighty power across the water from whom they secured protection, and acquired perhaps that exquisite artistry, akin to the ancient Khmers, that has survived to this very day.[21]

The west coast of Malaya during this Indianised period was for the most part subservient to the Indianised powers that expanded on the waters that joined it to Sumatra. There were more links in those days, more sharing of interests, between east Sumatra and west Malaya than with east and west Malaya. The waters between were far less of a barrier than the mountains; and even with the recent nineteenth century political division, this is partly true even today.

In Sumatra the power that exercised the most control over the western side of the Malay Peninsula was Sri Vijaya. This State rose to prominence during the later period of the 'Hindu Millenium' as Winstedt rather loosely calls it.[22] Sri Vijaya was essentially a maritime power. It was not interested in acquiring more territory, but from its capital near, it is thought (although without much evidence), where Palembang is today, its fleet established check points, small naval bases at strategic places,

---

[21] The ancient Khmer tongue still lingers in Kelantan and Trengganu today, together with this artistry, and with some Hindu ceremonies of great antiquity.

[22] R. Winstedt, *Malaya and its History* (London, 1951), pp. 24–31. When reading Winstedt, it is well to bear in mind the comment of the Dutch scholar, P. de Josselin de Jong, that "the overrating of Indian influence is almost a tradition in British studies on Malaya." *Bijdragen Tot De Taal—Land En Volkenkunde* ['Gravenhage (The Hague), 1960] Deel 116, p. 381.

similar to the Portuguese a few centuries later, so that it controlled the trade of the islands. Kalah became such a base, controlling, with Acheh opposite, the northern part of the Straits of Malacca. This control lasted until there was a devastating raid from South India in the eleventh century. Singapore (or Tumasik as it was called then) was also founded by Sri Vijaya as the guard to the other end of the Straits. By means of these bases and the revenue they levied, Sri Vijaya became very powerful, and was overthrown only when its fleets became quarrelling packs of pirates in the thirteenth century.

The state that replaced Sri Vijaya was Madjapahit, in Java. Madjapahit was much more cultured than Sumatra, it had absorbed Indian culture more deeply and had blended it with a stronger native culture, to produce a very characteristic art, some of which found its way to the Malay Peninsula. Madjapahit, by the fourteenth century, controlled most of the coast lapped by the Java Sea, and in addition secured tribute from both east and west coast Malaya. Indeed, when questioned as to the origins of their crafts and skills, east coast Malays today invariably refer to Java, even at times naming Madjapahit. It was not until the growth of Malacca in the fifteenth century and the acceptance of Islam by Malaya that this control was broken.

3

A great deal of the history of this Indianised period is unknown to us, and there is much examination and many exciting discoveries to be made. The outstanding scholar of this period is Professor P. Wheatley, who from a devoted and scholarly study of the Chinese, Arabic, Indian, Javanese and Malay sources has compiled *The Golden Chersonese.*[23] Although it is a brilliant book it is not a connected history for the author does not throw a continuous ray of light on the peninsula, but rather a quick flash, followed by darkness, and then another flash, and even deeper darkness. Many problems of Malayan history remain to be set, and answered. But if the history of this period is difficult

---

[23] P. Wheatley, *The Golden Chersonese* (London, 1960).

to discover and relate, the result of it, the cultural legacy passed on to Malaya, is still all around us, and it was with this legacy that Malaya entered the fifteenth century.

Perhaps the most important part of this legacy was the political aspect. The primitive political structure of the proto-Malays was added to and improved, and although its indigenous framework was maintained it became a real system. Under it all the other aspects of the Indianised legacy, the contributions to religion, to the economic and legal systems, and to literature and arts and crafts, were enabled to spread safely. Had the Indianised visitor not secured political control it is doubtful if much of his culture would have affected the local inhabitants; but by establishing this political umbrella, as it were, everything else was protected, as with the brief British régime, a thousand years later.

The Indianised state that arose took the old proto-Malay river chief and made him a ruler, a Raja. It elevated the rank immensely and made it hereditary. But the state went still further: it insisted on an elaborate ceremony when a ruler was crowned, investing it with a religious significance completely unknown before. To many the ruler became almost a god. This sense of semi-divinity has survived the centuries. The enthronement of a Malay Sultan today is still in essentials the same Hindu ceremony of 1500 years ago. The immobility expected from the ruler, the royal procession around the palace, the use of Sanskrit (the ancient Hindu language), and the anointment are all survivals from the past, and illustrate the great hold this Hindu ceremony secured over the politically conscious people of these river states.[24]

Along with the elevation of the chief to the impressive heights of Raja went an elaboration of his duties and an increase in his subordinates. Chief of these was his army commander, the *Bendahara,* who was primarily responsible for the defence of the

---

[24] In 1960, when this book was being compiled, Malaya witnessed the enthronement of the Sultan of Johore, and of the Yang di-Pertuan Agong, and these traditional elements were clearly apparent at each ceremony. By reading the morning newspaper one seemed to step back perhaps a thousand years.

river. Of great importance to the river states, far more important than in India, where river states did not exist, were the responsibilities of the *Laksamana,* for he was the Admiral, the officer in charge of everything naval; for when invasion came, it almost invariably came by sea.

It must not be thought, however, that every ancient political post connected with a Malay State is derived from the Indianised period. *Penghulu,* as has been shown, is of earlier origin, while others, as we will see, came after. The Malay State had created its essential structure before the Indians, Sumatrans or Cambodians came, and it continued to develop after they had gone; although it must be admitted that the most creative work were the refinements introduced by these political sophisticates.

Neither socially nor economically does it appear as if the basic indigenous structure was affected to the extent of the Malay political system. Socially the old class distinctions were perpetuated and probably accentuated between slave, commoner and royalty. Slavery persisted throughout the Muslim centuries. There was a very small middle class added to this, caused by the Indian enlargement of the simple economic activity, such as the fishing, sago cutting and possible padi growing, of the early period. The buyers of the gold, the sellers of the cotton, the middle-men, became the middle class; but as these tasks were almost invariably performed by Indians who merged with royalty, it simply meant that the aristocrats became more interested in trade than before, and not that a new social class emerged.

Of more importance than these was the legal legacy.[25] The Hindu element was very cruel, for its law was involved with religion, and being considered sacred it was never changed, never softened from the very remote, barbarous days in which it had been evolved. This rigid law was superimposed on ancient customs far more easy going and lenient. Some elements of the

[25] R. Winstedt, *The Malays: A Cultural History* (London, 1953) gives the best general treatment of the Indianised impact. However, recent research is inclined to give more emphasis to the indigenous element in Malay Culture than that allowed by the author, and to look to Java when he looks to India.

Hindu code persisted right up to the nineteenth century, softened both by the later Islamic law and the earlier proto-Malay custom, but not eradicated. In the beginning of the fifteenth century it was paramount.

Under this Hindu law death was the punishment for murder, stabbing, striking, robbery, theft, bringing false charges, perjury, and either betraying or opposing the royal command. Most of these offences are violent acts, and they reflect the violent age of A.D. 1400. Impaling, for example, was the Hindu mode of execution, the victim being left to die a lingering death, a gruesome custom which, although dispensed with by Islam, was persisted in by the Dutch in Java and Malacca until the nineteenth century.

Although it was a violent age, and a man was not an individual entitled to various rights but merely a follower of a Raja, the Hindu attitude to sexual offences was far milder than that taken subsequently by the Muslims. A man could kidnap a girl and marry her, although he had to pay a fine if she was engaged already. If a man committed adultery he was fined; but when Islam came he was stoned to death. Similarly, if a man seduced a married woman he would be fined by a benevolent Hindu, but stoned to death by followers of Islam.

Both in sexual and criminal offences it seems clear that the primitive Malay always tended towards ways by which the offence could be compounded. The strictness of Islamic sexual laws and of Hindu criminal laws were alien to the basic processes of the Malay temperament, which instinctively preferred a legal system fixed and humane, as its primitive customs had been. This made it easy for the British to introduce their Indian Penal Code in the nineteenth century and to sweep away the cruel vestiges of an outmoded law, and even now, although British political control has gone, British law remains extremely acceptable to the modern Malay.

In 1400 the religion of nearly all the peninsula in contact with the court was a mixture of Hinduism and Buddhism while the peasant in the kampong in all probability still clung to his primitive animism. Even today, after more than five hundred years of Islam in Malaya, traces of both that animism and that Hindu religion persist, in ritual and in practice, in words and in thought. This is not surprising. Pagans persist in Britain, and there are sun worshippers in Palestine. The three most elaborate Hindu rituals to survive are the enthronement ceremony of a Malay king, which is essentially a religious ceremony,[26] another religious ceremony is in the marriage of a Malay man and woman, and in the now almost discarded ceremony preceding the shadow puppet-play of north-east Malaya.[27] This is almost obsolete but the former two are part and parcel of modern Malay life, and to attend a Malay wedding, and to see a devout Muslim sitting motionless through a ceremony first brought here perhaps 2,000 years ago, is to realise again the strength of the Hindu legacy.

This religious debt is shown also in the language and literature. Many Malay spiritual words, such as religion itself (*agama*), heaven (*shorga*), and hell (*naraka*) are from Sanskrit, as are nearly all Malay words which express abstract ideas. The early Malay had a vocabulary of tangible things, solid objects that could be seen, but it was from the Brahmin that he learned the words for intangible things, and for abstract ideas and beliefs. He retained them along with such guides to his later literature as the ancient Indian classics, the *Ramayana* and the *Mahabharatha*, when another religion came in the fifteenth century.

It is centuries since art developed in any Muslim country, and most of the art, though not the culture, of the Malay was present on the peninsula by A.D. 1400. As a starting point in any examination of Malay arts, one can scarcely do better than study the *kris*, the Malay dagger. The Malay was to live through many dangerous centuries, and much of his character as well as his culture is personified in this weapon. There are many different types, some designed for strictly utilitarian

---

26 This is well brought out in R. Winstedt, *Kingship and Enthronement in Malaya* (JMBRAS, vol. 20, 1947).

27 For interesting comments on this see Anker Rentse, *The Origins of the Wayang Theatre* (JMBRAS, vol. 20, 1947); also A. H. Hill, *Wayang Kulit Stories from Trengganu* (JMBRAS, vol. 22, 1949).

ends, others for ceremony and display. The hilts of many, even when they have become heavily stylised, are fashioned after *Garuda, Vishnu's* sacred bird: that is, they are Hindu in origin, or at least they show Hindu grafting on to an indigenous idea, for the wavy shape of the blade seems quite non-Indian. The *kris* is typical of this period for although it appears to be an amalgam of two cultures, speculation still continues as to its origins.[28]

Kris manufacture still continues. Another Malay craft that also thrives today is silver-ware. Here again the pre-Muslim origin of this can be seen in the Buddhist petals and lotus flowers that devout Muslims beat onto bowls, bracelets and silver boxes, and weave by silver thread into the glorious Trengganu and Kelantan sarongs. In the Malay bronze work, too, this lotus motif can be observed, while it is possible to see in *Wan*, the giant kite-flying practised up the east coast, and in *Main Gasing*, the top-spinning game, perhaps other Buddhist survivals.

Some of the graceful dances of the Malay also perpetuate a tradition which, in the case of *Tari Labi-Labi* from Endau in Pahang (the turtle-dance), may be even of animistic origin. *Tari Sabong*, however, is thought to be a Sri-Vijayan dance, and the vigorous *Bergayong Ota Ota* came also from Sumatra to catch the enthusiasm of the young bloods in the courts of west Malaya.

The arts and crafts of any country are always an amalgam of old and new, of imported ideas and local adaptations, of indigenous genius and traditional craftsmanship; and this is so in the Malaya of today. The culture of modern Malaya, vigorously alive, is still being shaped and fashioned by a number of active factors. In this culture, which is no more than art plus life, the ancient Indian legacy is still evident.

It seems clear then that in A.D. 1400, when our study of this

[28] One of the world's largest collections of krises is to be found in the National Museum, Singapore. Here is also a collection of *parangs*, the large Malay chopping sword, but with them Indianised elements are not apparent. Can one surmize then that the *parang* is more indigenous, more ancient, than the *kris?*

modern Malaya begins, the inhabitants of the peninsula were already the inheritors of a complex cultural tradition, little explored as yet. To the politics, economics, religion, law, language and art of this culture, both indigenous and Indianised elements had contributed, overlaying and absorbing still earlier characteristics and customs that surely reached back to the Stone Age.

At present this pre-Islamic period is in many ways full of historical conjectures, speculations and possibilities. The darkness and confusion of these millenia need to be swept away by sustained research of many kinds: historical, archaeological, cultural, anthropological and linguistic research that should be intensely stimulating to all concerned, not merely because of the intellectual pleasure to be derived from throwing light upon a particular problem, but also because that light would help us to appreciate some of the attitudes of modern Malaya. As a way of understanding the present then, this pre-Islamic period, this incubation period of the peninsula in particular and South-East Asia in general, deserves our close attention.

2. THE MALACCA SULTANATE

By the end of the first millenium A.D. South-East Asia had become culturally homogeneous. The broad, pervasive influences of Buddhism and Hinduism had worked on the earlier animism to produce a way of life not markedly dissimilar throughout the entire area. Although its archaeological remains may seem to us diverse, this reflects a diversity within a wider unity. South-East Asia was more of a unit then than it is today; and an enclosed unit too, a separate culture complex that stood on its own feet, with a creative, dynamic element inside itself, owing little if anything to the outside world.[1]

This closed culture unit was characteristic at this period of world history not merely of South-East Asia, but of other parts of the world as well. India was separate, owing little to its neighbours; so too, for example was Western Europe, China and Central America. From this time onwards, however, the overall trend of history was for the high walls and the internal life of these units to be broken and disturbed, and increasingly for one world to appear.

This does not render less valid our framework of study, whereby we take the history of the peninsula as the unit of regard, a scrutiny that looks out from the peninsula, seeking those factors that have gone to create the State of today. It means, nevertheless, that we should remember that from the tenth century onwards, and even more from the fifteenth, while modern Malaya was evolving, so too was the modern world.

By the beginning of the fifteenth century, however, by the time of the Malacca Sultanate[2] (1402–1511), it is difficult to consider that South-East Asia was still a self-contained and

---

[1] In illustration of this, see the aptly named *The Culture of South East Asia*, by R. LeMay (London, 1954).

separate culture complex, since from well before A.D. 1400 the states of this area and the Malay Peninsula in particular were considering the applicability of a number of Asian developments which came increasingly from outside the region. Chief of these were the territorial ambitions of Siam, the influence of China and the spread of Islam, while in addition, breaking into the closed world of South-East Asia, was the increasingly effective European demand for spices.

The last of the great Indianised states in South-East Asia was Madjapahit, centred on Java. It became very powerful in the fourteenth century, under some leaders still honoured by the Javanese as national heroes. Kertenagara had founded the state at the end of the thirteenth century (1292), by securing the support of a Chinese expedition sent to the island by Kubilai Khan, which placed him in power. The great architect of the Empire, however, was Gaja Mada, the chief minister of the kingdom in the middle of the fourteenth century (1330–1360). Under Gaja Mada Madjapahit control spread, it is believed, from Java to Sumatra, South Borneo, Bali, Brunei and perhaps Singapore, or Tumasik as it was called then.[3] It maintained that empire, as Java maintains its empire today, and as all South-East Asian Empires have been maintained throughout history, by sea power, and it lost its grip on the area when its sea power was no longer effective.

At the end of the fourteenth century a Sumatran rebellion broke out. In this rebellion, which was suppressed, one of the leaders, as a doubtful legend tells us, was a young man named Paramesvara.[4] He was founder of the Malacca Sultanate. He

---

[2] For a general account of the Malacca Sultanate see R. J. Wilkinson, *The Malacca Sultanate* (JMBRAS vol. 13, pt. 2, 1935); and R. Winstedt, *A History of Malaya* (JMBRAS vol. 13, 1935, chapter 3); Both make use of the Portuguese 16th century chronicler, Tome Pires, *Suma Oriental.* (Hakluyt Series, London, 1944).

[3] For references to early Tumasik see R. J. Wilkinson, *Old Singapore* (JMBRAS vol. 13, pt. 2, 1935); and W. Linehan, *The Kings of 14th Century Singapore* (JMBRAS vol. 20, pt. 2, 1947).

[4] However Van Stein Callenfels in *The Founder of Malacca* (JMBRAS, vol. 15, May 1937) maintains that Paramesvara was a Javanese.

fled from the victorious Javanese, and sought refuge in Tumasik, another place that appears to have broken away.

The revolt of Sumatra and the break away of Tumasik both point to a weakening of Javanese control, and by 1400 the Madjapahit Empire was past its zenith. On the mainland of Malaysia another power was becoming powerful, and that was Siam. From Ayuthia, its capital, it spread south during the fourteenth century until by the beginning of the fifteenth century it was receiving tribute from Patani and the east coast rivers of Kelantan, Trengganu and Pahang, as well as from Kedah and Tumasik. It seems that Paramesvara thought that Tumasik should link itself to Sumatra, and not to Siam. He and his followers staged a sudden rising, and attempted a *coup d'état* by assassinating the ruler. Momentarily he was in command, but Siam's over-lordship was effective enough to force him to flee again, to the almost uninhabited west coast of the peninsula. He paused for a while at Muar, a little fishing village, and terminus perhaps for an overland route across the peninsula, and then sank to rest at Malacca.

At the time of Paramesvara's arrival Malacca was a small village, but possessing with Muar an overland link to the east coast that made it a trade terminus from China. None of the pre-fifteenth century travellers whose writings have come down to us—Marco Polo[5] or Fa Hsien[6] for example— mention it at all, and it must have been a most insignificant kampong when Paramesvara arrived; in fact it was probably why he stopped there, because it was insignificant, and it offered him a good hiding place. From the moment that he took refuge there, however, his fortunes began to change.

Among the outside influences affecting South-East Asia by the fifteenth century was the might of Ming China. This dynasty was founded in 1368, and by 1400 it was fully prepared to venture southwards in unprecedented strength in an effort to

---

5 Sir H. Yule, *The Book of Ser Marco Polo* (London, 1929).

6 See also J. Legge, *A Record of Buddhist Kingdoms; being an account by the Chinese monk Fa Hien of his travels in India and Ceylon* (A.D. *399–414*) (London, 1886). H.A.R. Gibb, *Ibn Battuta: Travels in Asia and Africa* (London, 1929), for a later traveller.

secure imperial recognition and tribute. A powerful fleet was assembled and the famous Admiral Cheng Ho given the command. Cheng Ho, a Muslim, set out in 1403 to exact tribute from the many states among the islands.[7] Here was the ally that Paramesvara needed. His organising ability had already made Malacca more prominent, and it was becoming a useful trading centre, particularly for those states in Sumatra that did not care for Madjapahit; but it was rather like a nut between the two arms of a nutcracker. Either Java or Siam might crush it at any minute. Paramesvara welcomed the magnificent junks of Cheng Ho, and entertained the visiting Chinese lavishly. He eagerly promised to send tribute to the Emperor in Peking, and he undertook to take it personally, provided that payment meant protection. It did, and Malacca was saved. There has been a temple to Cheng Ho in Malacca ever since.

Paramesvara was able to make good use of two great geographical advantages possessed by Malacca. These were its land isolation from Siam, separated by jungle and mountain from the foe that wanted to conquer it and so possess all the peninsula, and its sea location, where monsoonal winds made it a convenient stopping place for ships from India and China,[8] and the neighbouring states of Sumatra. Malacca grew to become a fifteenth century version of Singapore today, an entrepôt port, a storehouse for deposit and a commercial centre for the collection and distribution of imports and exports. That is to say Malacca was not a port exporting produce from its own hinterland, for the land behind it had little that was worth exporting: it merely served as a convenient storehouse for other countries, where goods could be re-exported. This needs one great factor: tranquility and the establishment of law and order. Paramesvara brought this to Malacca, this above all, and by so doing he took advantage of the great geographical assets possessed by the village, and made it a famous city.

Let us look a little more closely at this fifteenth century trade

[7] See J. V. Mills, *Malaya in the Wu-pei-chih Charts* (JMBRAS, vol. 15, pt. 3, 1937).

[8] V. Purcell, in *Chinese Settlement in Malacca* (JMBRAS, vol. 20, 1947) makes some interesting comments on this.

which made use of the security offered by Malacca. A much discussed but relatively unimportant feature in this trade was the demand for spices in far away Europe. From perhaps the beginning of the eleventh century, (A.D. 1000), Europe had begun to enjoy a rising standard of living. It was a very slow rise, but as the terrible invasions from the north and east stopped, as inter-European trade cautiously began, and as towns started to grow, each century saw a Europe that was a little more wealthy and a little more powerful. By the thirteenth century it was able to satisfy part of its demand for goods beyond Europe itself, and by the fourteenth century it was able to pay for select quantities of (in particular) spices from South-East Asia.

Spices were the most important commodity, apart from Christianity, that Asia ever exported to Europe: important not for their quantity, for even as late as the seventeenth century an annual cargo would consist of a few small ships, but for the train of results they initiated. They were needed to add to the European diet. During the long, cold winter in north Europe very few animals could survive, as the grasses were covered in snow. So they were killed when their food, such as hay, ran out. As the winter months went by the meat of animals thus killed became more and more foul. Spices successfully hid the taste, and the demand for them therefore increased tremendously until it affected most of Europe politically or economically.

It affected South-East Asia also, but not at all noticeably until the end of the Malacca Sultanate, and to read back into the centuries its later importance is to adopt a Europocentric attitude to Malayan history that is at variance with the facts. Of far greater importance to Malacca than the annual cargo or two of inter-continental trade was the bustling, vigorous intra-continental trade of sea girt Asia. It is Asian and not European trade that explains the growth of Malacca.[9] The merchants most closely involved both in the long trading link with Europe and the much more active India-China trade were either

[9] This is well brought out by B. Harrison, in his stimulating book *South-east Asia* (London, 1954), pp. 60–64.

from the Hadramaut and the coast of Persia, or the Indian sub-continent. These people had been sailing through South-East Asia to China, for centuries; now they stopped more often, and did an increasingly large proportion of their business in South-East Asia itself, in Malacca. But why in particular in Malacca? There were no spices there. Why not the spice islands themselves?

The reason may be political and not economic. Malacca was independent. It was neither under the control of Madjapahit, nor of Siam. Both these countries damaged trade by ill administered levies and taxes on visiting merchants, and by other restrictions. Malacca with its sensible 'come one, come all' was like an oasis in the desert, and the Indian and Arab traders came here throughout the fifteenth century in ever increasing numbers. So too did the merchants from China, for here they could buy pepper, tin and cotton, and sell their silks and porcelain, either to Indians going back to the Moghul Empire, or on to West Asia and Europe, or to the numerous traders of South-East Asia itself. Traders came from Burma, and west Siam, and from east and north Sumatra; most important of all, they came from all the islands of Indonesia restive under Madjapahit rule, in *prahus* loaded with peppers and spices. In Malacca they all met to buy and sell, perhaps to store, perhaps merely to tranship.[10] Malacca profited then not merely by its own assets, geographical and political, but by the mistakes of others, just as Singapore does today.

Among the commodities that arrived at Malacca was Islam. The most important role played by Malacca in the fifteenth century was not as the centre of the Malacca Sultanate but as the centre for the diffusion of Islam, and its political history has therefore left a less permanent legacy than its religious influence. Islam, however, had come to Malaya and to other parts of South-East Asia long before the mart of Malacca was founded. The earliest Muslim monument in this region is a gravestone in Java, near Surabaja, dated A.D. 1082. Another, in Champa, is dated

---

[10] For an absorbing study of this, see Van Leur, *Indonesian Trade and Society* (The Hague, 1955), pp. 1–117.

1039. Both were tombstones of traders from West Asia, and there are similar traces of Islam in south China at much the same time. Possibly they signify some indigenous conversion in the area as well. It is not until 1282, over two centuries later, however, that we hear of local people in west Malaysia being converted to Islam.

The Annals of China give clear evidence that Pasai in north Sumatra had become by then a Muslim State, for it records that in 1282 the ruler sent two ambassadors, who were Muslims, to China. Then ten years later, in 1292, Marco Polo records that the people of Ferlec in Acheh, a little further north, had recently been converted to Islam. Where had it come from? Learned scholars now tend to think that Islam was brought to Sumatra in the thirteenth century by Indian preachers, or missionary leaders of mystic groups, from the Bengal coast.[11] Later, in the fourteenth century, other religious and trading links were strengthened by Sufis from the port of Cambay in Gujerat in the north west, in what is now Pakistan. A steady stream of Bengali Muslims kept coming,[12] as their Hindu counterparts had for a millenia, during the fourteenth, fifteenth, and sixteenth centuries, while other commercial and religious movements came simultaneously from Gujerat, from Cambay in particular.

From about 1300 onwards for a full century, Islam continued to make progress in northern Sumatra, with Pasai as the important centre, but with the Hindu strength of Madjapahit still strong enough to confine the faith to the north. It was thus prevented from spreading south. Then at the beginning of the fifteenth century came the foundation of Malacca by Paramesvara, the same Paramesvara who, after the visit of the Muslim Cheng Ho in 1414, married the daughter of the Muslim Sultan of Pasai and changed his name to Megat Iskander Shah. Malacca had adopted Islam.

---

[11] From comments on this, see A. Johns, *Aspects of Sufi thought in India and Indonesia in the first half of the seventeenth century* (JMBRAS, vol. 28, pt. 1, March 1955); also see in particular the introduction to his *Malay Sufism* (JMBRAS, vol. 30, pt. 2, August, 1957).

[12] It is important to remember that East Bengal was the first coastal region in the sub-continent converted to Islam.

From Malacca the Muslim faith was to gain converts throughout the peninsula, driving underground the ancient Hindu and Buddhist beliefs, and it was to follow the trade routes to convert nearly all of South-East Asia. It was the only great expansion of Islam that was peaceful; everywhere else Islam had been spread by invading armies, but in South-East Asia it began and remains today a peaceful, non-aggressive religion, quiet and calm.[13]

Malacca was the heart of this expansion, but it was not the first place on the peninsula touched by Islam: that honour is accorded to the east coast, to Trengganu. A stone pillar with a set of regulations on family law and sexual offences has been found there at Kuala Brang, the earliest Muslim monument in Malaya.[14] It is dated A.D. 1303, much earlier than the foundation, let alone the conversion of Malacca, but close to Pasai's and Acheh's known conversion. Most previous writers refer to Trengganu as an out-of-the-way place, an isolated area, whereas it must be remembered that the east coast was very much the centre of things before the growth of Malacca, that here were the ancient states, not on the west coast, and here also was the greater part of the population. The people were remote from Madjapahit control, and largely independent, and therefore it was fitting for Islam to establish itself here, as in Acheh and Pasai. Although a Muslim community was apparently established under a hereditary ruler known as Telanai,[15] nevertheless when Islam spread throughout South-East Asia, it went out from Malacca over a century later.

But why was Malacca converted in the first place? And how? Many historians simply state that foreign Muslim merchants, Indian or Arab, converted the local ruler. This needs reconsidera-

---

[13] This should not obscure the fact that the spread of Islam, at least in the Malay Peninsula, went hand in hand with the armies of Malacca.

[14] H. S. Paterson, *An Early Malay Inscription from Trengganu* (JMBRAS, vol. 2, 1924). The author led a University of Malaya archaeological expedition to Kuala Brang in 1960, in search of further signs of early Islam. The expedition was fruitless, however.

[15] For some comment on this, see M. Sheppard, *A Short History of Trengganu* (JMBRAS, vol. 22, pt. 3, June, 1949, pp. 3–4).

tion, because it is illogical. We must remember the nature of early Asian trade. A wealthy important merchant hardly ever went on travels abroad himself. He stayed at home, investing his money in a ship, or the cargo of a ship, equipped for foreign trade. The actual trading was done by people who should be called pedlars rather than merchants. In foreign ports, Pasai for example, or Malacca, they set up their little stalls or booths in the market, or hawked their wares through the kampongs. Without doubt there was a great social gulf between the humble pedlar and the supreme ruler. It is most unlikely that the two ever met, or that the pedlar converted the king. It is therefore difficult to give credence to this theory.

What may have happened was that these Indian pedlars made converts among the tradesmen and shopkeepers with whom they did business. It paid to be of the same faith (as it still does, particularly in Asia), and possibly economic reasons played some part in making the change. In this way the number of Muslim inhabitants continued to increase.

Current research, however, is questioning the hitherto accepted importance of these pedlars or traders, and is focussing attention on the previously neglected work of the Sufi missionaries. Here, it is felt, is the basic difference between the first scarcely investigated signs of Islam during the eleventh century (which correspond to the Champa and Javanese pillars), and to the later waves that centuries later swept over and converted this vast area. There had been Muslim pedlars, Indian and Chinese, in both periods, but only from the thirteenth century onwards was there a new element, of great religious importance: devout missionaries, Sufis, preaching and converting. This is the vital difference.

This difference having been established, it may be maintained that in all probability the acceptance of Islam by the Malays (and the Indonesians generally), was not due primarily to economic reasons, nor to the political necessities also advanced, such as the search for allies and the fear of Madjapahit and Siam. We cannot explain this widespread acceptance of a new faith by referring merely to possible ultilitarian advantages that may have been secured by such a conversion. The Malay today is indifferent for the most part to economic pursuits, and it is unlikely that his attitude to life was any different 400 years ago. Indeed, in considering such materialistic reasons for conversion, we are in danger of overlooking the fundamentally religious character of the change, and of viewing the past through the secular eyes of the Christian in the twentieth century. In seeking an explanation, we should look more to the spiritual, emotional and sacred element, rather than to the materialistic or profane.

When anything as basic to a way of life as a new religion is accepted, in every case it is because the previous belief has been found insufficient. Economics and politics in this respect are remote from the cause of the change: it is a spiritual matter, an emotional satisfaction with a new religion which replaces, as the core of culture, an earlier faith that has become unsatisfactory, and is on the verge of collapse. In all great conversions, whether of an individual or a community, the new faith is accepted at a time when there is a deep rooted dissatisfaction with the old, and when the earlier belief appears increasingly inadequate to shoulder the framework of life. When man, confronted with new challenge, finds his faith insufficient, that is when he turns to a new supernatural solace; not with the thought of material benefit, but with the hope of calming his mind. That is why, surely, it was the religious persuasion of the Sufis, working in an atmosphere favourable to conversion, that transformed Malaysia, and why the economic and political arguments of their predecessors in the previous centuries had left such a small imprint. The Malay found little that he objected to in his economy; it was in his religion that he had lost faith, just as many South Chinese had in the nineteenth century, and Britons in the fifth. In each case a new faith penetrated to the heart of life.

Nevertheless, when we come to look not at the cultural collapse of the Indianised period, which explains the acceptance of Islam by the people of this area, but turn towards the history of the States of Malaysia from the fourteenth century onwards, we would be naive if we did not recognize that man is basically a political animal. He is more concerned with safety in this life than any possible salvation in the next, and irrespective of his faith he is determined to create a viable political state, which can protect and possibly advance him. Religion rarely plays a more important role in government than does politics. More often than not it has been the hand-maid of politics, not vice versa. Therefore it seems permissible to say that when one of the States of Java or Malaya or Sumatra adopted Islam, as distinct from individuals, it was in almost every case a political move based on a deep cultural transformation. It was a step by the ruler to secure allies, to obtain greater strength. When Pasai's ruler adopted Islam at the end of the thirteenth century, the political logic behind his move was fear of Javanese aggression, and the hope that the Indian Muslim state that traded with him would support him. When Paramesvara married the Sultan's daughter and became a Muslim in 1414 it was at least partly fear of Madjapahit, and Siam also, which influenced him and the hope that China and the Muslim states of Sumatra, which were trading extensively with him and providing Malacca with most of its food, would assist him. Similarly, when the faith spread through the peninsula and around the archipelago, the common people adopted Islam after listening to the eloquent Sufi missionary very largely because their earlier beliefs were inadequate and unsatisfactory. Perhaps economic as well as religious motives may have influenced a few, although this is doubtful. But then, after the ruler had swung over for political reasons, the remainder may well have followed their revered leader for the social advantages it brought. It was a phenomenon similar to the conversion of the early Christians in Europe, although not identical: Islam scarcely brought a higher civilization to the sophisticated Hindus of Java, for example, as it had to the Arabs, or as Christianity had to the Britons. Although it is correct that in most cases, politically, economically, socially, it paid to be Muslim, it does not explain either the acceptance, or the retention, of this new faith. These factors, surely, were no more than subsidiary, and do not explain the deep emotional satisfaction which Malaysians find in Islam. South-East Asia has stayed Muslim, not for these secular or materialistic reasons, but largely because of the appeal which the intrinsic qualities of

Islam has for the people, an attraction which may have been even more overwhelming then than now, and which must be borne in mind when we consider the causes for this basic cultural change.

Wherever Islam went in Malaysia the links with India were maintained. Islam in South-East Asia, as far as the masses were concerned, was not only of Indian origin, but maintained its Indian characteristics for several centuries. During the fifteenth and then increasingly during the sixteenth and seventeenth centuries the scholarly centre from which Malaysia derived most benefit was Gujerat, while in South-East Asia the principal centre of Muslim learning (as distinct from diffusion) was Pasai, and then Acheh.[16] Throughout this period and from all these centres the Sufi played a predominant role. The Indian characteristics of Islam in Malaysia can still be traced. In terminology, for example, various words are Indian in origin; a greater part of the religious literature in Malay is derived, not directly from the Arabic, but from Indian works, and the same applies to Malay religious legends. Most important of all, however, was the influence of mysticism, as spread by the Sufi. In Persia and India there arose schools of mystic philosophy, some of whose leaders came to Malaysia, and which gave rise to much of the most important Malay religious literature. The more important mystic brotherhoods had an enormous following, and doctrines and practices which in most Muslim countries were handed down as carefully guarded secrets were in this part of the world the normal form of religious knowledge and thought. Undoubtedly it was the work of these missionaries, forming their fraternities, that played a major part in the spread of Islam. This Indian hold did not begin to disappear until regular steamship lines were established late in the nineteenth century, permitting easy pilgrimage to Mecca for thousands of Malays,

[16] For a stimulating survey of the role of Pasai and Acheh in the study and spread of Islam, see B. Schrieke, *Indonesian Sociological Studies* Pt. 2. *Ruler and Realm in Early Java*, pp. 231–267, (The Penetration of Islam in the Archipelago); see also Van Leur, *Indonesian Trade and Society* (The Hague, 1955), for further pertinent comments.

Javanese and others. In Mecca the conservative teachings considered correct in the centre of the Islamic world were absorbed and brought back to Malaya, and many of the specifically Indian features, including the role of the Sufi, diminished in importance.

The spread of Islam through the Malay Peninsula was linked closely to the territorial expansion of the Malacca Sultanate. Indeed, the two are often difficult to disentangle. Following the conversion of Paramesvara in 1414, the new port increased in strength on the sea routes, but it was not to expand on land until later. Meanwhile the new wealth of the town increased the anxiety of Megat Iskander Shah (as Paramesvara now called himself) that he would be attacked, not by Madjapahit but by Siam. He was relying not only on his Muslim allies, but also on China, for protection. In 1414 and again in 1419 he journeyed to Peking, and persuaded the Emperor to warn Siam that an attack on Malacca would involve China.

But this was not very likely. Paramesvara seemed to have made an error of judgment. China was becoming rather remote and indifferent, and on Paramesvara's death in 1424 his son reverted to Hinduism. Perhaps this was for political reasons in the hope that Madjapahit would help. In 1413 a Siamese attack seemed very probable. Sri Maharajah, the new ruler, was saved by the reappearance of the redoubtable Cheng Ho, the Ming admiral. Madjapahit was unable or unwilling to assist, but Siam was again ordered by China to keep clear of Malacca. Siam, alone of the powers that have attempted through the centuries to conquer Malaya, was not sea minded. When it invaded the peninsula it did so very largely by land. Siam had no fleet with which to challenge Cheng Ho, and it never achieved its object, neither in the fifteenth century nor the nineteenth, of dominating the peninsula. Siam in fact retreated from the scene. Sri Maharajah died in 1444 at a time of peace, and in a port which was growing rapidly. The next fifty years were to be the greatest in the annals of Malay Malacca.

Following the death of Sri Maharajah in 1444 his infant son, Sri Paramesvara Deva Shah, was proclaimed ruler. But the Muslim community, led by Tun Ali, of mixed Sumatran and Tamil blood, revolted against the continuation of a Hindu régime.

He slew the young child, and placed on the throne another son of Sri Maharajah by another wife, who was Tun Ali's sister. Under pressure from his uncle Tun Ali, (who became Bendahara) the son, Raja Kasim, became a Muslim, adopting in 1445 the name of Muzaffar Shah. He turned immediately from palace intrigue to the threat of war with Siam, marching from Malacca to defeat their invading forces somewhere near the watershed of the Muar River. Thrown back, they did not appear again until 1456, eleven years later.

During this period Malacca was the scene of an internal struggle for power. The infant Sri Paramesvara Deva Shah had been cared for by the aged Bendahara, who had died shortly after the murder of the child. His post had passed to his nephew Seriwa Raja, and on the success of Raja Kasim, he committed suicide. Raja Kasim was a Tamil, but Seriwa Raja was a Malay, and in the struggle that followed the Malays largely supported his son, Tun Perak, while the Tamils and others supported Raja Kasim, or Muzaffar Shah as he had become. What had been a religious difference, with Hindus yielding to Muslims, became a racial quarrel, with Tamils yielding to Malays, led by Tun Perak.

Tun Perak was perhaps the greatest man produced by the Malacca Sultanate. Previously Mandulika of Perak, he had distinguished himself against the Siamese in 1445–46, and in an attempt to heal the breach that was dividing his state Muzaffar Shah courageously replaced Tun Ali by Tun Perak as Bendahara, who then as tradition demanded, supplied his sister as bride to the Sultan. Both sections, Malay and Tamil Muslim, were thus brought into the government. Muzaffar Shah by this brave act of statecraft had united the country just in time, for in 1456 Siam attacked again, this time by sea. Tun Perak was the saviour of Malacca, as he defeated the Siamese in a fierce naval engagement off Batu Pahat, and pursued them as they fled through the Straits of Johore. Then for over forty years (1456–1498) Tun Perak ruled Malacca although he never became Sultan.

In 1459 Muzaffar Shah died. Tun Perak as Bendahara ensured that fighting was kept to a minimum, and placed on the throne a cousin of his, whom he married to one of his sisters. This man, Mansur Shah, reigned for nearly twenty years (1459-1477). He reigned, but without doubt Tun Perak ruled. He ruled and with the help of Hang Tuah, the Laksamana, he conquered.[17] Pahang, for long a dangerous tributary of Siam, was invaded and subdued in 1459, and a Malacca princeling installed. Islam followed in his wake, and moved with Tun Perak to revive the Muslims of Trengganu as the Siamese retreated north.

The expansion of Malacca and the official acceptance of Islam had begun. Soon Johore, Benkalis, the Carimon Islands, Bintang and Muar were made part of the growing Sultanate, and the territories were given as fiefs to the relatives of Tun Perak and the Sultan. The next step was to expand on the sea-ways. Malacca was dangerously dependent on Sumatra for food; so by 1477 this food supply was in safe Malacca hands. The river states of Kampar, Siak, Rokan and Indragiri were subdued by the Malacca war fleets, and in 1474 Kedah too, Malaya's one granary of importance, received a Muslim Sultan.

Mansur Shah died in 1477, but Tun Perak, who had organised his imperial conquests, and the great Laksamana, Hang Tuah, who had performed them, lived on. Tun Perak was the king-maker, and he produced another, a younger son of the dead Sultan named Ala'uddin, who reigned for eleven years (1477-1488).

Ala'uddin's eldest brother had figured in a disgraceful although typical episode in his youth, when in a fit of pique he had slain the son of Tun Perak for the unpardonable offence of accidentally knocking off his headdress while playing *sepak raga*. Tun Perak, exercising considerable restraint, had banished him to Pahang, and he had died there in 1475. The great Bendahara found it advisable to send after him, shortly after the accession of Ala'uddin, another brother who had been passed

[17] Hang Tuah is perhaps the most famous personality in the Malacca Sultanate. His biography has appeared in Malay and English, and a most successful film has been made of his life. See R. J. Wilkinson, (JMBRAS, vol. 13, pt. 2), pp. 41–43, and M. C. ff. Sheppard, *The Adventures of Hang Tuah* (Singapore, 1958).

over in the line of succession. He seized the opportunity to proclaim himself Sultan Mahmud Shah of Pahang, and to murder the governor of Trengganu for paying homage not to Pahang but to Malacca. With difficultly Tun Perak kept the peace between the brothers, restraining Ala'uddin from war but permitting Hang Tuah in retribution to stab a relative of the murderer in front of the Pahang Sultan.

After the expansionist days of Mansur Shah this period was one of consolidation. This was the peak, or rather the plateau, of the Malacca Sultanate. Various states were rebuked and some were punished. Hang Tuah was sent to Siak, for example, to deliver a royal reprimand to its ruler for not obtaining Malaccan sanctions for the death sentences, while a fleet from Aru was dispersed, but no further conquests were made. Politically then, Malacca was quiescent; but culturally this was a most active period, with grave, learned Sufi moving along the trade routes to form their groups and propagate their faith throughout South-East Asia, often just a decade or so ahead of the Christian missionaries.

At home, in Malacca, the bustle and efficiency was maintained with some effort. It needed the public intervention of Ala'uddin himself to correct the abuses in the all important Temenggong's department. The Temenggong was Mutahir, son of Tun Perak's sister, and his incompetency was an ominous pointer to the future, for subsequently he became Bendahara.

The story as handed down by the *Malay Annals* was that "thieves were rife in the city of Malaka and people were being robbed night after night. So distressed was Sultan Ala'uddin to hear of the depredations of these thieves that one night having dressed himself like a thief he went in disguise with Hang Isak and Hang Siak round the city to see what was going on. On reaching a certain spot the king came upon five thieves carrying a chest slung on a pole. He set upon them and the thieves took fright and bolted, all five of them, and they threw away the chest." Sultan Ala'uddin pursued the thieves and killed two of them before they escaped. The next morning, the Annals continue, Sultan Ala'uddin appeared in the audience hall and addressed the Temenggong in front of the assembled court. "Was there a guard last night?", he asked. When the Temenggong replied that there was, the Sultan said, "we hear that a man was killed on the hill, and another at the entrance to the bridge. Who was the man that killed the two men?" And when the Temenggong replied that he did not know, Sultan Ala'uddin remarked scornfully, "Your guard seems to be of little use; we hear that thieves are rampant in the city."

He then had the chest he had recovered the previous evening brought in, and made Hang Isak and Hang Siak recount all that had happened: "Whereupon", says the Annals, "the chiefs did obeisance to Sultan Ala'uddin with fear in their hearts and their heads bent low with shame." From then onwards the Temenggong kept efficient watch for thieves; for "that was how Sultan Ala'uddin ruled in Malaka."[18] Unfortunately he died in 1488, and the decline had begun.

In 1488 Tun Perak made sure that another child, his great nephew Mahmud Shah, was made Sultan. For a decade all was well. Tun Perak, now an old man, was content to keep what he had. The state ran on the momentum of the past, although receiving new additions to its polyglot population in a migration of Chams from Indo-China, people similar ethnologically to the Malays, who had been forced to flee from their ancient land on its fall to Annam.[19] In 1498 Tun Perak died, the greatest man of the Malacca Sultanate. His story, and that of Paramesvara covers a whole century.

On his death in 1498 the great Bendahara was succeeded by a brother, Tun Puteh. He led Malacca on a last revival of foreign conquests, in which Manjong, Bruas and Kelantan paid homage. Tun Puteh died in 1500. Mahmud, the Sultan, was a mere figurehead. After the usual intrigue and struggle for the almost sacred regalia, power passed to the Temenggong, Tun Mutahir, who was promoted Bendahara. He epitomised the late stage of

---

18 C. C. Brown, *The Malay Annals*. pp. 113–115.

19 G. Marrison has written a most interesting article on these people: *The Chams of Malacca* (JMBRAS, vol. XXIV, pt. 1, 1951). See also his *The Coming of Islam to the East Indies* in the same issue, and *Islam and the Church in Malaya* (The Muslim World, vol. XLXII, no. 4, October 1957).

the Sultanate, being arrogant and inefficient, more concerned with display and with spending the wealth of this trading centre than in developing it. A lack of an internal vitality becomes apparent, as in the later days of the Roman Empire; but the State holds together.

By this time, by the end of the fifteenth century, the political structure of the Malaccan State had taken on a clear shape. Let us examine that structure. The Malay State, from before the Indian came until long after the Englishman acquired control, was based on the river. In this respect Malacca was not characteristic, and in its basic trading function it resembles more the Rhio-Johore Bugis Empire of the late eighteenth century. The States over which it acquired sovereignty, however, Pahang and Perak for example, were river states *par excellence,* and the river was their main artery of life, the very reason for their existence, until well into this century.

In Malacca and in the various river states the head of the political structure was the Sultan. Indianised influence, exercised during the first millenium, had created the Sultan from the river chief, and had elevated him to a high and noble regality. But it had not removed the indigenous attitude of the Malays towards him, a democratic attitude best expressed in their partial retention of the primeval right of the elders of the tribe to elect a chief.

The Sultan was never sure that the man he nominated as successor, the Raja Muda, would be accepted. Throughout the Malacca century, and right up to the present, the stability of any Sultanate has been threatened by what some historians claim to be a fatal flaw in Malay political thinking, and what others claim to be merely ill-organized democracy, the constant struggle by the relatives of the ruler for the highest post, a struggle that often burst into open fighting when the Sultan died. As Winstedt says "clearly, the choice of a Malay ruler by his chiefs was not a mere matter of form. And the exercise of this choice is still valuable."[20]

The line of succession was perhaps the weakest link in the

[20] Sir R. Winstedt, *The Malays: a Cultural History* (London, 1953), p. 71.

Malay political structure. Nevertheless, this structure endured for many hundreds of years, and vestiges of it remain to this day. For example, a comparison of the officers of a modern Malay State with those mentioned in the descriptions of Malaccan political affairs in the *Malay Annals*[21] show many similarities, despite the four centuries that intervene between the two.

The Chief Minister of the Malacca Sultanate, and of Kedah, Perak and the other river states, was the *Bendahara,* an Indian Sanskrit title, as were most of the other political titles. He was both prime minister and commander-in-chief, and was not merely the chief executive officer of the State, the man responsible for seeing that the Sultan's orders were carried out, but also the possessor of considerable independent power. He could order executions, for example, without reference to the Sultan, and it was he who on the death of the Sultan took charge of the royal regalia and who, after an interregnum, often a fateful one, invited the heir to be installed. No wonder that many a Bendahara became Sultan himself.

Apart from these considerable powers, which were exercised with great success by Tun Perak, for example, it was his duty to provide the Sultan with both palace and bride, the latter coming from his own family; and to preside, as the chief dignitary, at all court conferences and ceremonies.

Chief of the great men beneath the Bendahara was the *Temenggong,* the chief of police. The possessor of an ancient, non-Indian title, he retained his powers through the centuries, as those necessary for a man to maintain peace and order. He built prisons and arrested criminals; his men in Malacca patrolled at night between the wooden stilted houses, those of the chiefs being surrounded by rattan fences, and instantly slew any prowler. In the market by the sea shore their duties, originally merely to keep the peace, were enlarged of necessity to take responsibility for the accuracy of the weights and measures used there, probably the most common cause for any shrill argument and subsequent disorder.

---

21 *The Malay Annals,* Translated by C. C. Brown (JMBRAS, vol. 25, pts. 2 & 3, 1952).

With the creation of a modern Malayan Navy the role, if not the title, of *Laksamana* has been revived. There were active Laksamanas or Admirals in the Malay States until the nineteenth century, men in charge of the navy, whose main duty was to defend the river from attack by sea. There has been so called piracy in Malaysian waters for thousands of years; it still exists today. At times, as with the Lanuns or Achinese, the pirates or invaders were stronger than the individual states, and it was the constant preoccupation of the Sultan and the Laksamana to find a site for defence, a capital, far enough up the river to escape these piratical depredations, but close enough to the mouth to secure tolls on the produce coming down. As a result State capitals (apart from Malacca, which was uniquely powerful), constantly shifted, and no Malay State today has a capital of any historical significance whatever.[22]

An office that is still functioning at the mouth of every Malay river is that of *Shahbandar,* or Harbour Master. He was the collector of tolls and customs charges, and the controller of shipping in the port. The title is a Persian word, but without doubt the responsibilities it represented were well understood before the Islamic traders from the Middle East first ran their dhows up the sandy beach at Malacca. In Malacca the traders became so numerous that the Bendahara appointed four Shahbanders, to attend to the four chief groups: those from China and the East, from West India (i.e. Gujeratis), from Java and the islands, and from South-east India (i.e. Tamils).

Two other officers that deserve mention are the *Penghulu Bendahari,* the chief secretary, as it were, of the Bendahara, who dealt with court correspondence, and had charge of the ruler's household slaves and revenue. The other was the *Mandulika,* or Governor of an isolated outpost. He possessed civil and criminal jurisdiction but sent annual tribute to the Sultan.

Under these great men were minor chiefs, but their titles and responsibilities have not been the subject of sustained study,

---

[22] Alor Star, the capital of Kedah, may be the exception. Despite occasional sackings, it has remained the administrative centre of the State, owing to its strategic position, since at least the seventeenth century.

and it is difficult if not impossible to conjecture with any degree of accuracy what they were. They could not have been important, for as Winstedt writes "there was no expenditure...on any of the ends of modern civilised government. The only civil servants were police and tax collectors...(and) the only departments of government from which the peasant derived any benefit for himself were the departments of religion and magic..."[23]

The history of the fifteenth century, the story of the Malacca Sultanate, is culled very largely from the *Malay Annals*. It constitutes almost our first piece of documentary written evidence of Malayan history. In many respects it is unsatisfactory evidence, for it abounds in legends and obvious fables; moreover it is disjointed and does not follow a chronological pattern. Nevertheless, insufficient though it is as a history, it is a useful source book for the political structure of the State, and in addition tucked away in its pages are many glimpses of Malay life as lived in the Malacca Sultanate, small vignettes of social history that create a fascinating picture.

There are the two delightful stories of the Malay fops for example, that still ring true over the years.

> Now whenever Sultan Mahmud Shah went out for pleasure in the royal barge, he would stop on his way and send for the Seriwa Raja to accompany him. And though he would wait at the Seriwa Raja's landing stage as long as it takes to cook pot after pot of rice, still the Seriwa Raja did not appear. For it was his habit, when a royal summons came, to go into his house and have a nap! Not till he was roused by the Raja's messenger would he get up, ease himself and have a bath. After his bath he would have a meal. After his meal he would don his sarong and he would undo it twelve or thirteen times until he had got it to his liking. Then would come the jacket and the head-cloth, and the process with the sarong would be repeated with them until they too were to his liking. With the scarf also the same thing would happen; it would be put on and then undone again fourteen or fifteen times until it was to his liking. After that he would get as far as the door of the house when he would go back to his wife and ask her to tell him if there

[23] *The Malays: a Cultural History*, pp. 77–79.

> was anything amiss with his clothes. If she said that there was something not yet altogether right, he would undo the offending thing and set it to rights. Then at last he would leave the house...

Both in this case, and in the following story, note how the supposedly downtrodden Malay wife ruled the roost, and how the husband turned to await her judgment. Note also the reference to the use of glass.

> Bendahara Sri Maharaja was endowed by nature with good looks and he was moreover a great dandy. He would change his clothes seven times a day; he had a thousand jackets of one sort or another; his headcloths stood ready tied on blocks, twenty or thirty of them in constant use; and he had a full-length looking-glass. When Bendahara Sri Maharaja was dressing, after he had put on sarong, jacket, cresses and scarf, he would ask his wife, "Which headcloth do you think would go best with this suit?" And the Bendahara Perempuan would say, "Such and such a headcloth would go best", and her advice would be taken by Bendahara Sri Maharaja.

Down through the centuries the Malay has played his version of football, *sepak raga.* It is the same today as in the days of the Malacca Sultanate; but what twentieth century Sultan can emulate the Raja of the Moluccas?

> He was an expert at Malay football (sepak raga) and the young nobles of Malaka played football with him, he being the leader in each game. When the ball came to him, he would kick it himself a hundred or even a hundred and fifty times before he passed it to someone else; and he would indicate to whomsoever he proposed to give the ball and then pass it without once making a mistake. Then he would sit down on a chair to rest and be fanned by men in pairs, while the young men went on playing. Then when he resumed playing and the ball came to him, the Raja of the Moluccas would kick it himself for as long as it takes to cook pot after pot of rice and the ball would stay up in the air until he wished to pass it to someone else: such was his skill at the game.

A story with a moral, advising us to attend closely to our own affairs, is the sad tale of the defeated and imprisoned Maharaja Sura.

> It happened one day, after Maharaja Sura had been imprisoned for some while, that the elephant Ya Kenyang was led past the prison-cage on his way down to the river to be bathed. Sri Maharaja Sura called him and when the elephant came up to him, he examined him and perceived that one of his nails was missing. And he said, "To think that after all these years this is the first time I have looked at my own elephant like this! No wonder I lost my country!"

There are many other small word pictures in the *Malay Annals* that portray that boisterous age far better than many a text book that concerns itself with the chronology of Sultans and the coming of the Portuguese. There are the descriptions of the ceremonial and etiquette at the court, the savagery and treachery of Hang Tuah and other warriors, the diplomatic exchanges of needles and sago with China, the arrogance of the visiting Muslim Sufis, and much else.[24] All this ends when:

> there came a ship of the Franks from Goa trading to Malaka: and the Franks perceived how prosperous and well populated the port was. The people of Malaka for their part came crowding to see what the Franks looked like; and they were all astonished and said "These are white Bengalis!" Around each Frank there would be a crowd of Malays, some of them twisting his beard, some taking off his hat, some grasping his hand.[25]

This was in 1509. The Portuguese, content no longer to buy from others and animated by visions of God, glory and gold, had come to the spice market. Tun Mutahir failed to welcome them as yet another contribution to his polyglot city, and tried by deceit to seize their ships. Nearly all escaped, carried the news to their Admiral in India, D'Albuquerque, and returned two years later.

Tun Mutahir, who had isolated himself by his capricious and arrogant conduct, had been killed in 1510 when attempting to overthrow the Sultan. Now Mahmud Shah was overthrown by the Portuguese. The Malays fought well, but many Javanese,

[24] Another contemporary account of Malacca is printed in vol. 1, no. 2, *Journal, South-East Asian History*, "A New Account of Malacca", by P. de Josselin de Jong (September, 1960).

[25] C. C. Brown, *The Malay Annals*, JMBRAS, vol. 26, pt. 2, 1952, p. 157.

Indians and Chinese in the town, that is the bulk of the merchants, were either apathetic or openly on the side of the Portuguese. Malacca's internal disunity was fatal for its defence, and the city was captured on 24th August 1511. Mahmud was forced to flee overland to Pahang, then to Johore, and finally to the island of Bintang. The Sultanate at Malacca had ended, and a new period had begun.

As with the downfall of all Empires, nationalistic historians find it easier to attribute the collapse to external foes, and to ignore internal weaknesses. Without doubt the Portuguese attack of 1511 was successful, and so the Malacca Sultanate collapsed; but if we are to learn anything from history we must remember the internal weaknesses, the illness of the body politic, that permitted this success. Glaring inadequacies had developed in Malacca that made it an easy prey. By 1500 the foreigners were already drifting away to places such as Acheh, Bantam, Patani and Brunei. With the Chinese in particular resorting to Patani, and the Indians to Acheh and Bantam, there are indications that Malacca had reached the summit of its power before the end of the fifteenth century. Its internal troubles would most probably have brought about a dismemberment of the Malacca Sultanate whether the Portuguese came or not.

The fifteenth century was a glorious page in Malayan history, when for once the peninsula was independent, and its capital was a world city, propagating Islam throughout the Archipelago. It deserves to be remembered; but let us also remember the causes of its collapse, and avoid the errors committed then.

3. ACHEH, THE MINANGKABAU AND THE BUGIS (1500-1800)

In nearly all the books on Malayan history so far written, the three centuries that the following chapter attempts to cover, the sixteenth, seventeenth and eighteenth, are divided neatly into two: the sixteenth century is dominated by the Portuguese, and the seventeenth and eighteenth by the Dutch. In the case of Malaya, (for this division of the centuries is applied generally to all South-East Asia), the dividing line is taken as 1641, when the Dutch drove out the Portuguese from Malacca.

This conception of the centuries is a basic historical mistake. Historical writing is perhaps less open to factual errors than many others, for the historian is trained to be accurate; but it is always prone to bias, and the bias in nearly all the earlier works on Malayan history is a European one. Nearly all the authors have been Europeans, brought up in the late nineteenth or early twentieth century historical attitude of surveying the world in a Europo-centric manner. The predominant theme in Asian history, (or African), is European expansion into that continent, Europeans in Asia, not Asia itself. This is out of date; but it has always been incorrect, and to think of the Malay Peninsula during these three centuries as experiencing a Portuguese and a Dutch period is to be very wrong. It is a one-sided point of view. Asia, not the European in Asia, must be our theme, which we must study from within, looking outwards. If that standpoint is appreciated, the Portuguese and Dutch will be seen to share the South-East Asian stage with others. Only in this way can a more balanced story be told.

Long before the sixteenth century the Malay Peninsula had become one of the cross roads of Asia. This was made clear in our study of Malacca in the previous chapter.[1] The Malay States

[1] An impression of the bustling activity of this Asian centre is given in a Portuguese account of the trade, commerce and character of the Malays, and of Malacca, and much else: J.V. Mill's translation in JMBRAS,

were constantly exposed to outside influences and pressures. The cause of these influences and pressures was usually commerce, inter-Asian commerce constantly exceeding the ancient but minute trade with Europe. The Portuguese pressure, when it came, was therefore but one of many, and even so not the most important. Neither on the seas, as an external influence, nor on the land, as an internal pressure, did it ever affect Malaya very much. Indeed it was not until the late nineteenth century that the Malay Peninsula was affected internally by Europeans. Until then it was the influence of other Asians: Indians, Achinese, Minangkabau, Chinese and Bugis in particular, that was far more significant. Each had far greater internal effect than the few sea-bound Portuguese or Dutch. The sixteenth century is properly the Achinese century in Malayan history, not the Portuguese.

The fall of Malacca to the Portuguese in 1511 has often been claimed as the end of Muslim trade, and as the cause for the collapse of the Malacca Sultanate. This is indicative of the attitude that attaches an excessive importance to the Portuguese, and neither claim can be justified. The Malacca Sultanate although declining before 1511, survived its loss of a capital, and continued to exist aggressively in Johore. The Portuguese contributed to its diminution of power, but only as one of many other factors, while the inter-continental and inter-Asian Muslim trade was not cut off and ended by the few fidalgos and the few small ships a year of trade they secured at Malacca. It was dispersed and diverted, by the Muslim and Chinese traders intensifying their preference for four new emporia, because even before 1511 it seems as if they had begun to move to Acheh in north Sumatra, facing India; to Bantam in Java hard by the short Sunda Straits; to Patani, on the northeast coast of Malaya; and to Brunei in northwest Borneo. The Portuguese were able to exercise only a very vague control over the Asia-Europe trade, and they themselves secured only a trifling portion of it. They were a few infidel voyagers in a Muslim sea, and although their achievement in reaching Asia after a century of endeavour was

Vol. 8 (1930) of *The Description of Malacca, Meridional India and Cathay*, by the Portuguese Eredia, written in A.D. 1613.

a brilliant feat of national effort, and all honour to them, they did not influence Asia very much; rather the contrary: Asia influenced them.[2]

A Portuguese squadron under Diego Lopes de Sequeira had arrived at Malacca in August 1509; it had received an unfriendly reception, and this in turn led to a punitive expedition from Goa by the Viceroy, the Supreme Commander in the Eastern Waters, Alfonso d'Albuquerque. After an unsuccessful attack in July 1511, the Portuguese finally captured the city on the 10th August 1511. The Sultan, Mahmud, retreated upriver, then across to Pahang, going up the same trans-peninsular route that was mentioned earlier, and then finally, in early 1513, to Bintang in the Rhio Archipelago.[3]

Although driven from his capital Sultan Mahmud still retained considerable power,[4] for although the Sultan of Kampar went over to the Portuguese, Lingga, Indragiri, Siak and Aru still paid homage to him, and on the peninsula itself Muar, Rembau, Sungei Ujong, Klang, Manjong and Bruas, Pahang, Trengganu and what is now Johore recognized him as overlord. The Portuguese, by seizing Malacca, had captured perhaps a square mile of land, and had secured the possession of a fine bay; but this by itself was by no means a decisive victory, and more often than not the Portuguese at Malacca were on the defensive in the century that followed, firstly against Mahmud and his successor, then against Acheh, and finally against the Dutch. Certainly they never dominated the waters of South-East Asia;

---

[2] For an examination of the Portuguese voyagers, and the manner of their living, see I. A. MacGregor, *The Portuguese in Malaya* (JMBRAS, vol. 28, pt. II, May, 1955); and R. Cardon, *Portuguese Malacca* (JMBRAS, vol. 12, pt. II, August, 1934).

[3] We have reached the stage in Malaya's history where we can call to our aid, and enjoy, the contemporary account. For this, see W. Birch (ed.), *The Commentaries of the great D'Albuquerque* (London, for the Hakluyt Society, 1927).

[4] For example, he attacked Malacca in 1518–19 with such strength that when relief came from Goa the Portuguese had been reduced to 30 men. For eye witness accounts of the numerous attacks on Malacca, see R. Cardon, *Old Malacca—Tranqueira and Gajah Berang* (JMBRAS, vol. 21, pt. I, 1948).

in fact with one post in Malacca, isolated and remote from Goa in India, and another post 2,000 tenuous miles away in the Moluccas, and numerous enemies in between and all about, they were in no position ever to do so.

The one permanent result of the Portuguese conquest of Malacca was the establishment of the royal houses of the two new sultanates of Johore and Perak. Mahmud died in 1528 after two powerful but unsuccessful attacks on Malacca and was succeeded after the usual palace intrigue by his youngest son, Ala'uddin. He married a daughter of the Sultan of Pahang, and in 1530 he established his capital up the Johore River, moving from place to place, until he became firmly established and grew in strength at Johore Lama, from 1540 onwards.[5]

This river, flowing powerfully southwards into the Johore Straits that run between Singapore and the mainland, was well placed for an independent existence. Contact could be maintained with Sumatran allies, as well as with Pahang, while the Portuguese men-of-war were too few to restrict contacts between Ala'uddin and his elder brother, Muzaffar, who had established himself as the first sultan of Perak. Johore, Pahang and Perak combined against the Portuguese, provoking two raids by the Portuguese up the Johore River in 1535 and in 1536. However, Ala'uddin had realised the impossibility of recapturing Malacca, and was inclined to accept the status quo and to establish friendly relations with the little band of Europeans, particularly as a new danger had arisen.[6]

For in North Sumatra an ambitious power was emerging: Acheh. This state had been created by Ali Mughayat Shah in the first few decades of the sixteenth century. Before his death in 1530 he had united by force and fanaticism the small river states of Pedie, Daya and Pasai. For long a centre for Muslim

[5] For this, and subsequent capitals of Johore, and their history, see the modestly written but detailed account in C. R. Gibson Hill, *Johore Lama and other ancient sites* (JMBRAS, vol. 28, pt. II, May 1955).

[6] For a detailed examination of the Johore Sultanate at this time, and its relations with the Portuguese and Achinese, see I. A. Macgegor, *Johore Lama in the Sixteenth Century* (JMBRAS, vol. 28, pt. II, May, 1955).

learning, Acheh attracted to its river mouth, a convenient assembly point before the dangerous ocean passage to India and to West Asia, many of the Muslim traders from India or Bagdad who formerly had traded at Malacca. Free of the vexatious exactions of Malacca, Acheh grew in strength, and began extending its control down the Sumatran coast. This brought it into conflict both with the Portuguese, who secured much of their pepper trade from here, and with Johore, which still held suzerainty over the south Sumatran rivers.

This clash of interests between Acheh and the Malayan powers, Johore and Malacca—for so the Portuguese must be regarded—was brought into the open when the aggressive Ala'uddin Riayat Shah al Kahar ascended the throne in 1537. In that same year his Achinese war fleet sailed into Malacca Bay, and the Portuguese were forced on to the defensive, sheltering behind the stone walls of their massive fort.

Twenty years before, the Portuguese, few in number, had captured Malacca by their greater valour and purpose. This advantage they no longer possessed. The Achinese were just as determined as their rivals, and there was no apathy with them. Cannon were used by all warring parties, and although kris and sword were the usual personal weapons, shoulder arms were also used. In equipment neither was supreme. The Portuguese were saved in 1537 and again in 1539 and 1547, when Ald'uddin Riayat attempted a night landing, by the thick stone walls of their fort, and by the trained discipline of their small force. This alone distinguished them from their rivals. Nevertheless, although their power was not extinguished, it remained ineffective.

The forces of Acheh, failing to capture Malacca in 1537, sailed south down the Sumatran coast and in 1539 made an attack on Aru (Deli), an important pepper island and a subsidiary member of the Johore Sultanate. Johore endeavoured to retaliate, and a family alliance of Johore, Perak and Siak sailed forth in 1540 to recapture the island. In an effort to prevent any further defection the queen of the island was married to the Johore Sultan.

A great man, Francis Xavier—perhaps the most famous Christian ever to visit East Asia—now moves into this scene, for he landed at this time at Malacca. A Spaniard, who with Ignatius Loyola had founded the Jesuit Society in 1539, he had come out to work among the Portuguese. He spent several years in Goa, and then moved on to Malacca, landing there in 1545. In 1546 he visited the Spice Islands, but he continued to work in the pauper hospital in Malacca, amid much opposition, for a further two years (1547–48). Among much good work, he founded here in 1548 a school, St. Paul's, linked to the St. Paul's Church built on the hill by d'Albuquerque in 1511, at the same time as he ringed it with his mighty fort, *A Famosa*. Eredia was one of the famous men educated at this school.

Francis Xavier sailed to Japan in August 1549, but he visited Malacca again in 1552. He died in December of that year, off the coast of China. The body of this outstanding and venerated missionary was brought back to Goa, where it was laid to rest.

The fort of Malacca, inside which he worked, of which now only a few remnants remain, has been described, along with much else of great interest, by Barretto de Resende. It contained, so he said,

> Six bastions, including the breastwork, each one called by the name written on it. All the walls have parapets, and each bastion occupies a space of twenty paces...The circumference of the whole wall is five hundred and twelve paces...The bastions contain forty-one pieces of artillery, of twelve to forty-four pounds iron shot. All are of bronze, with the exception of nine iron pieces, and there is sufficient powder and ammunition in His Majesty's magazines for their supply.[7]

Most of the accounts of Malacca of this period deal at length with this great fort. While obviously it was the outstanding point of interest (and its ruins are still very impressive today), it was nevertheless more a symbol of defence than attack. The

---

[7] W. G. Maxwell (ed.), *Barretto de Resende's Account of Malacca* (JMBRAS, vol. 60, December 1911). This account of Malacca written perhaps in 1638 is only part of a lengthy manuscript now in the British Museum. It seems a great pity that it has not yet attracted the attention of the Hakluyt Society, or some other body interested in securing its publication.

massive stone walls erected by d'Albuquerque sheltered the Portuguese and provided them with a defence. There is no mention of a sally port in these walls, and in fact, Malacca under the Portuguese and also under the Dutch later, was a solid rallying ground, a place largely of consolidation and defence. It was not the Portuguese who attacked and few chroniclers refer to their ships, the essential for aggressive moves.[8] In this period the dominating aggressors, whether potential or actual, were the Achinese, and to their activities we must now return.

In 1564, by-passing much raided Malacca, Acheh struck again at Johore. A powerful fleet swept up the Johore River, with tide and wind behind it. Johore Lama was savagely destroyed and the entire royal family, caught completely unawares, was carried captive back to Acheh. Here the old Sultan was put to death, but his son, Radin Bahir, was sent back to rule Johore as Muzaffar Shah.

Docile and obliging though he had been in Achinese hands, once back in Johore he ventured defiance and in 1568 he sent forces to help withstand an attack on the Portuguese, for Malacca was useful as a buffer between Acheh and Johore. Acheh endeavoured to re-establish authority, burning along the Johore River in 1570 and forcing the Sultan to move his capital up-stream to Seluyut. In 1570 Muzaffar Shah, the last representative of the old Malacca-Johore Sultans, was poisoned, and a usurper from Pahang, Ali Jala Abdul-Jalil, succeeded to the throne. He continued his state's opposition to Acheh.[9]

Affairs went differently for Perak, the other member of the family alliance, for it lacked the presence between it and Acheh of any resilient buffer, such as Johore possessed in Malacca. In 1575 its great river valley was devastated, and its Sultan and his children carried off to Acheh. Here they attracted

---

[8] For a scholarly account of an exception to this, see I. A. Macgregor, *A Sea Fight near Singapore in the 1570's* (JMBRAS, vol. 29, pt. III, August 1956).

[9] Johore-Achinese relations are examined by Sir R. Winstedt, *A History of Johore* (JMBRAS, vol. 10, pt. III, 1932); See also I. A. Macgregor, *Johore Lama in the Sixteenth Century* (JMBRAS, vol. 28, pt. 2, 1955).

the attention of the Sultan. One of the sons was elevated to the Achinese throne as Mansur Shah, while a younger brother was sent back to rule Perak. Thus was Achinese control established over Perak, a control that lasted for half a century, while its influence, political and economic, continued for several centuries.

As a result of these successes over Johore and Perak, Acheh now dominated the field. It was barred from further conquests by the alliance of Johore and Malacca, Portuguese and Malays both fighting for their vital interests against a common foe. In 1582 the Portuguese were able to beat off another Achinese attack on Johore, but this so reduced the external threat that Johore, feeling that Acheh need no longer be feared, then fell on Malacca. In retaliation the Portuguese sacked Johore Lama in 1587, and the capital shifted to Batu Sawar. Thus the interminable three-sided struggle dragged on to the end of the century, Acheh fighting Johore, Johore sometimes with Malacca (as in 1582), and sometimes against her (as in 1586). It was not European against Asian, or Muslim against Christian: the reasons for the warfare were attempts at political domination and economic control. It was a struggle without a real victor, for none of the powers had an absolute supremacy. They all had the same weapons and the effectiveness of their ships was about equal. The Portuguese, besieged by the Achinese in 1568, 1570 and 1573, and by Johore in 1586, were far fewer, but a little better disciplined; otherwise there was little difference: Acheh always the menace and the aggressor.

The struggle continued into the seventeenth century, with an additional complication: the Dutch arrived. Back in Europe the Dutch had been the main distributors to the western countries on the Atlantic or North Seas of the spices brought back to Lisbon from the East by the Portuguese. The Dutch were very conveniently placed to penetrate from their North Sea coast to the German, Belgian and French lands that radiated behind them. But towards the end of the sixteenth century their economic links with Portugal were snapped by Philip II, the Emperor of Spain, who in 1580 secured control of Portugal, and who a few years before had controlled Holland. He brought pressure to bear on the rebellious Dutch in 1594 by closing the port of

Lisbon to them. By doing so he hoped to weaken their opposition to Spanish rule. They retaliated by sailing direct to South-East Asia.

The various commercial interests of the Dutch were grouped into a United East India Company, under the control of the government, and in 1596 the Company succeeded in gaining the necessary base it needed for the spice trade in Bantam in Java. Shortly after its establishment the British arrived too, in 1602, similarly formed into an East India Company, although not under government control. This Company also built warehouses and established a small base at Bantam, alongside the Dutch. The British displayed a very minor interest in the spiceless Malay Peninsula, and although a factory was established in 1612 at Patani, and there was intermittent trade for some time with Kedah,[10] its efforts were puny. One ship a year or perhaps two or three at most sailed back to London from South-East Asia, and the East India Company's appearance on the scene had very little significance. By the end of the century the Company had transferred its activities to India. The Dutch, however, were in greater strength, and their dislike for the Portuguese is the one constant factor in Malayan history for forty years. But these two European powers rather cancelled out each other's efforts: they merely complicated, and in no appreciable way altered, the confused Malayan scene.

The Dutch tried to overthrow the Portuguese, and they looked to Johore and Acheh for effective support. But these two Malayan powers were old enemies. How could they consider combining to attack what was becoming an insignificant third? They never did; and the Dutch never secured much support from them individually either. In 1606 the Sultan of Johore signed a treaty with the Dutch Company, and assisted it in an attack on Malacca. But he soon discovered that the Dutch wanted Malacca for themselves, and that in any case their military strength was quite inconsiderable, and of little help to him. When they failed

---

[10] See R. Winstedt, *Notes on the History of Kedah* (JMBRAS, vol. 141, pt. III, December 1936), which gives an account of one of these seventeenth century private traders, a Mr. Lock.

to grant him support against Acheh (which had by now the lion's share of the Indian trade), and Patani (which had the China trade), his assistance slackened, and following their unsuccessful attack on Malacca in 1606, which was dispersed by a Portuguese fleet, the Sultan lost all interest in them.

The Dutch then turned to Acheh, signing a treaty with them in 1607, and immediately the Portuguese from Malacca sent ambassadors round to Johore in an effort to redress the balance. With the Dutch refusing to assist the Sultan, yet trying to secure a site for a fort, Malacca and Johore concluded an amicable treaty in 1610, and the Portuguese were free to face Acheh and the Dutch.

The Europeans, never predominant, became rather the junior partners in the Acheh-Johore rivalry. Dutch interests were concentrated on the Spice Islands far to the southeast, and on its factory established at Batavia in 1619. The British had retreated to India. The Portuguese at Malacca, at times less than two hundred fidalgos, were a spent force. But not so Acheh, and the first half of the seventeenth century is its grand period of expansion.

In 1607 Iskander Muda became Sultan, and soon the war fleets were assembling. Five years later the old subject of contention over which Johore and Acheh had quarrelled before, Aru felt the full force of Achinese imperial might. He sailed on and across to the Malay Peninsula, to sweep through the Johore Straits and up to Batu Sawar. It was burnt and plundered in June 1613, and again the Sultan of Johore and his family were carried off to Acheh.[11] Charged specifically with attacking the old bastions of Malacca, a younger son was sent back to the throne of Johore, but as he made no effort to do so a punitive expedition destroyed his capital again in 1615. The Sultan, Abdullah Maayat Shah fled from the Achinese krises, pursued all the way from Bintang to Lingga to the Tambelan Island, where he sought refuge and died in 1623.

---

[11] This is described in a contemporary record, *P. Floris, His Voyage to the East Indies in the Globe, 1611*–1615, ed. by W. Moreland for the Hakluyt Society (London 1934).

Acheh then turned on Pahang. It was completely crushed in 1617, Achinese prahus carrying destruction far up its rivers. The Pahang royal family were once more carried as hostages back to Acheh, where one of them, Iskander Thani, subsequently (in 1636) was to assume the throne.[12] Kedah, until now left alone as falling within the Siamese sphere, was attacked and defeated in 1619, and its Sultan too was taken as hostage over to Acheh. Finally Perak, which had shown signs of independent activity, was re-conquered in 1620. Acheh, ruthless, vigorous and ambitious, had thus secured an unquestioned suzerainty over the Malay Peninsula. This rule was maintained unchallenged until Iskander's death in 1636, and although weakened during the rule of Iskander Thani (Johore attacked Pahang for example in 1638–39, and allied itself to the Dutch in 1640), it did not end until after his death in 1641, and the beginning of a long line of queens. Until then Acheh had been the dominant power, the whirlwind of the peninsula, and to think of this as the 'Portuguese Period' is fanciful, for these hundred years (1540–1640) were Acheh's greatest century.

Dutch power in the eastern archipelago, unlike their influence in the Straits of Malacca, had grown steadily during this time. Although its main interests remained focussed on the Spice Islands and later on Java itself, the geographical position and the economic importance of the Malacca Straits insisted that, when the Dutch had strength enough, they should endeavour to establish their control there. In addition to these motives, which have influenced all South-East Asian invaders throughout history, the Dutch were also led to intrigue, ally and fight in Malayan waters by their antipathy to the Portuguese. These factors combined to make a European clash inevitable.

By 1633 the Dutch Company felt powerful enough to blockade Malacca. Year after year the few Portuguese waited in vain for a relieving fleet, and failed to secure Johore or Achinese allies. By 1640, when the Dutch began to attack in strength, they were in desperate plight, and although for some months

[12] For this see W. Linehan, *A History of Pahang* (JMBRAS, vol. 14, pt. II, June 1936).

they withstood the siege in which Johore participated with the Dutch, they finally surrendered in 1641.[13] By this time the town had lost much of its importance. Its main arteries of trade had long since left it. The spice trade, the China trade, the India trade—all had been diverted elsewhere. The Dutch therefore acquired a moribund town into which they now endeavoured to breathe new life.

The Dutch attempted to revive the town in three major moves: by forcing all passing vessels into Malacca; by treaties with Acheh, that divided the tin production of Acheh's subordinate, Perak, a major centre for Indian traders; and by treaties with the other tin producing states of the peninsula.

They had come to meddle in Malayan waters mainly because of the increased trade in tin, and their efforts were aimed very largely at funnelling it into Malacca. Their efforts failed. The Dutch acquired by right of conquest the former Portuguese suzerainty over neighbouring Naning, and from here and from Rembau, a vassal of Johore, a thin trickle of tin resulted. However, armed intervention was necessary in 1646 and in 1678–80 to ensure even that trade, while no practical success whatever was achieved with the tin states further afield—states that were trading actively with private British merchants in India.

A treaty was signed with Kedah in 1642, which promised to exclude non-Dutch ships, and to send half the country's tin to Malacca. This was a dead letter. The Dutch spent the remainder of the century attempting an intermittent blockade of Kedah in an unavailing effort to enforce it, and to keep out the Indian and English merchants. Ujong Salang, (Phuket), the tin island to the north, signed a similar treaty in 1643, which it treated in as cavalier a manner as did Kedah. The Dutch managed only slightly better in Perak, managing, through the good offices of Acheh, to secure a tin-monopoly treaty in 1650, by which it shared with Acheh the export of that commodity. This treaty had to be

---

[13] For a detailed and contemporary account of this, see Mac Hocobian's translation of P. A. Leupe, *The Siege and Capture of Malacca from the Portuguese in 1640–1641* (JMBRAS, vol. 14, pt. I, January 1936).

renewed in 1659, by which time the ability of Acheh to control Perak had long vanished, moreover the Dutch had to maintain a fort on the Dindings until 1690 in order to exercise even a nominal enforcement of their treaty. Thus it is thought that the Dutch did not secure much tin even from Perak.[14] Malacca was run on the cheap, always at a loss, and it remained an expensive outpost of the Company, beaten by the free flow of trade all round it. To the Portuguese Malacca had been one of their few but one of their main bases in South-East Asia, and when they went they left both a faith and a community. To the Dutch Malacca became very quickly an almost redundant port, on the flank and not at the heart of their operations, and the impression they made was negligible.[15]

With the decline of Achinese power, and the non-belligerent presence of the Dutch, the Johore Empire began to grow again. Efforts were made to recover the Sumatran rivers that once had been in the old Malacca Sultanate. In 1662 Siak's independent life was replaced by direct control from Johore, the Sultan sending a Shahbandar to rule for him. By 1669 Indragiri too had accepted a Johorese governor; while after an intermittent thirteen year war of raids and ambuscades (1666–1679), Jambi was also brought within the fold.

In the face of this expansion the Dutch traders at Malacca endeavoured to secure some economic advantage. The Dutch throughout the archipelago were completely opposed to territorial gains, for they were there merely for trade, as shown most obviously in the humiliating conditions they accepted in Japan. In 1689 they managed to sign with Sultan Mahmud of Johore yet another of the monopoly treaties that characterised their economic policy. It was no more effective, because the Dutch lacked the means of enforcing it, than any of the others; in any case, it was completely ignored after the murder of Mahmud in 1699,

---

[14] For this see W. E. Maxwell, *The Dutch in Perak* (JMBRAS, vol. 10, 1882), and R. Winstedt and R. J. Wilkinson, *A History of Perak* (JMBRAS, vol. 12, pt. I, June 1934).

[15] For an account of late seventeenth century Malacca, see C. O. Blagden, *Report of Governor Balthasar Bort on Malacca, 1678* (JMBRAS, vol. 1, August 1927).

and the ascent to the throne of one of his murderers, Abdul Jalil Rayat Shah.

Achinese domination, which had terrorised Malayan waters for a tumultuous century, had ended in 1640, and despite the Johore war with Jambi the following fifty years were comparatively quiet.[16] The Dutch burghers busied themselves with their books, while junks and prahus of all descriptions sailed with their cargoes, either bulky goods of low price, such as rice or coffee, or small collections of costly ware, such as silks and porcelain, across the waters of South-East Asia, to India or to China. It was a comparatively peaceful time, the second half of the seventeenth century, and the virtual vacuum of power in the Straits of Malacca permitted the migration from west Sumatra of the Minangkabau people, an Asian movement of considerable importance to the Malay Peninsula.

These sturdy and well organized peasants were great agriculturalists. In search of land they moved down the rivers to the Straits of Malacca and crossed to the Malay Peninsula. They had long sent their padi to Malacca; now they settled on the lands behind it, cleared and cultivated it, and grew their padi there. Good peasants make good fighters, as Rome and Russia have shown, and the Minangkabau were sturdy warriors. They brought a stiffening, a discipline, that was unknown in south Malaya before. They brought also a unique matrilineal outlook. Property, the line of descent, much authority—all descended through the female, not the male. An embryonic democracy too was in their possession, their political unit being a small group with a leader freely elected. This combination of assets produced a number of small states behind Malacca, populated with hard working men and independent minded women: characteristics that have lasted in the Negri Sembilan (The Nine States) to this very day.

---

[16] For three most interesting descriptions of the Malay Peninsula at that time, see J. J. Sheehan, *Three Seventeenth Century Visitors to the Malay Peninsula* (JMBRAS, vol. 12, pt. II, August 1934). See also the fascinating and detailed account of Acheh and Kedah in T. Bowrey, *The Countries Round the Bay of Bengal, 1669–1679* (London, for the Hakluyt Society 1905).

2

The eighteenth century in Malayan history is the Bugis century. As with the Achinese and the Minangkabau, the history of these Asian people has been neglected, while the study of the relatively unimportant Portuguese, and the Dutch, has been pursued with comparative vigour. We still wait for detailed historical studies of these races, but enough is known at least of the Bugis to trace the outline of their century of conquest, and to see their influence on the Malaya of today.

The Bugis have been compared to the Norsemen in Europe. Both were adventurers who forsook their largely agricultural pursuits and migrated on the seas, to raid, pillage and settle other countries. Like the Norsemen, the Bugis were possessed of organizing powers, and a strength of character greater than their neighbours. In Europe the well governed state of Normandy arose as the Norseman's contribution to Atlantic civilization, and perhaps Selangor and Johore are the best examples of Bugis occupation and organization in South-East Asia. There is probably scarcely a member of the Johore Civil Service today who has not Bugis blood in his veins, and Johore's independent and competent progress in the nineteenth and twentieth centuries is largely explainable by the migrations of the eighteenth.

There had been Bugis traders in Malayan waters for centuries. In the sixteenth century Malacca knew well their *pajalas,* their large prahus with a distinctive tripod mast and a deep oblong sail, and it was from Malacca, a few short years before the Portuguese came, that they took Islam back to their home ports in the Gulf of Boni, in the South Celebes. The Bugis copied their craft from the Portuguese, and the *pajala* was adapted into the famous *palari,* which at first glance, as it sails into sight today in the waters of Singapore, is remarkably like a miniature seventeenth century fore and aft rigged galleon.

In this craft those Bugis that took to the sea continued to trade on the waters of South-East Asia, and probably beyond, for there are many reasons for believing that they voyaged south to the tropical coast of northern Australia as well, there to gather sandalwood and *bêche de mer* for the Chinese market. Macassar, although not originally within the highly argumentative and aggressively independent Bugis states of the south Celebes, became their main assembly port. It grew throughout the seventeenth century, not merely because of its geographical advantages, centrally situated as it was in the Java Sea, but also by reason of a certain lack of regulation and taxation, of freedom from restriction on trade, characteristic advantages which later helped an infant Singapore.

To and from Macassar and the ports in the Gulf of Boni the regular monsoons aided the arrival, through the centuries, of the junks, prahus, *paduakans, palaris,* and other island craft, and many European vessels as well; until in 1667 the Dutch stamped on this independent trade; and under the leadership of Speelman, they captured the port although it took four months of desperate fighting. So the old grey fort, built about 1634 with Portuguese help, became Fort Rotterdam for the next three hundred years. It still stands today, wide and massive, close to the prahu harbour and the busy ocean wharves, guarding the manuscript and palm leaf material which records the past of the Bugis and is now mouldering away almost untouched within its walls.

The fall of Macassar was not of itself decisive enough to drive the Bugis to migrate, yet it is from this period, the later stages of the seventeenth century, that the Bugis abandoned trading to establish permanent settlements overseas. They were not organised as colonists in the European fashion, for they did not set forth as Pilgrim Fathers (although religious intolerance may have played some part in their movement), but they were firm of purpose and united in their brotherhood. They helped each other, as bands of *condottieri,* in a kind of loose association of adventurers; and although as with the Vikings, there was little communication with, and no control from, their homeland, the Bugis colonial experiment enjoyed remarkable success. They made themselves felt in Kedah, Perak and Pahang. In Selangor a Bugis became Sultan, and in Johore they eventually obtained complete control.

Their intervention here dates from early in the eighteenth century. In 1699 the mad Sultan Mahmud was murdered at Kota Tinggi, and in the disturbed conditions that followed a young Minangkabau of Siak, Rajah Kechil (rumoured to be Mahmud's son), determined to capture the throne. He turned to a Bugis leader, already famous—Daing Parani—little realising that he was mounting a tiger. With his help Johore Lama was attacked in 1717, the Sultan was reduced to his previous rank of Bendahara, and Raja Kechil, based at Rhio, assumed the throne of Johore and Pahang with the title of Sultan Abdul Jalil Rahmat Shah.[17]

There was immediate trouble. Daing Parani and his chain-armour clad followers felt that their reward was inadequate. They joined forces with the deposed Sultan, and although the latter was killed at the mouth of the Pahang River, his son, Sulaiman, carried on the fight, driving Raja Kechil back to Siak. Once Sulaiman had been proclaimed Sultan, an alliance between him and Daing Parani was confirmed by a treaty in 1722, by which the chief adventurers were elevated to the highest ranks of the nobility.

This early success is characteristic of Bugis political infiltration on the Malay Peninsula in the eighteenth century. They did not overthrow established states so much as infiltrate and occupy the great positions of power, usually by alliance with a discontented and rebellious section of the state.

Not merely in Johore were the Bugis becoming the power behind the throne. Their success was most marked in Selangor where they secured the throne itself.[18] Before the middle of the seventeenth century this small river had offered a livelihood to very few; it had possibilities in trade, however, particularly in tin, and as early as 1681 a Bugis settlement at the river mouth was troubling Kedah to its north. By 1700 a Bugis Yamtuan was

---

[17] For this dark page in Malay History see R. J. Wilkinson, *Mahmud II and Abdul Jalil III* A.D. *1687–1720* (JMBRAS, vol. 9, pt. 1, 1931); also A. Hamilton, *A New Account of the East Indies* (London, 1727).

[18] For the Bugis colonisation of Selangor see R. Winstedt, *A History of Selangor* (JMBRAS, vol. 12, pt. 3, October 1934); and see also his *History of Negri Sembilan* in the same issue of the Journal.

reigning there over a population growing under his firm protection. Selangor joined with the Bugis-dominated Johore to fight the irrepressable Raja Kechil supported by the Minangkabau. He had attempted to place an ally on the throne of Kedah in 1723; invited to participate by a rival candidate, the Bugis, despite the death of Daing Parani, drove him back to Siak, installing meanwhile their own supporter. They interfered in the dynastic squabbles of Perak as well, led by Daing Parani's brother, Daing Merewah and his nephew Raja Luma.[19] After driving away a Minangkabau fleet commanded by Raja Kechil's son, Raja Luma proclaimed himself on the death of his father, Daing Chelak, in 1745, the first Sultan of Selangor.

This usurpation of power by the Bugis was bitterly resented by the Malays, particularly in Johore, while the Dutch regarded the turmoil in the tin states with horror. These two joined forces when the Bugis under-king of Johore, Daing Chelak, died in 1745. Sulaiman, the Sultan, was able to make a bid for his lost freedom. He acted swiftly. In the hope of securing Dutch help against his enemies, he ceded Siak (over which he had lost all authority to Raja Kechil), and promised tin-monopoly rights to the Dutch in Selangor, Klang and Linggi. He gave away something which was not his, and to no advantage; nor did it benefit the Dutch.

By 1748 the Bugis had re-established their position in Johore. Daing Camboja had become the new under-king, with headquarters, characteristically enough, in Rhio, for the Bugis were far more interested in trade than were the Malays, and Rhio was far more suitable for this purpose than any Johore River. In Siak the position was chaotic. Raja Kechil had become insane and his sons were fighting over the succession. Wisely the Dutch refrained for some years from interfering, but in 1755 they decided to secure what had been pledged them—Siak, whose tin and pepper might revive Malacca. In the following year Sulaiman signed another treaty, again pledging the tin monopoly of Selangor, Klang and Linggi in return for assistance in removing his Bugis lodgers. It took the Dutch six hard years to conquer

---

[19] The son of yet another of Daing Parani's brothers (there were five of them), Daing Chelak.

Siak. Sulaiman never lost his Bugis, and shortly after his death in 1760 Daing Camboja was firmly established in Rhio as the actual ruler of Johore. For his deputy he appointed Raja Haji, brother of the Sultan of Selangor. A succession of Sultans passed above them, but these two and their supporters held on very securely to the reins of government.

Meanwhile the Bugis were assuming power elsewhere in the peninsula, and the Dutch saw their tin contracts vanishing and felt their sea authority, which restrained breaches of their policy of trade monopoly, sorely weakened. They had become a nominal factor, as the Bugis again expanded the empire of Johore. In 1770, Raja Haji with Daing Camboja secure in Rhio, sailed with his brother, the Sultan of Selangor, up the Perak River. He ignored the Dutch garrison at the mouth, persuaded the local ruler to marry his daughter to the Sultan of Selangor, and with that alliance secured he fell on Kedah. Here he burnt Alor Star, the capital, to the ground, in retribution for a non-payment of debts. Earlier he had forced Jambi and Indragiri to renew their old allegiance to Johore, which thus controlled the Straits again. On the death of Daing Camboja in 1777, he secured the succession as the new under-king of Johore. He was the heart, the driving power of late eighteenth century Bugis imperialism. His biography has yet to be written.

With nearly all of the Malay Peninsula subjected to the rule of the Bugis, there remained only two centres of resistance. In Malacca the impoverished and neglected Dutch sat quiet amongst their ledgers, and wished that trouble would pass them by too,[20] while in the pocket states of what is now the Negri Sembilan the Minangkabau stoutly refused to pay tribute, and in 1770 sent to Sumatra for a prince of their own to lead them. The Bugis carefully avoided this threat and left it alone. But Malacca was too tempting altogether, and Raja Haji gathered all his forces for its destruction.

By this time, the late eighteenth century, Daing Camboja and

---

20 For impressions of this, see B. Harrison, *Malacca in the Eighteenth Century; two Dutch Governors' Reports* (JMBRAS, vol. 27, pt. 1, May 1954).

Raja Haji after him had increased not merely the political strength of the Rhio-Johore Empire but also its commercial wealth. Basically the Bugis were traders, and when Penang came to be founded in 1786 the Bugis fleet was always welcomed, for it was recognised that they came to trade, not to pirate; and this attitude of mind is reflected in the growth of the Rhio Archipelago as a leading trading centre in the latter decades of the eighteenth century.[21]

The constant accounts of fighting that fill the last few pages may have been misleading if it is not realized that along with the Bugis battles there went also consolidation and development. While Raja Haji was sacking Alor Star, Daing Camboja was keeping healthy the heart of the enterprise, the Rhio Archipelago. During the latter half of the century the capital, Rhio itself, almost as convenient as Singapore was to become, became even more popular.

Rhio was independent of the Dutch, and it practised a liberality of trade and a freedom from exactions that was in complete contrast to all the ports dominated by them. It was honest, peaceful, and the centre of an important tin area; and because tin was the commodity above all demanded by the European traders, who, in ever increasing numbers, infiltrated into South-East Asia in the late eighteenth century, Rhio boomed. By the imposition of restrictions and controls in Java, Sumatra and elsewhere the Dutch sought to stop all local trade with this flourishing port. It was in vain: their efforts merely assisted its growth. It became the great bazaar of the islands, the great centre of independent life.

By the 1780's the decisive challenge between Bugis and Dutch could no longer be avoided. Raja Haji was raiding off Malacca, Rhio was far surpassing it as a trading centre, and all the Dutch interests west of Java were imperilled. The Dutch attacked Rhio in 1782, but their forces were beaten off, while their base,

---

[21] This is illustrated clearly by B. Harrison, *Trade in the Straits of Malacca in 1785; a memorandum by P. G. de Bruijn, Governor of Malacca* (JMBRAS, vol. 26, pt. 1, July 1953). Several contemporary books also enlarge upon Bugis trade based solidly at Rhio. See for example T. Forrest, *A Voyage from Calcutta...* (London 1792).

Malacca, was attacked by Bugis from Selangor. Raja Haji followed his Dutch opponents back to their exposed base, and with his brother, the Sultan of Selangor, he laid siege to the ancient fortress. The Selangorese had devastated the northern shore before he arrived, and were based solidly on Tanjong Kling. He landed with his warriors at Telok Ketapang, five miles south, and together they closed their ring.

Malacca, shrunken, aged and almost abandoned by the Dutch, was near its end. Dutch power was negligible, and in fact the whole Dutch system of government in the East, a Company that had lasted for nearly two hundred years, seemed rotten through and through. It lacked the stimulus that sustained the British in India, a vigorous and profitable trade with China, and it was like a sinking ship, kept afloat only by its pumps.

In Europe, Holland had been involved in a war with Britain, 1780–1784. Through that war the Dutch had lost all their ancient outposts in India, and they had seen their isolated possessions on the west coast of Sumatra, the Indian Ocean side, taken over without difficulty by the British East India Company. Furthermore the Dutch had been saved from more critical, perhaps fatal, injury in South-East Asia only by the brilliance of De Suffren, the naval commander of their ally, France, who had kept the British at bay in Indian waters.[22]

Most alarmed at this, the Dutch made a national effort to revive their fortunes, and after peace was declared they despatched to the east a strong force of ships and men, commanded by Van Braam. It was planned that this fleet not only would re-establish Dutch authority among the Spice Islands, where lay the main Dutch interest, but would also bolster Dutch control in Java itself. However the fleet arrived at Batavia just as Malacca was about to fall. The fleet hurriedly sailed there, poured reinforcements into the fort, and in June 1784 launched a counter-attack on the exultant Bugis. Amid fierce fighting outside the walls the Bugis broke and fled, leaving Raja Haji dead by the river bank. Hot on their heels Van Braam pursued them north out of

---

[22] For a general outline of this see V. Harlow, *The Founding of the Second British Empire, 1763–1793* (London 1952).

Selangor, and then smashed into Rhio in October 1784.

Here the Sultan, Mahmud, was freed of his Bugis Yamtuan Muda, (under-king), but was forced to accept a Dutch Resident instead, whose duty from 1785 onwards was to control trade. Control meant death, and Rhio rapidly lost its commercial importance. In 1795, however, revolutionary France in Europe overran Holland, while four years later the Company collapsed completely and the Dutch outpost on Rhio was removed. The Bugis again assumed their paramount position. By 1803 there was a Bugis under-king again, Raja Ali; but by 1819, when the British came south from Penang to find a base more convenient for trade, there was a Bugis Temenggong, Daing Abdul Rahman, in Singapore. His grandson, the great Abu Bakar, was the first new Sultan of Johore. Even today the governing and ruling class of Johore is separate and can be distinguished from other classes for although the old structure of government is much the same as before the Bugis came, with local chiefs and headmen, the infiltration of the Bugis into this structure is complete, and their values have been adopted. The same picture is seen in Selangor. The Bugis element in Malaya is one of the more important elements in its national character, and its story and their character warrant detailed study.

3

In some respects the end of this chapter leaves us almost where we began. When we survey the centuries of barren strife, how has the peninsula advanced? What has changed? If we regard the history of the Malay Peninsula during the three centuries which we have covered here, and search for developments that can help us explain the Malaya of today, there is a considerable amount of sterile detail that can be passed over. In this characteristic its history is similar to that of South-East Asia as a whole, where, by and large, the political, social and economic standards of life remain unchanged. In all these big divisions of human endeavour, although there is much to record (particularly perhaps in political history and in the details of trade), there is little in any development of these three centuries that can be claimed to be pertinent today, while there is little that we know of Islam that warrants recording.

The changes in the Malay Peninsula that are of relevance, and which help explain how the Malaya of today came to be fashioned, are not these elements therefore, but the ethnological changes. We need attribute little importance to any political, or social, or economic development during these three centuries, and we should consider the religious impact as yet unproven; but we should note above all the big migrations that occurred. The movement of Minangkabau introduced a matrilineal element into the peninsula which has still a considerable impact, felt in many ways; while the Bugis migration is of even more relevance, and of far more importance than the many wars and the almost senseless struggle between Achinese, Malay, Portuguese and Dutch.

While, however, these are the main developments within the peninsula, we should remember also the great events which were occurring outside; in particular in Europe where the current of history was beginning a steady flow whose influence was to affect Malaya profoundly.

At much the same time as d'Albuquerque reached Malacca, that is at the beginning of the sixteenth century, the modern age was beginning in Europe. From the sixteenth century onwards we can see in Western Europe a conscious rivalry between national states. There comes the disruption of the western Christian Church, with the Reformation, and the establishment of lay, non-secular, national authority. Both the new world, in America, and the old world, in the culture of ancient Hellas, are discovered, the latter leading to the brilliant awakening and flowering of men's minds with the Renaissance; and this in turn is part of, and encourages, as a fundamental attitude all over western Europe, a widespread, increasing demand for a critical, scientific treatment of data.

This rejection of dogma, this challenge to accepted modes of thought, this insistence upon enquiry and rational belief, is perhaps the outstanding factor of the modern world. In all countries that share this modern world, to think, and not to accept, is the common outlook on life. It is fundamental to progress. It had not been a common characteristic of the European, any more than of the Asian, before the sixteenth century, for dogma held too powerful a hold. By the nineteenth century progress itself had become an unchallenged dogma, as the countries of the world came ever closer together.

With the lay scholar supreme (a victory achieved not without a long struggle), with the acceptance of a critical, enquiring attitude as necessary for the progress of the national state, the development, consolidation and expansion of the west European state occurs. So while we peer closely at the Malay Peninsula, do not forget that behind our back western Europe is transforming itself. As Johore struggles with Acheh, a Reformation and a Renaissance are occurring. Men are learning to think for themselves, with happiness and progress as their goals. An economic revolution begins, with commerce, king for centuries, yielding in the eighteenth century to industry, while in England in particular, democracy begins to alter the structure of the national state.

These social, economic and political developments reached out from Europe in the nineteenth century to Malaya and to the rest of the world. Of them all, perhaps the most fundamental development of these centuries which came to Malaya was the attitude of mind. It was not until the twentieth century that the peninsula accepted this outlook, and became curious, to enquire after new knowledge, and to challenge the validity of old thought; and it was just in time: for a country without curiosity is like a man without initiative doomed to drift at the mercy of others. The danger is that in becoming critical and sceptical, a man may lose his faith, and doubt the religion of his elders; and to have no God is to have no hope. Religion and reason struggle for reconciliation in Malaya even today.

4. PENANG AND THE NORTH

The founding of Penang in 1786 is often taken to be the beginning of modern Malaya, and since this marks the beginning of British rule over the country there is some element of truth in the assumption. Nevertheless the British on Penang exerted an influence which was for some time no greater than that of the Portuguese in Malacca, and far less than the Bugis in Rhio. Thus we should not attribute to 1786 the much greater British influence that came later.

In some respects Penang is more important not as a beginning but as an end. It is an end, or nearly the end, to the British search for a trading base in South-East Asia. Many earlier historians thought that Penang was founded for reasons of naval strategy.[1] The British in India, so the reasoning ran, needed a naval base from which to guard the Bay of Bengal during the north-east monsoon, when the waters off Madras were untenable, and the Navy sailed away from the dangerous lee shore. This was often the time when the French appeared, and, as under De Suffren in 1782 and 1783, they menaced the British trading posts in India, unprotected while their fleet lay in Bombay. To counter this threat, so many have said, Penang was founded.

All this is based on an error of fact. Penang was never a naval base. The Navy found existing bases sufficient, firstly the large and well equipped port of Bombay, and then later Trincomali in Ceylon.[2] It never established itself in Penang, and played no part whatever in its settlement. The only power that ever used Penang as a base was Germany, in the Pacific War. German and Japanese submarines operating from Penang in 1943 sank more ships and a greater tonnage—over half a million tons—than all the submarines sailing from all the bases along the coastline of Europe from Norway to France in the same year. More

---

[1] For example, see D. G. E. Hall, in his *History of South-East Asia*, p. 421.

[2] For a short, unhappy, period (1789–1796), it established a base also on the Andaman Islands.

damage was inflicted on the allies in this year from this one port than from all the English channel ports combined.[3] But it was never a British naval base, and it was founded purely for commercial reasons.

What were these commercial reasons? To find the answer we must look not at the Malay Peninsula but elsewhere, at the general position of the British in Asia. During the eighteenth century two great developments had occurred among the British in the East. Firstly in India the Company had been transformed, owing to the victories of Clive and Hastings, from a commercial enterprise, making modest profits on the borders of collapsing Empires, to a great political power, heavily embroiled in the government of millions of people. Secondly, Britain had developed a large tea trade with China. The consumption of this beverage became a national custom in Great Britain during the later half of the eighteenth century, and the demand for tea steadily rose, particularly after Pitt passed his Commutation Act in 1784, whereby the duty payable on its import dropped from over 100% to 12½%. The East India Company, with a monopoly over its importation and sale, reaped an ever larger profit. This profit was vital for its existence, as it had failed to adjust its management in India from a commercial concern to a political state, and it was heavily in debt, just as were the Dutch in Java. Government is very costly, and the East India Company was able to govern in India only by its profits from China.[4]

All efforts were directed towards increasing the China trade. There was, unfortunately, a stumbling block. Although the British wanted all the tea they could secure, there was scarcely anything they offered in exchange desired by the Chinese. It became more and more obvious that China was almost self-sufficient. The Chinese had hardly any need for any outside commodity whatever. If the British wanted tea, they had to pay for it very largely with silver bullion, valuable all round the world, and,

---

[3] This little known use of Penang is described in S. E. Morrison, *The United States Navy in World War II* (Oxford, 1956), vol. X, p. 274.

[4] This is brought out clearly in C. N. Parkinson, *Trade in the Eastern Seas 1793–1813* (Cambridge, 1937). See also H. Furber, *John Company at Work* (Harvard, 1948).

unfortunately for Britain, acquired mainly from Spain. When Spain was at peace with Britain the silver from its great mines in Spanish America could be acquired through trade and then sent to Canton; but when it was at war with Britain, as for example when it participated with France, 1779–1785, in the American War of Independence the supply of silver dried up, the China trade suffered, and the government of India became most precarious.

This silver bullion was however supplemented in Canton by a few other commodities desired by the Chinese. Chief of these were tin and pepper. They were acquired in South-East Asia not by the Company itself, for it had become too large and too heavy for the adroitness needed for private trade, but by the efforts of the country traders, in the many ships that sailed to Rhio. They were captained by such men as Bowley, Lock, Forest and Light, to name a few, and it was to improve their operations, to give them a bazaar more stable than their shifting decks, that a search was made for a secure base where they could acquire commodities that would assist the China trade.

In their search for such a base the British were hampered by the presence of their old rivals, the Dutch. Although they did not physically occupy much of Malaysia, the Dutch had secured a considerable control of the region. This they had done, by treaties with numerous local rulers, re-inforced by a navy that endeavoured to maintain as a Dutch preserve the lands on the shore of the Java Sea. The control was such that the intrusion of another power in the eighteenth century would have precipitated international repercussions of a gravity far exceeding any possible advantage likely to be gained.

Under normal circumstances Holland provided a very useful buffer in Europe against France. Britain had no quarrel with the Dutch and as Holland abstained from interference in India an invasion of its sphere of interest in South-East Asia would have been tantamount to an act of aggression, unthinkable alike to the authorities in India and to Parliament in London. So Britain's policy was to look for a base in an area that fulfilled three specific requirements; it had to be remote from the Dutch; it had to assist the trade with China; and thirdly it had to be safe in an area that was politically stable.

These three qualifications, of remoteness, utility and stability, eliminated most of the mainland of South-East Asia. Ava, Siam and Cochin China were each ruled by a sovereign hostile to Europeans, arrogant in attitude and unstable in manner. Each was constantly warring with its neighbour; and besides, there was no tin. No base could thus be considered there. Nor could it be found in the far south-east of the islands, for although it could claim remoteness from the Dutch it was remote also from everywhere else, particularly China; and again there was neither tin nor pepper. The centre of the area, the Java Sea, was Dutch, and there remained but two areas in South-East Asia, the northwest, (that is north Sumatra and the north of the Malay Peninsula), and the north-east, (North Borneo), where the qualities necessary for success might exist. These were therefore examined.

They were examined in the first instance by Madras. After Clive the British in India held three great areas, designated Presidencies. There was Bengal, where lay the wealth, which was the heart of India, controlled after 1765 by Fort William at Calcutta. On the west coast the original seventeenth century foothold at Surat had given way to Bombay, where the finest naval base in Asia maintained the Company's fleet; and on the east coast there was Fort St. George, or Madras, the centre of the private or country traders, who looked seaward to South-East Asia for sustenance.

In London in 1767 the decisive step was taken. The Company, faced with the increasing drain of silver to China, and frustratingly aware of the profits that could be gained if it could only increase its tea sales, decided that steps had to be taken by India to acquire more goods for sale in China. More funds had to be made available in Canton for tea purchases. From this decision stems all that follows.[5]

A few years after this decision was taken, but while it was

---

[5] The vital importance of the country trade in maintaining Britain's position in the East is shown clearly by M. Greenberg, *British Trade and the Opening of China 1800–1824* (Cambridge, 1952).

still unimplemented, London learned with surprise that a group of private traders, Messrs. Jourdain, Sullivan and De Silva of Madras, had established a trading base at Acheh, in north Sumatra, where they were dealing extensively in pepper. The Madras officials, aware of the 1767 decision, decided to intervene, and when the private traders informed them that they had established another agency in Kedah, in the north of the Malay Peninsula, the Madras officials decided to take over this base as well. Accordingly the Company in 1772 sent two young favourites (Desvoeux to Acheh and Monckton to Kedah) to legalise and then to assume control over these two private trading centres, both of which it decided would assist the China market. In both enterprises it failed dismally. In each case the local representative of the Madras association, Harrop in Acheh and Francis Light in Kedah, was treated with scant respect by the uninformed Company official, and his advice was ignored. In each case the local ruler was antagonised by the unimaginative and heavy handed Company approach, and in the face of much hostility the missions were withdrawn by early 1773.[6]

So much for the north-west. It had been tried and found wanting. There remained the north-east, the North Borneo region. Could a trading base be established there? This area had an outstanding advocate, Alexander Dalrymple, a prominent Company official from Madras, skilled in cartography and experienced in South-East Asian waters. He had long been recommending such a base, particularly in reference to the uninhabitated island of Balambangan, off the North Borneo coast, which he had secured for the Company in 1764. When the Company decided in 1767 to move into South-East Asia his was the only plan before it, and it was accepted. A base would be established there. Numerous arguments with Dalrymple delayed the expedition, however, and it was not until 1773, a little later than the Madras missions to Acheh and Kedah, that a settlement without Dalrymple was made on Balambangan.

---

[6] This episode is treated briefly by H. Dodwell, *The Nabobs of Madras* (London, 1926), and in rather more detail by A. Wright and T. H. Reid, *The Malay Peninsula* (London, 1912).

It was in vain. Balambangan was a green desert. No trade came there, no town grew up, and in 1775 it was over-run by Suluk pirates and burnt to the ground.[7]

In that year, 1775, Hastings was appointed Governor-General of India. Faced with the rapidly rising tea trade, and the even more desperate search for funds with which to finance it, he launched several expeditions in search of a useful base. Despite his drive, he was quite unsuccessful, and his efforts assisted the China trade in no way whatever.

In 1778 he sent an expedition to Cochin China, but it failed. An attempt to create a favourable balance of trade with China through Tibet collapsed; while a further visit to Acheh, in 1784, was ruined by the anarchic condition of the State.

In 1782 Forrest, an experienced ship's captain, was sent to the Moluccas, and although he cautiously kept away from this wild area, where Bugis bands clashed impartially with one another and with the Dutch, he did secure, on his way back, the offer of a base in the Rhio Archipelago, just south of the site of present day Singapore, and in the heart of the actively trading, independent, Bugis empire. Hastings deliberated and decided to accept the opportunity despite the challenge it constituted to the Dutch. Forrest was sent back in 1784, with orders to establish a base there; but again Hastings was foiled. Swift intervention by the Dutch War of 1780–1786, had deprived the Bugis of their independent status, and Forrest was too late.

In Calcutta at this time was the trader Francis Light. He had left Kedah, and was one of a number of Eurasian and European traders based on Phuket, or Junk Ceylon, an island rich in tin that lay off the Kra Peninsula. He and his friend James Scott recommended that the Company establish a post there. The officials in Calcutta considered the idea, but in 1785 it was overrun by the Burmese and savagely mauled in one of their constant struggles with the Siamese. Hastings lost interest:

[7] Dalrymple, who failed to secure this expedition, failed also to lead the Royal Society's expedition to the South Seas. Selected originally, he quarrelled with the Society as he had with the Company, and the command passed to a Lieutenant James Cook, R. N., who went on to a brilliant career of discovery in the Antipodes.

the Company wanted no base in a cockpit of war. There remained only the alternative suggestion of Light, the uninhabitated island of Penang, offered to the Company by the Sultan of Kedah. After the departure of Hastings, Light, brought into the service of the Company and leading a small force as Superintendent of the settlement, landed on the island on 17th July 1786. The long search had ended.[8] A new town had begun.

Trading vessels began calling at Penang as soon as the settlement was established. Within the space of a year the register of prahus, junks, snows and East Indiamen conformed to a pattern of trade that has remained constant ever since. There were the big ships from India, waiting to unload piece goods and opium, while jostling all round these solitary monsters, like chickens round a squatting hen, were the diminutive vessels both from the mainland near by, from north Malaya and south Siam. These were trans-shipping their small cargoes of tin and Straits Produce, as it came to be called: the edible birds' nests, rattans, damar and other produce of the jungle, and from Acheh and north Sumatra opposite, with cargoes generally of pepper. This circle of trade has remained for a hundred and seventy years the regular stand-by of Penang: it is still its main field of interest today.

It was a circle of trade that played an ever decreasing role in the Company's affairs in China, and the irony of the long search for a commercial base in South-East Asia is that by the time it succeeded, when Penang was established, the search was found unnecessary. The country traders had found a substitute for tin and pepper, and in opium they had discovered the answer to all their problems. Opium, easy to grow and to ship from India, and yielding greater profits in China, was replacing the illusive South-East Asian commodities in Canton by the nineteenth century. By the 1830's, China, instead of receiving, was paying out large quantities of silver for the privilege of smoking

---

[8] In H. P. Clodd, *Malaya's First British Pioneer* (London, 1955), we have one of the few biographies of a Malayan personality. Although more material has come to light since this was published, it is still a most interesting account of Francis Light and the early years of Penang.

opium.[9] The balance of trade became ever more favourable to the Company as opium came on to the market in steadily increasing quantities. On the other hand there was a gradually decreasing need for an intermediate base in South-East Asia, and although Penang, and later, Singapore, throve on their own particular circles of trade, and remained useful as entrepôt ports, the replacement of tin by opium explains why they remained isolated outposts. With tin no longer desired there was no Malayan counterpart to the gradual British occupation of India. The Malay states remain Malay States. It is not until the Suez Canal was opened bringing these states hard against a vast and unprotected trade route, that they were regarded seriously, and any annexation of the hinterland of Penang and Singapore was considered.

From 1787 until the founding of Singapore in 1819, over thirty years later, the Bugis traders from Rhio and the Celebes broke annually into Penang's circle of trade, to exchange their gold, sarongs and Straits Produce for piece goods and opium. They were a welcome sight, for they came to trade, not raid, and from them it is thought that Francis Light borrowed their idea of a free port. Until crushed by the Dutch in 1667 the Bugis port of Macassar had been one with only inconsequential levies or tariffs. Goods could be imported and exported virtually free. This was in direct contrast to the Malay practice, where at the fickle whim of a ruler, random and extortionate taxes were exacted from any visiting ship. The Dutch too had a long list of taxes and various controls, which at least were standardised and known; but all these restricted trade. Light cut through all this nonsense, and in 1786 proclaimed a port free of all charges, open to all the world. Like Macassar a hundred years earlier, or Rhio a mere decade before, the effect was magnetic. The small craft that had been sailing to half a dozen ports before were now drawn to Penang, while a steady migration of settlers began.

In an effort to supplement this trade, and to provide a revenue that would make the island self-sufficient, Light encouraged

---

[9] This is shown most clearly in the Opium Appendix in Greenberg, British Trade and the Opening of China 1800–1824, pp. 220–1.

the clearing of the jungle covered island and actively assisted the Malay, Chinese, Indian and European pioneers who introduced the planting of various spices. In the early days land could be had for nothing, and a nice confusion was created by Light's liberality; but it led to the spread of pepper and clove estates all down the eastern side of the mountainous island, where stretched a plain some five miles wide. By the 1810's and 1820's stately homes, linked to bustling Georgetown by shady avenues, stood serenely amid acres of crops.[10] Their export however, never provided more than a minute portion of the revenue necessary for the cost of government, and Light and his successors relied far more on what was a traditional mode of revenue raising in South-East Asia: the taxing of the pleasures of the Chinese.

This was done by 'farming', that is by selling to the highest bidder the right to run a gambling den, or the sole right to retail opium, or tobacco, or pork. These so-called farmers provided their own supernumerary staff to ensure that their privileges were maintained, and did everything possible to see that they made a profit from their position. This farming system, which did away with the government's need for a large staff, and which provided it cheaply with a sizeable revenue, lasted throughout the nineteenth century, and for over a hundred years the opium farm gave the administration by far its largest single item of revenue. The opium farmer was also almost invariably the leader of the dominant Secret Society, by which alone he enforced his monopolistic rights.

Penang has often been described as a failure, in that India was forced from the beginning to make good the deficit caused by the local government's inability to secure funds sufficient to pay for the annually recurrent costs of administration. But historians who take this deficit as proof of a failure have been misled by peering too closely at government reports to the exclusion of many other factors. Government is not the totality of life, and

---

[10] For a contemporary description of Penang, compare E. Trapaud, *A Short Account of The Prince of Wales Island* (London, 1788) with J. Wathen, *Journal of a Voyage in 1811 and 1812 to Madras and China* (London, 1814); see also F. G. Stevens, *A Contribution to the early history of Prince of Wales Island* (JMBRAS, vol. 7, 1929).

although the government never made the profit, nor the Navy the use, that the Company expected of Penang, yet trade from the very beginning was attracted to Georgetown, its business enterprises expanded steadily, and its private citizens continued to increase. These inhabitants reflected in their racial structure the new Malaya, the Malaya of today. Malays, Chinese, Indians, Eurasians and Europeans all mixed and worked together as the first streets of the new town took shape, and as the canvas tents of the soldiers on the point were replaced first by wooden huts and then by brick buildings. Long before the first brick was laid, Penang was a success, and it is still a success after the last wooden hut has long since vanished from the town.

Malaya lacks social historians. It would be interesting to have a detailed examination of the way of life, the modes of dress, and the manners and customs of the peninsula in past centuries. How lived the people that drifted past the fort in Georgetown, a hundred and fifty years ago? On reading the early records of Penang what is perhaps most surprising is to discover that possibly the greatest change that has come in 150 years has been that of the social status of the average European.[11] Today nearly all Europeans in Malaya are largely middle class people. They do not work with their hands in shops or in fields, nor are they aristocrats living on landed wealth. Most of them hold positions of varying responsibility in British firms and banks. In 1800 this was not so. There were two European merchants then in Penang, James Scott and the American Samuel Tufts; the remainder were tavern keepers, blacksmiths, coopers, caulkers, carpenters, clerks and boat builders. There was no British money supporting large firms, and in Penang in 1800 the British were very largely working class people.

If the position of the European has changed, there are some aspects of early Penang that have a very contemporary ring indeed.

---

[11] For the social historian the most interesting of these early records is the newspaper, *The Prince of Wales Island Gazette, 1805–1827*, which has many revealing paragraphs.

The only resemblance to a theatrical representation among the recreations of the Malays is a raree or puppet show, the only difference being that in a puppet show the figures are seen and in this their shadows are. It is called *Wyang Kulit* or leather puppets. It is exhibited in a rough shed which has a flooring raised about three or four feet from the ground; the building is enclosed on three sides, the front alone being open. Across this opening a white sheet is stretched on which the shadows of the puppets are thrown and seen through by the audience; the latter sit or stand in the open air.

The show seems to be of Hindu origin; it is probably obtained from Java. The figures, bearing strong resemblances to the representations of Hindu gods and goddesses, are made of buffalo hide, and the arms alone are movable. The figures are perforated to represent the eyes, shape of the dress, etc. At the back of the shed, concealed by the sheet, sit the musicians who keep up an incessant din on drums and cymbals. . . . Also a show called *Myong* is exhibited by men and boys, the latter disguise themselves as women so successfully that Malay youths have been known to fall in love with them, forsake their kampongs and wander for days in the train of the actors. The Myong appears to be of Siamese origin, none but natives of Siam engage in it. . . .[12]

The Chinese were soon the most numerous of the peoples of Penang. Already their most distinctive social organization had been noticed. Light wrote in 1794, "They are a valuable acquisition, but speaking a language which no other people understand they are able to form parties and combinations in the most secret manner against any regulations of government which they disapprove."[13] Secret societies are with us still. So too is the Chinese theatre, described by Wathen in 1814 thus:

The stage was elevated from the ground to the height of one storey in the front of the house, and was covered with green baize. A curtain was drawn across, and anon the play commenced. The performers, dressed in the most extravagant costume, came forth from behind the curtain, and proceeded to declaim with great vehemence, accompanied with panto-mimic gestures. . . .

---

[12] J. D. Vaughan, '*Notes on the Malays of Pinang and Province Wellesley*', *Logan's Journal*, vol. (N.S.) II, 1857. See p. 110, note 12.

[13] *S. S. Factory Records*, vol. 2, Light to Bengal, 25th January 1794.

> I confess that I could not make out the story, or discover the plot. The audience in general however, were delighted beyond measure with the exhibition.

As Captain Lennon wrote in 1796 of a similar play, "I doubt not if people of the same rank of life in a distant country town in England, were to attempt getting up a play, they could hardly outdo the exhibition of the sort we saw at Penang, on a stage erected for the purpose in the streets."[14]

Although inexperienced of government, Light was given no instructions on administration. On the contrary; India requested him, Light, the ship's captain, to supply it with his ideas on how it should be policed and administered. At the same time authority necessary for the administration of justice was denied him. He was refused authority over Europeans, he was unable to try acts for which the penalty was death, and he was not empowered to try acts of piracy. This crippling restriction on his power, and the lack of directions given him, are in great contrast to the powers and authority vested in another ship's captain whom Britain chose in 1788, less than two years after Penang was established, to form another settlement. Captain Phillip founded Sydney with complete and absolute powers, and with the most detailed of instructions. But when it founded Penang the East India Company had thought of it merely as a more stable country ship, as an anchored emporium, and it had not visualised the problems that quickly came crowding in. Light had to face them alone.[15]

In his efforts at administering justice he was assisted by his sturdy common sense. As soon as Georgetown came to assume its polygot appearance he followed Dutch and Malay practice and appointed 'Capitans' of the various communities, with authority to hear all breaches of the peace and petty crimes

---

14 W. C. Lennon, *Journal of a Voyage through the Straits of Malacca* (JMBRAS, vol. 7, 1881).

15 Two historians who deal with this are A. Aspinall in *Cornwallis in Bengal* (Manchester, 1931), where a lengthy appendix treats Penang, 1786–1793; and H. Dodwell in 'The Straits Settlements, 1815–1863', a chapter in vol. 2 of *The Cambridge History of the British Empire* (Cambridge, 1940).

committed by their community. Where people of more than one race were involved, or where it was a major crime, then it was he who tried it. He used his own rough and ready sense of justice in deciding the case, and although he kept asking the authorities in India for a written code of laws, they kept replying that they could not do so without authority from England. As that authority never came, Light was left to make the best of it he could.

Francis Light died in 1794, having just secured the promise of an assistant. No real improvement in administration occurred, however, until 1800, by which time Penang was sixteen years old, lusty and healthy, and obviously in need of parental aid if it was not to become a juvenile delinquent. It was decided at last to establish the administration of justice on a regular footing. A Lieutenant Governor replaced the Superintendent, and a trained lawyer, John Dickens, was appointed as Magistrate. The Lieutenant-Governor was instructed by Wellesley, the Governor-General, to draw up a report suggesting the best means of administering justice to the various races and religions on the island, and although the Lieutenant-Governor (Sir George Leith) and the Magistrate are noted for their quarrels, nevertheless they co-operated in this. Soon their draft regulations began to move backwards and forwards between Penang and Calcutta like some stately man-of-war as it was discussed, amended and revised at either end.

By 1805 these regulations had become embodied in a draft Code, which had not, however, been finally accepted in London. London, however, had completed plans for expanding the administration of the island. It decided after all that Penang would be the site for a naval base. Instead of the few hard working officials, a whole flock of fresh young men, including a Mr. Thomas Stamford Raffles, descended on the town.[16] From the Bombay dockyard came Philip Dundas (nephew of the great Lord Melville, Pitt's right hand man), to be the new head, while the adminis-

[16] For Raffles in Penang, see C. R. Wurtzburg, *Raffles and the Eastern Isles* (London, 1954). Here is collected a rough treasure trove of original materials relating to this period.

tration was elevated to the status of a Presidency, to rank at one stroke of the pen with Calcutta, Bombay and Madras. There were now plenty of men to administer justice (particularly as no naval base was built),[17] and there only remained the question of what justice to administer. The answer to this came in 1808.

The Charter of Justice, which Penang was called on to administer in that year, brought to the Malay Peninsula perhaps England's greatest gift, a legacy destined to remain long after its political control has vanished. British law, with its concepts of individual freedom, of a man being innocent unless proven guilty, of habeas corpus, of equality before that law, no matter how high or low a person be in the state, of the right of appeal even to the Ruler—all this and more came to Penang with this Code, together with the organisation of its administration, of courts separate from the government, and a Judge to superintend that administration. The actual laws were those evolved by the British in India, and well they have served, amenable to modification, but ever the protector of the community and the basis of justice. British law now rules in parts of the world from whence its administrators have long since departed. That law came to Malaya in May 1808.

Penang was never a particularly lawless place. The most difficult people were the South Indians. In 1810, for example, a typical year, 8,800 summons were issued for offences to be heard in the courts, and over 7,600 were in the Tamil language. A little under 400 were issued in Malay, 300 in Chinese and 400 in English. Over four-fifths of the arguments in court were conducted in Tamil. Yet the South Indian numbers were no larger than the Malay, less than a third of the population. Many a twentieth century magistrate must be very thankful that politics and trade unions now provide alternative platforms for this popular pastime of oratory and debate.

Light and his successors had suffered constantly from a shortage of instructions. One order, however, constantly repeated, had a greater effect than the lack of many others. This was the rule, first given to him when he sailed for Penang in 1786, which

[17] For an explanation of this, see the following chapter, pp. 94–5.

had been incorporated by William Pitt in his India Act when he re-organised the East India Company in 1784, placing it more directly under state control. The Company was never to be a party to any measures likely to involve it in border warfare. There were to be no political engagements with neighbouring States. It was to remain aloof, neutral it would be termed today, at all times. The East India Company had become embroiled in India through disregarding this; and if it was to make a trading profit out of its Eastern venture it must not meddle in Malayan politics. Defensive alliances, treaties of friendship, call them what you will, Pitt had said, they inevitably brought the same result: the expensive despatch of British troops to quell some disturbance over the frontier. The Directors adopted an attitude of *laissez-faire* for nearly a hundred years; and Malaya was left to suffer its troubles and misfortunes alone.

The most dangerous if not the most immediate of these troubles was Siam, the menace of the north. The main reason why the Sultan of Kedah ceded Penang in 1786 had been the hope of securing British protection from his enemies. To the south Selangor was hostile; to the north lay Siam. In a rather vague way the Sultan was a vassal of Siam, and Kedah had been in the habit for perhaps several centuries of sending a token tribute, a small golden tree, or *bunga'mas*. Any supervision that Siam maintained over this extremity of its empire was exercised by Ligor, the southern state entrusted with this task. Following the victories of Burma in the eighteenth century, however, and its climax in 1767 by the destruction of Ayuthia, the Siamese capital, Kedah stopped even the sending of the *bunga'mas*. It had been virtually independent for a century or more as Siam declined; and now it did not maintain even this gesture. In 1782, however, Bangkok was founded, and a new Siam began to rise from ashes. The Sultan of Kedah, in his conversations with Light, always referred to the Bugis in Selangor as his enemies, and his father had been sheltering in Perlis from them when Monckton called; but without doubt he was casting glances over his shoulder at Siam as well.

The Sultan of Kedah was apprehensive of Selangor and Siam and envious of Penang. Across the water he could see it, rapidly developing, with traders neglecting his rivers for the safety and security of its bazaar. The 1786 Treaty of Cession had never been completed, and relations became strained. The Company troops he had hoped for had not come. The question of a money payment remained unsettled, and while the Company endeavoured to keep the coasts clear, as it had agreed to, it naturally avoided any land commitment, where it had no responsibilities whatever. He therefore resolved to take back the island, and to sack the new settlement. This attempt was the first serious threat to Penang's existence. In 1791 the Sultan summoned a fleet of Lanuns to assist him. A combined force gathered in the Prye river, and watched the bustling port across the way. Its strength and confidence increased. Light had only a few hundred Indian troops, and he had been strictly instructed never to make any aggressive moves. At the last moment, as the Prye mob, numbering thousands, prepared for an attack on the following day Light struck first. On 12th April 1791 his small, disciplined force crossed before dawn, and hit the assembled flotillas as night ended. Completely surprised, the enemy broke and fled northwards along the coast. Light had won a decisive victory.

The Sultan then signed a Treaty of Cession (1791).[18] No promise, however vague, of support on land was made. A payment of $6,000 per annum was accepted. The Sultan was still hostile, if a little subdued, and began an intermittent blockade of the island. Penang has always depended on Kedah for its food. The rows of lorries that now queue each morning for the ferry across from Butterworth are only the twentieth century substitutes for the prahus and junks that formerly carried to Penang from the Muda, Merbok and other rivers the buffaloes, rice and vegetables lacking on the island. Cut off this food supply and Penang will quickly starve. This the Sultan attempted.

Another irritant was the blatant piracy. The prizes in Penang harbour were so good that more and more Malays moved down to the Prye river, or lurked among the islands nearby, and

[18] This Treaty, (and all other Malayan Treaties of importance), is given in full in W. G. Maxwell and W. S. Gibson, *Treaties and Engagements affecting the Malay States and Borneo* (London, 1924).

with increasing audacity fell on the small ships as they neared Penang. It reached the stage where sailors, rowing in to the jetty at Georgetown after anchoring their ship, were captured. Many a seaman, going back in the evening after a night ashore, was taken not a hundred yards from the shore, and sold as a slave somewhere down the coast.

In 1800, to counter both the food shortage and the prevalence of piracy, a strip of land on the mainland opposite the harbour was secured from the Sultan, and a further $4,000 per annum paid him. The purchase had been recommended amongst others, by Light and Leith, and by Coloned Wesley (later Wellesley), an influential if junior army commander. He was waiting in Penang in 1797 with a force for the fleet that was to take it to capture Manila. He never did go to Manila, but he did become the Duke of Wellington, the greatest soldier Britain produced in the nineteenth century.[89] His brother, as Governor-General of India, was busily expanding British influence there, in aristocratic disregard to Pitt's India Act, and for once the instructions were disregarded here too. Province Wellesley, as the newly acquired territory was called, helped to clear the harbour of pirates, but it was marshy, swampy and uninhabited, so Penang continued to rely on Kedah for its food. It did not receive a population until 1821, when thousands of Malays fled there to escape from Siam.

All this time Siam was growing steadily stronger. By 1800 it was beginning to assert its ancient suzerainty in the Kra Peninsula, and its voice was being heard again in the attap huts by the river banks of north Malaya. The *bunga'mas* went again to Ligor, and on to Bangkok. But was this sufficient? Should not the diplomacy of Kedah have included a search for allies? It had no friends to the north. Siam was in its most imperialistic mood, and was already talking of peninsula dominance, reviving its old fifteenth century dream. In 1818 it felt strong enough to instruct its southern overseer, Ligor, to see that Perak was punished for not sending the *bunga'mas*. Con-

---

[19] Britain's greatest sailor, Nelson, was also in Malayan waters for a time, shortly before Penang was founded.

temptuously, Ligor passed on the order to Kedah.

The Malay States were fatally divided. There was no leader of any stature whatever in the early nineteenth century, no Tun Perak, no Raja Haji, for all were little men, jealous of one another. Kedah made no attempt to win friends to the south either, rather the contrary, and in 1818 it turned on Perak, and forced Perak to send north the *bunga'mas*.

Then in 1821, isolated north and south, Kedah suffered a crippling invasion. The forces of Siam swept down the coast and up the slow rivers. Alor Star the capital, went up in flames.[20] The Sultan fled over-land, hotly pursued. Thousands of refugees poured across the Muda River into British territory. Flushed with victory the Siamese forces followed, to meet the disciplined fire of a Company of troops. The Siamese fled back into Kedah, while the Sultan sought safety in Penang.

The Raja of Ligor, sending a detachment still further south to Perak, to prepare the way for the next step, demanded the Sultan's return. It was refused; but so too was a request by the Sultan for troops to regain his territory. Penang adopted the traditional attitude of Britain, which has always welcomed refugees and émigrés, but which nevertheless has refused consistently to meddle in the affairs of their abandoned homelands. Penang was strengthened in its attitude by its awareness of considerations of greater importance to the British in the East than the collapse of Kedah, in particular of the possibilities of trade with Bangkok.

For a hundred years Siam had abandoned its seventeenth century tolerance of Europeans, and had turned a contemptuous and indifferent back upon them. Early European adventurers had not prepared the way, as they had in India and Java, for the establishment of trading factories and for the growth of European control. Rather the story must look to Japan for an example, as by the early nineteenth century Siam was a

---

[20] An eye witness to this was Anderson, a Penang officer, and his vivid description can be read in T. J. Newbold, *A Political and Statistical Account of the British Settlements in the Straits of Malacca* (London, 1839). It should be remembered, however, as the reader wades through the account of bloodshed, that he was violently anti-Siamese.

country almost as mysterious and as unknown as Zapangu; but not quite, and among the traders in Penang and the officials in India the possible opportunities, should friendly relations be established, were considered with some interest.

In 1818 Penang had sent some gifts to Siam, and when their receipt was acknowledged by the ruler himself it prevailed upon India to despatch in 1821 a mission to Bangkok, headed by a former Penang official, Dr. John Crawfurd.[21] He was asked to obtain from Siam assurances that the produce of Kedah would be permitted to flow to Penang, and that the Sultan of Kedah could come back to his throne, while in addition he was charged by India with obtaining commercial advantages, such as the removal of the generally haphazard and arbitrary levies exacted at Bangkok on British vessels. While in Bangkok he concentrated on the latter assignment, but in all that he attempted he failed. He left Siam in October 1822, not having advanced Britain's position in any way. In consequence India's interest waned.

Ligor, the lackey of Siam, returned to the attack, and while its troops systematically looted Kedah (beating off wild attacks by the Sultan's sons in the process), it maintained its pressure on Perak, and began casting expansionist eyes on Selangor, the state still further south, in readiness for yet another move.

The Malay Peninsula was saved from Siamese domination by Robert Fullerton, who arrived as Governor of Penang (and Malacca and Singapore) in August 1824, and who completely reversed the earlier British attitude of acquiescing in the pretensions of Siam. Previously Siam had been looked at from India, and had been regarded as a possible friend or counter to the aggressive tendencies of Burma. Fullerton for the first time brought a Malayan outlook on to the scene, and he set out vigorously in a manner similar to Raffles, to protect and to expand

---

21 Crawfurd, later to become Resident of Singapore, has left an account of this mission, in *Journal of an Embassy from the Governor General of India to the Courts of Siam and Cochin China*, 2 vols. (London, 1830).

British interests in the Malay Peninsula and to stop the Siamese.[22]

He quickly discovered that Ligor, having taken possession of Kedah, was preparing for the invasion of the ancient but momentarily weak state of Perak. In early 1825 large numbers of prahus were being fitted out in the rivers of Kedah and to the northward. He acted with swift resolution, and in a manner quite contrary to his instructions. The Penang squadron was sent to patrol off the river mouths, and Fullerton informed Ligor that should its fleet sail south it would be regarded as an act of war. The bluff worked. The fleet stayed on the beaches, and the first check had been made.

Fullerton had acted in defiance of his instructions, for India did not consider that Penang should attempt to protect the southern Malay States. To explain his attitude Fullerton sent to Calcutta a representative, Captain Burney, who so convinced the Governor-General of the utility of his actions, and so impressed him with the need to re-open negotiations direct with Bangkok, that he was named the leader of another mission to Siam.

The authorities in India had sent Crawfurd to Siam in 1822 largely for commercial reasons. Burney went in 1825 to argue the case of the British in Malaya. In 1822 the Supreme Government had regarded Siam not merely as a possible centre for British trade but also as a possible ally or check against Ava, which had been acting in an aggressive and irresponsible manner against the British in Bengal. By 1825 interest in both these possibilities had waned, but both Penang and the new bustling Singapore were clamouring for direct contacts with Siam; so Burney sailed.

He achieved a first success before he ever reached Siam. He was induced by Fullerton to sail up the Kedah river and to negotiate with the Rajah of Ligor. The Sultan had become aware of the different atmosphere. Fullerton was of very different

[22] Fullerton is well described by L. A. Mills, *British Malaya, 1824–1867* (JMBRAS, vol. 3, 1925). This paper was a pioneer attempt, based on the original despatches preserved in the India Office Library, and it has remained the standard work on this period for over thirty years. It has lately been re-printed.

metal from his predecessors, and India no longer was so completely pro-Siamese. The Sultan had hesitated in Kedah, contemplating Perak and Selangor, for some six months. Now in July 1825 he welcomed Burney and signed a treaty, by which he agreed to withdraw his fleet from Kedah and his small pressure group from Perak, and to abstain fom attacking either Perak or Selangor.

In Bangkok Burney was treated with great suspicion. The Siamese entertained the most extravagent fears of British pretensions. In nearby Burma a British war against Ava was bringing them to the Siamese border. Burney was still in Bangkok when the Treaty of Yandabo (1826) ceded the coastal provinces of Tenasserim and Arakan, as well as Assam and Manipur to the British, and the wildest rumours of British designs on Siam also made his negotiations most difficult. Suspicious and sensitive, the proud Siamese were determined not to yield on any matter in which their position, pride or prestige was involved.

Burney was concerned with stabilising the chaotic affairs of the Malay Peninsula. Five states were involved, each one varying in actual dependence on Siam, all claimed by it as part of its empire. Kedah was completely engulfed, Perak but partly, and Selangor scarcely at all; while on the east coast Kelantan and Trengganu sent a *bunga'mas* and bothered no-one. The extreme position of fiery Fullerton was that all must be wrenched away; but Siam clung to all the states. Burney, after five months of patient negotiation, assisted by his fluent Siamese, and by his friendship with the Rajah of Ligor and the moderate group around the emperor, secured a compromise treaty that was so vaguely worded that no-one lost face, but which permitted either power, depending on who was the stronger, to interpret it as it saw fit.

Burney was quite unable to persuade Siam over Kedah. The Raja of Ligor, the court, the emperor—all were united. Burney asked that the Sultan be restored, his relatives and followers be released, and that the Siamese troops be evacuated. In return he promised that the *bunga'mas* would be sent, together with $4,000 annually. It was quite unacceptable. Ligor was obtaining $30,000 annually from Kedah as it was, and over a 1,000 Malays were in Bangkok as slaves. Obviously it was not to Siam's advantage to terminate the occupation, and Kedah remained under the control of Ligor.

Burney was more successful elsewhere. Siam admitted that it had never received the *bunga'mas* from Perak before 1818, and agreed that henceforth Perak could send it at its pleasure. Selangor, it was also agreed, could govern itself as it saw fit. On the east coast too Burney persuaded Siam to retreat, and to state that provided Kelantan and Trengganu continued sending the *bunga'mas,* it would interfere there no more than at that moment, and would not interrupt their trade with Singapore. Here again face had been saved. Burney had realised that it was impossible, indeed not politic, to force the Siamese by written treaty to abandon publically their pretensions; but by inducing them to accept an Agreement (June 1826) deliberately worded so loosely that various interpretations could be placed on it, he drew a broad line across the peninsula.[23]

In India Burney's negotiating skill was recognised and his treaty was applauded. British relations with Siam had been placed on a sounder footing, both politically and commercially, so he had done well. Fullerton had expected more, but he too appreciated the opportunity it gave him, and he acted swiftly in the Malay Peninsula to implement the treaty.

Ligor, in defiance of the 1825 Agreement, had been reinforcing its band of armed men at the court of Perak. Fullerton sent Captain J. Low at the head of a mission, to inform Perak of the Burney Treaty, and to tell the Sultan that he was a completely independent sovereign.

Low sent the Ligorians fleeing through the jungle. They had established an almost overwhelming control of the court, and many of the leading Perak chiefs, including the heir to the throne, had sworn allegiance to Siam. Low acted swiftly. The Raja Muda had his claim to the succession formally annulled, a new list of ministers was announced, and a treaty with Perak

[23] This Mission is dealt with in detail by *The Burney Papers* (A collection of official records relating to the Mission), 5 vols. Bangkok, 1910–1914; See also W. F. Vella, *Siam Under Rama III, 1824–1851* (New York, 1957), where Siamese sources are used.

was signed (October 1826) acknowledging its complete independence, stating that no despatch of any *bunga'mas* was necessary, and pledging British assistance should it be troubled by Siam, Ligor or any other state.

This treaty was in complete defiance of Company policy, and it went even further than Fullerton had envisaged. A *fait accompli* had been achieved however, and Fullerton, although he received a reprimand from India, supported Low's action in pledging British support. He carried his case although the treaty was never ratified, yet when the Sultan of Perak appealed to Penang for aid in 1844 and 1853, the terms of the treaty were accepted as binding. In 1874, when the policy of installing British officers as Residents in the Malay States was inaugurated in Perak, it was Low's Treaty that was cited as the authority.

These two treaties of 1826 and the military effort that accompanied the latter mark the end of Siam's southward ambitions. They therefore had more effect on the Malay Peninsula than the far better known treaty which had been signed two years previously, the Anglo-Dutch Treaty of 1824. This had been an Agreement between two European powers that to a very large extent merely recognised and rationalised what already was in fact. It tidied up the European map of South-East Asia, but it did not alter in any significant way the internal position of the Malay Peninsula. The Burney and Low Treaties however had momentous results. The long creep south of Siam, which easily might have over-run the whole peninsula, was checked decisively. Siam came no farther.

Fullerton had stopped Siam, but he had not restored the Sultan of Kedah, and he had to endure another sixteen years in the wilderness of exile in Penang and Malacca. His followers invaded Kedah in 1830, 1838 and 1841, each time unsuccessfully. Finally the old Sultan succumbed. His son pledged loyalty to Siam in 1841, Britain brought pressure to bear in Bangkok, and in 1842 he was accepted again in Alor Star.[24] Henceforth for the rest of the nineteenth century the *bunga'mas* went to

---

[24] The pocket state of Perlis was separated from Kedah by Ligor before he returned.

Bangkok, and Kedah royalty received their education there, until in 1909, when Britain acquired Siamese rights, the twentieth century saw the despatch of the last of the golden flowers, this time as Kedah's coronation present to King George V of Great Britain.

5. SINGAPORE AND THE SOUTH

Shortly after the founding of Penang, the excesses of the French Revolution precipitated a war between Great Britain and France. Penang, which had been founded to assist the trade with China, participated in that war to protect it. Its inadequacies in that role, and the determination of the British to maintain and augment that trade, lead us step by step south to the founding of Singapore.

Although the war with France did not begin in Europe until 1793, there was skirmishing and fighting in the East from 1789. The British fleet, which guarded the Bay of Bengal, suffered severely through Admiralty indifference during this period, and Britain maintained its position in the Indian Ocean only because the French colonies and Navy were reacting in confusion and indecision to the French Revolution. Penang for example remained almost entirely defenceless, and even when the war began in earnest, in 1794, it was not a naval base, nor had it a fort adequate to defend its harbour.[1]

In January 1795 the French overran the Netherlands, and by establishing a revolutionary Republic, which concluded an alliance with France, brought to bear a new threat on the British. Whereas before the main French base was the island of Mauritius, now all the Dutch possessions in the East could be utilised as well. The British Navy moved swiftly to defend the vital India-China trade. In August 1795 Malacca was captured without loss, and remained British throughout the war, being administered at first by the Army and then from 1804 by Penang.[2]

Another eastward campaign was mounted by the Navy in the following year, in 1796, when the fabled Spice Islands, the

---

1 This naval war between Europeans in Asian waters is covered in detail by C. N. Parkinson, *War In The Eastern Seas, 1793–1815* (London, 1954).

2 An interesting account of this unheroic campaign is given by G. Irwin: *Governor Couperus and the surrender of Malacca*, 1795. (JMBRAS, vol. 29, pt. 3, August, 1956).

Moluccas, were attacked and captured. The establishment of control took some time, but in late 1796 Robert Farquhar was installed at Amboyna as Resident, and a supply of spices was sent to both Penang and India for planting and cultivation. In 1797 for the third successive year the British Navy carried the war eastwards, when an expedition set out from Madras to capture Manila. It assembled at Penang, but heard there that Napoleon had concluded a peace with the German States, and was turning his interest towards India. The expedition was cancelled and the divisions sailed back to the threatened Presidencies.

For the next few years both Penang and Malacca played unsensational but important roles as most convenient assembly points for the convoys that travelled each monsoon to India or to China. French, Spanish and Dutch privateers and men-of-war sought to disrupt and interfere with the Canton traders, and if the facilities of Penang and Malacca had not been available the lumbering East Indiamen would have faced a lonely, enemy infested strait without any naval port at all. Yet when peace came in 1802, bringing a momentary lull with the Treaty of Amiens, no decisive aggressive step had been taken against either the French on Mauritius or the Dutch on Java. Thus the grave threat to the British-China trade remained.

Appreciating this, Lord Wellesley, the Governor-General of India, took the initiative, when hostilities began again, to abandon the Spice Islands and in 1803 he established Farquhar on remote Balambangan Island where he had decided to build a naval base on the flank of the China trade. When news of his actions reached the Company in London, however, it was horrified. China ships were being but rarely attacked, the convoy system was working admirably, and the founding of a distant outpost at a time when Britain faced formidable foes inside India itself, apart from encounters on the waters near its coasts, and when major enemy bases were uncaptured, was a step too rash to be authorised. Farquhar was recalled to govern Penang, and the base was abandoned in 1805.

The Company in London was controlled by the great Dundas, Lord Melville, who in addition had become First Lord of the Admiralty, and his plan for protecting the China trade was to build a base on Penang. In April 1805 it was decided to make the island a Presidency, to build a naval dockyard and fort, and to establish a fleet there. Dundas' nephew arrived in November 1805 to execute these instruction, but in the months that had elapsed Dundas had resigned from the Admiralty to stand impeachment and to vanish from public life. However, the battle of Trafalgar had been fought in October 1805, shattering the combined fleet of France and Spain. The need for a base had gone, and although two ships were built, a frigate in 1809 and a 74 gun ship of the line in 1811,[3] the great hopes and plans for Penang died away as retrenchment and economy replaced extravagance and expansion.

Among the young men brought out from London in 1805, when Penang became a Presidency, was Thomas Stamford Raffles. By marrying the discarded but troublesome mistress of a senior member of the Company his salary had risen from £150 to £1,500 a year, and by coming to the East he left a name that has made him an historic figure. Ambitious, clever and energetic, he soon found that his restless spirit was cramped by the small settlement and dampened by the restrictions of expenditure and the reductions of staff that followed the optimistic ideas of 1805. His opportunity came in 1808 when he visited Malacca, and learned from William Farquhar, the administrator, that it was to be destroyed, so that if Holland ever again occupied it, it could not be reconstituted as a rival to Penang.

The decision to destroy and to abandon Malacca was the result of muddled thinking by the Penang administrators, who thought that if this was done all the trade of Malacca and all its settlers would be attracted northwards. A port however, is a living entity, the heart of an area, and neither the heart nor the body it serves can survive a wrenching apart of the two. In a brilliant despatch, cogent, eloquent, comprehensive and irrefutable, Raffles demonstrated the futility of the operation. Penang and more important, India, were convinced. Although the great fort was destroyed during 1807, the order to evacuate was cancelled and Malacca remained.

---

[3] Named the *Pinang* and the *Inglis* respectively.

By his despatch Raffles had attracted the attention of Lord Minto, Governor-General of India, who was anxious to prosecute the war against France to a successful finish. Minto had been the personal friend of Lord Nelson, and he shared his liking for decisive aggressive action. Under his leadership a two-armed sweep south from India was planned, one south-west to capture the major French base at Mauritius, and the other south-east to capture Java and so remove all danger to the China trade. Raffles was employed at Malacca for this latter attack, establishing there a centre of espionage and information.[4]

In 1810 the French base of Mauritius was captured from India, and the following year Minto accompanied a large invasion force that sailed for Java. It assembled at Penang, then at Malacca, where Raffles joined Minto, and finally off the coast of Borneo. The expedition which landed on 4th August was well led by General Gillespie, and the French and Dutch and local forces on Java could offer little resistance. Java capitulated on 18th September 1811. Leaving Raffles behind as Lieutenant-Governor, Minto returned to India.

This victory thrust Penang ignominiously into the background. After 1811 the China or India bound ships could safely use the short Sunda Straits between Java and Sumatra, and so avoid, in any passage between the Indian Ocean and the South China Sea, the long Straits of Malacca, with its variable winds and pirate packs. Penang was thus by-passed. In addition the liberal trade attitude of Raffles attracted to Batavia (the present day Djakarta), the Bugis and other island traders who previously sailed north to Penang.

Disadvantageous though the victory was to Penang, nevertheless the general position of the British in the East was greatly strengthened by the collapse of Java, and the establishment of peace over the waters of South-East Asia. This improved position was threatened in 1814, however, when the Anglo-Dutch Convention was signed in London. The war with France was nearing its

[4] There is a delightful eye-witness account of Raffles at Malacca in Munshi Abdullah's *The Hikayat Abdullah*, Translated by A. H. Hill (JMBRAS, vol. 28, 1955).

end. Britain was determined to create the Netherlands as a strong buffer state that would stand between it and any new continental threat. The stability and strength of the Netherlands depended upon its colonial possessions, so Britain restored to it all the factories and establishments it had lost in South-East Asia. Thus Java and its dependencies, Celebes and the smaller islands situated in the Straits of Macassar, the Moluccas, Malacca and various minor posts on Sumatra reverted to the Dutch. Britain retained merely Ceylon and the Cape of Good Hope.

After the battle of Waterloo in 1815 the war with France ended, and the Dutch began coming back to the East. They moved immediately to re-establish their former superiority, adopting, although with more vigour, their former system of monopoly and exclusion. They refused to recognise any treaties that the British had made with the local rulers; foreign vessels were refused permission to call at the minor ports of Java; and a heavier duty was imposed on them than on Dutch vessels at the one port at which they were permitted to trade, while all local craft had to acquire passes before being permitted to sail. Regulation followed regulation, and so too did occupation, so that by 1818 the Dutch had not only re-occupied all their former establishments but had extended their sway over almost the entire Indonesian Archipelago.

This was the situation that confronted Raffles on his return to South-East Asia in 1818 to assume his duties as Lieutenant Governor of Bencoolen in west Sumatra, an ancient outpost that the Company had maintained since the seventeenth century more through policy than profits, as a toe hold in an otherwise Dutch preserve. It was crumbling and minute, yet it was all that Raffles, with his complete lack of Indian experience, could hope for. He was sustained by his hatred of the Dutch, and it was they who gave him his opportunity.

He was aghast at the depreciation of Britain's position in the East brought about by Dutch implementation of the Anglo-Dutch Convention. He set to work immediately to check them, but almost invariably his suggestions fell on deaf Company ears, for he was, after all, a very minor Company official with little standing in India, and his actions were disapproved and countermanded. He urged the appointment of a British representative to protect British trade and to protest at injustice; the establishment of a chain of stations to limit the Dutch sphere of interest; and the drawing of a line that would give all islands south of the Sunda Straits to the Dutch, with all islands north of it becoming British. All this was ignored. He then moved from words to action, and in 1818 attempted to found a station on the Sumatran shore of the Sunda Straits, in Sumanka and then Callambyan or Forrest Bay. His actions caused grave alarm among the authorities in Java who acted swiftly, and intense annoyance in India. The post he had established was withdrawn, and the Sunda Straits became Dutch. His efforts to secure the Sultan of Palembang also failed, as the Dutch advanced there too. In all that he did he was checked, and it was as a despondent and frustrated man that he decided to seek official support and sailed to Calcutta in late 1818.

Here he found a tide of opinion flowing slowly against the Dutch. As the nineteenth century progressed Britain was becoming a great industrial country, and was moving upward to a long plateau of immense power. It was becoming the greatest nation in the world. Influential Chambers of Commerce were viewing the world's markets, and were becoming critical of any attempt to restrict British trade. In India itself the threat of the Dutch to the broad artery of trade that flowed to and from China, and the growing British markets in South-East Asia were increasingly recognised. In this awakening the sober but alarming despatches from Penang, as well as the more hysterical communications from Bencoolen, played their part. Hastings, the Governor-General, recorded in 1818 that "we are now exposed to the hazard of being totally shut out by the Dutch from all participation in the commerce of those seas."[5] The time had come for action.

---

[5] India Office Records; Raffles Collection. Minute of the Marquess of Hastings, 25th October 1818, quoted by J. S. Tay in *The Attempts of Raffles to Establish a British Base in South-East Asia, 1818–1819* (Journal, South-East Asian History, vol. 1, no. 2, September 1960, p. 42).

Hastings was anxious that British trade with China and with the islands should be protected and that Dutch influence should be kept south of the equator. He decided that this could be done by obtaining possession of the Straits of Malacca. Following a mission by Farquhar in July 1818 to Siak, Lingga, Rhio and Borneo, Raffles was despatched in December of the same year to conclude a Treaty with Acheh, which would give Britain control of the northern entrance of the Straits. In addition he was instructed to have Farquhar establish a new post at Rhio, which is on the equator, at the southern entrance. Hastings further considered that by exchanging British-held Bencoolen for Dutch Malacca the entire Straits might become British.

On his arrival at Penang Raffles discovered that the Dutch had re-occupied Rhio that year, and that the planned southern base was in danger. Correctly appreciating that the main threat to any British trade was there, at the exit from the Straits, and not at Acheh in the north, he secured Farquhar as his assistant, and sent him south to search for a substitute to Rhio. Despite the disapproval of the island's administrators, anxious not to be involved with the Dutch, he then followed. They inspected the Carimon Islands which lie on the horizon from Singapore. They were unsuitable, and guided partly by advice and partly by his own historical interests (for he knew of Tumasik), he went directly to Singapore, which lies hard by the one clear channel cut through the myriads of islands that cluster at the end of the Malay Peninsula. It had a broad sandy bay where a small river provided a suitable place for a settlement; and it had no Dutch flag flying over it.

Raffles and Farquhar found the island almost uninhabitated. There were piles of human skulls on the foreshore, but there was only one kampong of Malays and *orang laut* at the river mouth, presided over by the Temenggong of Johore, and another in the ancient, concealed channel nearby that was later to become Keppel Harbour. One or two other kampongs were situated on the other side of the island in the Straits of Johore, where the Changi and Selatar Rivers flowed in, and in the jungled, pathless interior there were a few groups of Chinese, in all perhaps thirty, working gambier. Apart from that the island was empty. The *de facto* ruler of the island was the Temenggong of Johore, Daing Abdul Rahman, and with him on 30th January 1819, the day after he landed, Raffles concluded a treaty which gave him, in exchange for $3,000 annually, the right to establish a factory on the island. The Temenggong, however, had a superior, and although he was virtually independent, Raffles, to make Britain's position secure, particularly in the Chancelleries of Europe, felt it necessary to secure a treaty with the Sultan of Rhio-Johore, the nominal over-lord. Here arose both an obstacle and an opportunity.

The death in 1812 of the previous Sultan, Mahmud, had occurred at a time when the eldest son (in Malay: *Tengku Long*), Hussein, was absent in Pahang, and he was not able (or more likely, not willing) to venture south until twelve months had elapsed. During this time the Bugis under-king, who controlled the Sultanate, appointed a more pliable younger son, Abdul Rahman, and Hussein was thrust aside. Thus by 1819 Abdul Rahman, the Sultan, was under Dutch control (for the Dutch had returned and by a Treaty signed on 26th November 1818 they had recognised him as Sultan). However, there was his discontented elder brother claimed both by the Temenggong and the Bendahara, who since Mahmud's death in 1812 had been ruling Pahang in a similar independent manner, as the rightful Sultan. Quickly and secretly Hussein, then living in obscurity in Rhio, was brought to Singapore and recognised by Raffles as Sultan of Rhio-Johore. Then on 6th February 1819, in return for $5,000 annually, he confirmed the earlier treaty, and gave to Britain the sole right to build a factory on Singapore Island, the port of which was placed under the immediate protection of the British authorities and was subject to their regulations. Thus Singapore was founded.

Singapore was a free port, from the beginning, and Raffles has received perhaps undue praise for what was merely a continuation of an earlier Penang practice. No clarion call announced his policy, no free trader was he, as may be seen from the cautious instructions on duties that he gave to William Farquhar on 6th February, as he hurried north to Acheh. "It is not necessary at present to subject the trade of the port to any duties—it is yet inconsiderable; and it would be impolitic to incur the risk of obstructing its advancement by any measure of this nature."[6] Free trade, begun almost timidly, rapidly became essential. Despite minor setbacks and much criticism, Singapore is still today a free trade oasis in a desert of restrictions, quotas and tariffs.

William Farquhar, left behind on the beach at Singapore, prepared grimly and not a little apprehensively for war with the Dutch. Fortunately for Farquhar it was a paper war. Raffles' speedy action had secured for Britain a legal right of possession, or at least an arguable right. The administration of Farquhar made that right worth arguing. The presence of a modicum of law and order by the river mouth, the British flag and troops, the announcement of free trade, the efficient arrangements for a port, combined with its geographical advantages, made the settlement immediately popular. As the young James Matheson wrote in May 1819, his China-bound ship having been diverted to Singapore by the outpost established on St. John's Island by Farquhar, "I have formed the highest opinion of Singapore as a place of trade...I am of the opinion that a person settling here might carry on business to great advantage."[7]

His opinion was shared by thousands of others who flocked to Singapore. Estimates vary, but it is possible that by the end of 1819 5,000 people had already settled by the river mouth, with hundreds arriving each month. A steadily increasing proportion of these were Chinese, from Malacca, Java, elsewhere in South-East Asia, and from China itself. Singapore has developed as a Chinese city under the Union Jack. Both were vital to its success.

Britain reacted at once to this settlement. Raffles had moved in opposition to those small men of Penang frightened of the Dutch and of the future for their own island, and he had been officially unaware of belated instructions from India cancelling the pro-

[6] Initial instructions of Raffles to William Farquhar, 6th February 1819, quoted in C. Wurtzburg, *Raffles of the Eastern Isles* (London, 1954), pp. 403–404.

[7] Quoted in J. C. Edgehill, *British Trade and the Opening of China* (London, 1951), p. 97.

ject. For a time their views influenced London officials who in any case were irritated by what seemed yet another unnecessarily belligerent act of Raffles. Dutch hostility too for a time made the Company waver, but as the sensational news of its success poured in and as Singapore rapidly became not merely a Company outpost but a national asset, the government's attitude hardened. The Dutch objected. A pity, thought the politicians, particularly as their goodwill in Europe was desired; for Holland was very useful as a friendly buffer against any continental tyrant. Could not some compromise be arranged? It was so decided.

Discussions begun in 1819, and delayed by the British for some time, ended in 1824 when the governments of Holland and Great Britain signed the Anglo-Dutch Treaty. The Dutch agreed to pay some outstanding debts to the British (the settlement of which had caused most of the discussion), and agreed further to relinquish to the British their remaining outposts in India; while they ceded Malacca on the Malay Peninsula. Their old tin treaties and agreements with the various Sultans, which they had vigorously attempted to renew after 1814, also lapsed. The Negri Sembilan, or parts of it (Rembau, alongside Malacca, in particular), had been brought vaguely under Dutch suzerainty. This passed to the British. Selangor had been forced in 1819 to renew an old Dutch treaty by which tin went to Malacca. The old Bugis Sultan had never abided by this, and had declared himself independent, as in fact he was. Perak had withstood a Dutch attempt in 1819 to renew an old tin treaty, and it too was independent. Thus all that Britain gained in the East in effect was the decaying port of Malacca, and a few delapidated harbours in India; in Europe however, Dutch goodwill was won.

In return the British agreed to vacate their equally useless Fort Marlborough (Bencoolen) on Sumatra, and promised not to make any settlement or conclude any treaty with that island. The Dutch withdrew from the Malay Peninsula, and the British from Sumatra, and the Straits of Malacca was between them. In addition Singapore was recognised as British, but the Dutch were promised that no further settlement would be made on any other islands south of the equator[8].

The treaty dealt not merely with territorial matters: it attempted to settle the commercial rivalry as well. It was of fundamental importance to both Penang and Singapore that there should be no attempt by the Dutch to impede local craft sailing to these ports. The Dutch were induced to promise that they would never restrict the free passage of these *kolehs* and other small vessels of the Eastern Archipelago, no matter what port was their destination. Both also agreed never to impose unequal duties, never to tax the trade of the one higher than the other, and never to attempt, by treaty with a local ruler, to exclude the rival's ships. They mutually agreed to grant each other most favoured treatment. All this looks well on paper. In practice however, the Dutch south of the equator and the British north of it somehow managed to look after themselves to the detriment of the other. But this too, of course, was merely a logical development of what had been happening before.

Finally the two powers promised to co-operate in suppressing piracy in Eastern waters. This they never did, in fact the Dutch and the British failed to co-operate in Eastern waters until it was far too late, in 1942, when their co-operation merely ensured that their ships sank together under the gun-fire of the common enemy, the Japanese.

The treaty made no startling changes to the position of the European in South-East Asia, nor did it affect particularly the Asian himself. The Johore Empire had stretched across the equator, with the Rhio Archipelago south, and Johore and Pahang north of it. When this was divided into two fields of interest, Dutch and British, the Sultanate was divided too. Mills, in his *British Malaya, 1824–1867,* goes as far as saying, "the result of the Treaty of 1824 was the dismemberment of the Empire of Johore".[9] Here again, however, the treaty merely emphasised

8 The Anglo-Dutch Treaty is treated in G. Irwin, *Nineteenth Century Borneo* (The Hague, 1955). He brings out clearly that the major part of the preceding discussions were occupied with questions of finance, with the settling of debts incurred in Java and elsewhere. It seems that the British occupation of Singapore was not seriously challenged by the Dutch after 1820.

9 Mills, *British Malaya, 1824–1867* p. 79.

what was happening already. The Sultanate had broken up before 1824. From the death of Sultan Mahmud in 1812 the peninsula states of Pahang and Johore under the Bendahara and Temenggong had become, in practice, completely independent by reason of their non-recognition of Abdul Rahman. The Sultan and his Bugis strong men had been on the Rhio Archipelago. Their nominal control over the mainland had not been strengthened by the return of the Dutch in 1818, and the complete dismemberment of the Sultanate was imminent and inevitable. It would have occurred,—it virtually had occurred—without the 1824 treaty.

The other states involved likewise experienced no dramatic change and suffered no significant result, and they continued on their way, either within the influence of Britain or Holland. This European influence steadily grew stronger as Europe expanded round the world, but the treaty merely marked a tidying up. It can be compared to the re-grouping that occurs on a football field after a goal is scored, when the players sort themselves out and go to their respective ends. Britain had scored the goal with the settlement of Singapore; the umpire's whistle acknowledging this had been the Anglo-Dutch Treaty of 1824.

In that same year (1824) the East India Company secured the full cession of the entire island. Raffles, it will be remembered, had in 1819 secured permission merely to establish a factory, and after his departure the Temenggong, with some semblance of legality, had levied exactions upon the *prahus* that flocked to the new port, on the grounds that Singapore remained a Malay port subject to his laws. Both he and the Sultan practised their levying in a manner scarcely distinguishable from what a westerner would term piracy, but it was impossible to punish them or their followers. Raffles returned to Singapore in 1823 and signed a Convention with Sultan Hussein and the Temenggong. In return for $1,500 a month to the Sultan and $800 a month to the Temenggong, they each gave up all right to levy dues upon *prahus* and other local craft, or to act as judges.

Crawfurd, who replaced Farquhar as Resident in late 1823, concluded a Treaty in 1824 with the two Malay chiefs that filled in the gaps left by the 1823 Convention. In return for $33,200 and a pension of $1,300 per month promised to the Sultan, and $26, 800 and $700 a month to the Temenggong, Crawfurd secured a treaty that placed British sovereignty over the entire island of Singapore beyond dispute. The Sultan and Temenggong ceded the island of Singapore "together with the adjacent seas, straits and islets lying within a radius of ten miles, in full sovereignty and property" to the East India Company, its heirs and successors for ever.[10]

During these early years of occupation both Farquhar and Crawfurd were faced with the same problem of administration that bedevilled the first few decades of Penang, namely the lack of any Code of Laws that was legally binding on the polyglot population, and the absence of any legally constituted courts. This made the task of the Resident most difficult. Until 1827 Singapore was lawless, in that it had no law to administer. Its first riot, which broke out between rival Malay groups in 1823, was quelled by the small military contingent; but it was a pointer to the future which Farquhar regarded with foreboding.

In 1823 Raffles quite illegally but most helpfully appointed twelve prominent merchants as magistrates, bringing them into the government with a role similar to that of the English Justices of the Peace, in which post they did good work. He issued some general regulations on the administration of justice at the same time, which were useful, but also illegal. Farquhar had established a minute police force of twenty or so men, and had introduced the well tried 'Capitan' system. By 1823 there were two Chinese Capitans or headmen, and a Bugis, while the Malays relied on their Temenggong and Sultan. These leaders merely dealt with internal offences, crimes that concerned one race only. In the case of interracial offences the Resident had to arbitrate, but by what law?

Crawfurd, as Farquhar and Light had done, endeavoured to administer by enforcement of the general principles of British law, tempering it wherever necessary, and yielding to Chinese or Malay practice whenever their own institutions or customs were affected. Strictly speaking, however, he acted illegally for only the Crown could establish a Court. British law ever since

[10] For this Treaty see Maxwell and Gibson, *Treaties and Engagements affecting the Malay States and Borneo* (London, 1924).

the conflicts in medieval days was the King's law and only the King's law. As no-one in the realm could dispense justice without the Crown's consent; as the Parliament of Great Britain did not formally recognise Crawfurd's Treaty and accept sovereignty over Singapore until 1826; and as the island's first Charter of Justice did not arrive until 1827, the island, strictly speaking, was until then outside the law. The Charter was the Penang Charter writ large. Singapore had been joined to Penang and Malacca in 1826 as the Straits Presidency. Each unit of this Presidency was visited by the Penang judge who travelled on circuit with the Governor. When he was not in the settlement the Resident had the responsibility of hearing and judging all the minor cases. In 1837, ten years later, the courts so established in the three settlements, were given the right to hear Admiralty cases, that is, crimes such as piracy committed on the High Seas. This was in addition to the civil and criminal cases they already were hearing. This long sought right, however, played little part in suppressing piracy, for the culprits were scarcely ever apprehended. Endemic piracy vanished when the steamships came, not when the courts were established.

The Presidency so established by the East India Company was never able to pay for itself. Despite the rapid growth of Singapore and the steady increase of Penang, the mode of revenue raising adopted, that of taxing by farms the pleasures of the Chinese, never yielded sufficient to pay for the salaries and services of the government. The Chinese saw to that. Each year India had to meet a deficit; either it or Britain paid for the Straits Settlements to remain British throughout most of the nineteenth century. By 1829 Singapore had a population of perhaps 15,000. Its civil servants numbered three. There were a dozen at Penang, and two at Malacca. They and their subordinates and supernumeraries were costing India far too much. The Presidency was therefore abolished, and the Straits became a Residency, with an official establishment of eight. Today this would be inadequate to administer one Rural District in Singapore. In 1829 it had to administer Britain east of India. In 1832 the capital of this Residency shifted from Penang to Singapore, by this time the greatest of the three.

Singapore became and has remained great by reason of its trade. This trade consisted firstly of Straits Produce: the rattans, birds' nests, gutta percha, sago, damar and other jungle exports, brought on the south-west monsoon by an ever increasing number of small *prahus* and Indonesian sailing craft from as far away as Macassar and Ambon. Secondly, there was the produce of China: the tea, dried fish, pottery and innumerable other articles that were shipped during the north-east monsoon in the heavy Chinese junks.

Perhaps the most important 'export' from China was the Chinese. The southern states of Kwantung, Fukien and Kwangsi had had links with the *Nanyang* since at least Ming times. The Imperial edicts against emigration were quite ignored. Cheng Ho, when he visited Malacca early in the fifteenth century, met many of his countrymen there; but it was not until the civil wars of the Manchus (in the late eighteenth century) and the increase in population pressure in the nineteenth, that migration southwards became considerable. Naturally enough the Chinese then migrated to those places that were safe and profitable. Penang and then Singapore above all else fulfilled those requirements. So in the Chinese came, many from China itself in the famous five-masted Pechili junks, vessels that Marco Polo described in the thirteenth century, and last seen in Singapore early in the twentieth. Their vigour should not be forgotten when assessing the reasons for Singapore's success.

British traders from Canton also used Singapore not merely as a trade centre where silk and tobacco could be sold, but also as a most useful entrepôt port where goods for England could be trans-shipped. Until 1833 the East India Company maintained a monopoly of trade between China and Britain. The numerous private or country traders could engage in commerce between China and the islands, or India and China: indeed they were encouraged to do so, for by their transactions funds were provided in Canton for the Company. But the merchants could not take part in the direct trade from China to England. This kept them out of the all important tea trade. Quickly, however, such firms as Jardine Matheson and Co. and others realised the advantage of Singapore as an entrepôt port. Goods, particularly tea, were sent from Canton to Singapore. This was quite legal, and the East

India Company did not interfere. These goods were then transshipped at Singapore, and sent to London. This too was legal. In this way the monopoly was broken. Singapore's establishment, in fact, was one of the main reasons why the Company's monopoly was abolished in 1833. This in turn led to a further tremendous increase in trade with China and the acquisition of Hong Kong.

Another large section of the trade with Singapore came from India. Piece goods, rolls and rolls of cloth, went into the godowns[11] and shops, to be re-exported in smaller quantities to the islands. Opium too came from India, hundreds of chests of it, again to be re-exported. Singapore was the essential link that had hitherto been lacking, the centrally situated retailer, which acquired the bulk purchases and which broke them down into small units.

This was done also with goods from Britain, for many years an inconsiderable part of Singapore's trade, but which accounted for one item of some importance, iron. British iron came out to Singapore as cargoes on ships by-passing India and going direct to China. It had a ready sale in Singapore, the centre of an area where for over a thousand years, virtually until the establishment of Penang, the use of metal had been confined to a man's weapons and little else. The heavy bars and hoops of the metal used as ballast on the outward sailing tea ships were beaten, broken and fashioned by Chinese workers to suit a vast range of uses. Subsequently the metal exports from Britain widened to include manufactured articles of steel in an incredible assortment that has increased constantly ever since.

The bulk buying and selling of the commodities that flowed into Singapore from Europe, India, China and South-East Asia was arranged to a considerable extent by European firms or entrepreneurs. Singapore, far more than Penang, became the centre of a powerful European business community that became established there, not merely because of the Free Trade policy but because of developments in India and China also. In 1813,

[11] Warehouses. The origin of this word is obscure, its use among Europeans in Malaya being at least four hundred years old. According to Hobson-Jobson, *Godown* is derived from the Tamil. See *Hobson-Jobson: A Glossary of Colloquial Anglo-Indian Words and Phrases...* by Col. H. Yule and A. C. Burnell (London, 1903), p. 381.

six years before Singapore was founded, the East India Company lost its monopoly of the India-England trade, and the private merchants were free to compete in this lucrative business. As a result there was a rapid increase in the number of merchants in Calcutta and Madras, and many were quick to appreciate the possibilities of business in Singapore. Again, in Canton, the company's grudging acceptance of private traders had led to their growth. They too looked eagerly for agents in Singapore. They were not disappointed.

The first British Agency House established in Singapore was Messrs. A. L. Johnston and Company, formed in 1820 by Alexander Johnston, who had landed on the island the previous year. The second notable merchant to arrive was Alexander Guthrie, who in 1821 began a business that has survived and prospered to this day. If its progress could be narrated, it would form an economic history of Singapore. Messrs. Syme and Company was formed in 1823, while in 1826 the enterprising surgeon of a Portuguese man-of-war enlarged his medical store to form Messrs. J. d'Almeida and Sons. The flourishing twentieth century Agency House of Paterson, Simons and Company began in 1828, with Boustead and Company in 1830. In 1837 the Singapore Chamber of Commerce was formed.

The youthful vigour, the dash and the enterprise that marked these young men, who in these early days worked in their small offices by the crowded river, or who matched their wits against the Chinese *towkay* or the Bugis trader in the packed godown, has survived in the almost venerable but most active establishments that now grace the Singapore foreshore. It is indeed on the survival of their business acumen, and on that of their Chinese associates who handled then, as they do now, the retail selling and much of the buying of the commodities brought in, that Singapore still depends.

Singapore hoped, as had Penang before it, that its trade would be reinforced by the products of its own soil. For centuries the British had envied the Dutch, with their control of the spice trade with Europe, and immediately after the founding of Singapore steps were taken by the Europeans to grow a variety of tropical crops. Without exception they failed.

Raffles sent nutmeg and clove seeds and plants to Farquhar from Bencoolen in 1819. They were planted out and had an initial success, particularly in the Serangoon area a few miles inland, where a few tracks penetrated the wilderness. By 1840 there were some twenty small plantations struggling to survive; but twenty years later they were all dead. Cloves also had been introduced in 1820, but they never flourished. Sugar planting was tried and abandoned. Coffee shrubs were planted in the 1820's, while several Europeans experimented with cotton in the 1830's; both crops failed.

The soil of Singapore is very poor, a red laterite that nourishes little apart from a non-demanding jungle that thrives on a humid atmosphere and a hundred inches of rain a year. These were the qualities that killed all the experiments and hopeful beginnings of the ignorant Europeans.[12] These same qualities sustained the widespread activities of the Chinese, who from before the time of Raffles were planting and cultivating pepper and gambier. This agricultural pursuit, always combined, became by the 1830's the main staple of export from Singapore.

The cultivation radiated out from the Singapore settlement in a fan-like pattern across the island towards the Straits of Johore. It offered to hundreds of Chinese each year, mainly Teochews, with a sprinkling of Cantonese and Hokkiens, the opportunity to make a living denied them in Singapore town. One at least, Seah Eu Chin, from Swatow, made a fortune from it, although nearly all the plantations were started by individuals without any finance of their own, supported by advances and credit from a trader in town, and resold when a modicum of capital had been acquired. They would squat in the wilderness, seize and clear perhaps fifty acres, and maintain alongside it a virgin patch of jungle of a similar size. This supplied the firewood for the constant boiling of the gambier plants necessary to extract the commercial product, while the refuse left over provided the manure for the pepper vines that were interspersed between the gambier

[12] These various experiments were described, often enough, in the *Journal of the Indian Archipelago*, more familiarly known as *Logan's Journal*, which, beginning in 1847, ran for thirteen fascinating volumes, to close in 1862.

rows. Once the jungle had been felled and burnt the farmer had to move on, as his means of sustenance had gone. Both pepper and gambier relied on that jungle patch. In this way, ignored by the government, fighting and quarrelling, being mauled by tigers (one a day by 1840), or being involved in fierce secret society exactions, but frantically working, gambling and smoking, the Teochew, clad in shorts, jacket and broad bamboo hat, pushed down the jungle and moved across Singapore island. From the early 1840's, faced by a shortage of timber and with the soil exhausted, the planters had begun to move across the Straits into the Malay Peninsula. The part they played in opening up Johore will be outlined in the next chapter but one.

The early 1830's, which had seen on Singapore the gambier and pepper industry at its height, witnessed also at Malacca the one disastrous and foolhardy war ever fought by the British against the Malays. The Naning War (1831–1832) was a shocking blunder; two military expeditions whose exploits bordered on the farcical, and which secured an additional revenue for the Company, at the cost of $800,000, of perhaps $100 per annum.

Naning was a small inland state just outside Malacca. When in 1824 the British took over Malacca from the Dutch (to whom it had been returned in 1818), they inherited Dutch treaty rights and obligations here, and although most of these treaties, with Perak for example, or Selangor, were quite obviously inapplicable, having lapsed some time before, the officials in Malacca pretended to believe that an ancient arrangement with Naning, by which a nominal yearly tribute was paid, was still active. In fact it had lapsed, but Lewis, the Superintendent of Lands at Malacca, the evil genius behind all this, was anxious to implement every possible British right he could discover. Fullerton was the Governor of the Straits, a man of vigorous and determined character as we saw previously. He never received the correct facts, he was misled by his subordinates into thinking that Naning was an integral part of Malacca territory, and in 1829 he demanded of Naning that the nominal tribute should revert to the even earlier arrangement (pre 1765) of a tenth of its crop. The *Penghulu,* Abdul Said, refused and began open defiance.

Fullerton's successor, Ibbotson, arrived to find chaos and with instructions from the Directors in London to re-impose authority over Naning. In July 1831 a small force expecting little or no opposition, was sent out from Malacca town to Taboh, Abdul Said's capital. The narrow paths through the undulating jungle provided ideal traps for the Minangkabau, who had called to their aid men from Rembau nearby. The column was harassed, its lines of communication were cut, guns had to be abandoned and it was forced to retreat to Malacca.

This most unexpected reverse led to a re-appraisal. The Dutch records at Malacca were consulted again, and it was discovered that Naning had stopped paying any tribute to the Dutch long before and that it had always been what Abdul Said had claimed, independent *de facto* if not *de jure*. Stubbornly it was decided, however, that the loss of face must be recovered. A much larger expedition plunged into Naning in 1832 at the incredibly slow rate of three miles a month. Taboh was reached in June (the force left Malacca in March) by which time the resistance of the thousand Minangkabau had collapsed. Naning's 200 square miles were brought directly under the administration of Malacca.

This foolish and costly enterprise benefited no-one except Abdul Said, the defeated leader of Naning. He surrendered on the promise of a pardon. The Company gave him a house, a garden, an adequate pension and security for life. By waging a war that cost his enemies £100,000 ($800,000) he obtained an assured income larger than he had ever had before. He lived happily in Malacca, in growing wealth and sanctity, venerated by his followers, and he died, naturally enough a great believer in the British, in 1849.

The Naning War may have had an importance far greater than its petty character might lead one to suppose. From 1833 no further attempts were made by the British to interfere with the affairs of the Malay Peninsula. The next forty or so years witness a great growth, particularly in Penang and Singapore, but after the Naning War the Malay States, from Kedah to Johore, were left well alone. The British had burned their fingers only slightly, but that was enough to reinforce the Indian directive which insisted that the Straits Settlements mind their own business. To this consideration we must now turn.

6. SINGAPORE, 1833-1873

In many respects Singapore was a neglected city during this period, for in 1833, the year after it became the headquarters of the Straits Settlements Residency, the British Government took away from the East India Company its monopoly of the China trade, the extremely profitable tea trade to London. The Straits therefore ceased to offer any hope of commercial profit to the Company. Indeed the transport of Indian opium to Canton had already made the settlement largely superfluous from the Company point of view. In the late eighteenth century the Company had been sending annually large quantities of silver, together with all the tin and pepper it could secure, to Canton to buy tea, but by the nineteenth century the Chinese were paying back that silver together with all the tea they could secure in return for the privilege of smoking themselves into insensibility. The growth of the opium imports into China and the exports of silver to buy that opium is illustrated by the following table, compiled from Greenberg.

	Opium Imported to China	Silver Exported from China
1819	4,000 chests	$ 850,000
1829	16,000 "	6,650,000
1833	20,500 "	unknown
1839	40,000 "	unknown

Singapore and the Straits Settlements generally were retained through broad factors of national importance, not through any narrow Company desire, and the Company endeavoured throughout this period to see that its custody of the Straits Settlements cost it as little as possible. It was not interested as a Company in promoting British trade as a whole, and although many of its Directors were national leaders, the Company as a body saw no reason why it should encourage the activities of those same groups of merchants that were under-mining or had overthrown its monopolistic position in India or China. From 1833 onwards its one aim, therefore, was to keep the Straits deficit as low as possible and so Singapore was ignored.

Singapore suffered much, in the way of neglect, as did the other two towns. It suffered too on the occasions when Bengal noted its existence, for example when it endeavoured by its Currency Act of 1855 to push the Indian rupee into an area where the Mexican dollar and cent were a standard currency, trusted throughout the archipelago. This was rare however, for usually the Straits were left to suffer alone. But there were many compensations for this lack of Bengal interest. After 1826 there were virtually no problems of foreign policy, as Siam and Holland had both been eliminated from the area; neither were there any commercial problems, apart from piracy, which were beyond the powers of the merchants to settle. Strong government leadership, therefore, in this age of *laissez-faire,* was not called for in the Straits at this time.

Although the Straits ports never yielded a profit to the Company, many fortunes were made there by enterprising private merchants, and it was during these decades that a most spectacular increase in the trade and the prosperity of Singapore particularly took place. While Malacca stagnated, and Penang grew steadily, in Singapore the absence of import and export duties, the security, the efficient arrangements and the steadily growing accumulation of skills and specialised services offered by European, Indian and Chinese firms around the harbour attracted trade from all over the archipelago, and from China, India and Europe. Singapore, as Raffles had foretold, became the hub of trade in the Eastern Seas, despite the efforts of the Dutch to force trade into their own harbours.

European and Asian merchants flourished alike in a society devoted to making money. All appreciated the absence of official restraints, the unrestricted immigration of labour, and the freedom from all taxation upon commerce, upon incomes, even upon the luxuries of life. Only man's vices were taxed; the government remained largely inactive, its administrators being too few to do much at all. Occasionally India attempted to impose port dues or harbour taxes, as in 1856, so that the annual deficit might be overcome; but however small, the suggested tax was bitterly attacked as an infringement of Singapore's freedom of trade. This was the town's sacred cow; kick that and the whole population objected.

Singapore's trade, assisted by a number of external developments, grew rapidly. One external development of great importance to Singapore occurred in 1842, when James Brooke became the ruler of Sarawak, on the southernmost and wildest river of the impotent but ancient Sultanate of Brunei in Borneo. Born in 1803, Brooke had served in the East India Company, being wounded in 1825 in the first Anglo-Burmese war. He had resigned from the Company in 1829, and on inheriting £30,000 from his father he had purchased a schooner and had sailed to South-East Asia on a romantic mission of exploration and enquiry.

He had visited the west coast of Borneo first in 1839. Kuching, the village on the Sarawak river, was nearly as small then as the kampong which Raffles had found on Singapore island. It consisted of a hundred or so Malays, three Chinese shops, and a minute trade with Singapore in antimony ore, dug by forced labour, the trade being restricted by the pirates that prowled the seas in between. In the jungles behind the village the Dyaks were in rebellion against the ruler, Raja Muda Hassim, the uncle of the Sultan of Brunei, and when in late 1840 on a second visit Brooke succeeded in quelling the revolt he was offered and accepted the government of the river settlement. This was confirmed by the Sultan in 1842.

Brooke turned immediately to the establishment of law and order along his river, and to the suppression of piracy off-shore. On a brief visit to Singapore he met Captain Keppel, whose ship, H.M.S. *Dido,* had participated the previous year (1842) in the first China War. The two returned to Sarawak, and a determined sweep was made against the strongholds of the Borneo pirates. Subsequently Brooke was able to secure other units of the Royal Navy, which continued the attack in this wild area, attacks which in 1845 culminated in the destruction of the main pirate base in Marudu Bay, at the extreme northern tip of Borneo, and in

1846 in cession by the Sultan of Brunei of the minute island of Labuan, later to be joined to the Straits Settlements.[1] Its establishment, and the steady acquisition by Brooke and his nephew, Charles, who succeeded him in 1868, of the lawless west Borneo rivers, almost eliminated piracy from that area, and so reduced considerably the source of Singapore piracy. At the same time the spread of law and order internally permitted the country to develop, and provided Singapore with a new market. In 1833 Sarawak's trade with Singapore was nil. Forty years later (1873) it was worth over half a million dollars.[2]

Singapore trade was also increased by another British acquisition, the establishment of Hong Kong in 1842. Canton had long been found inadequate as the sole base for foreign trade, even in the eighteenth century, and British relations with China had grown increasingly unsatisfactory. An embassy headed by Lord Macartney, despatched in 1793, seven years after the founding of Penang, had made fruitless representations to the emperor, and a further mission in 1816, led by Lord Amherst, charged by the East India Company to secure some easing of the restrictions upon residence and trade at Canton, was equally unsuccessful. The basic reason for the failure of both missions was that the Imperial Court, encouraged by the Cantonese merchants, regarded the foreigners at Canton as tributary vassals, as barbarians, and contemptuously refused to admit that the Europeans were representatives of independent and sovereign states. Events moved towards an impasse that could be broken only by war.

In 1834, following the abolition of the East India Company's monopoly of trade, and in response to a Chinese request that a 'headman' be appointed to control the British community in Canton, Lord Napier was appointed as superintendent of trade

---

[1] Labuan, ceded to Great Britain in 1846, was a separate Crown Colony until the end of 1889. It was administered, 1890–1905, by the British North Borneo Chartered Company. In 1906 the Governor of the Straits Settlements became also, and one suspects, reluctantly, Governor of the island. It was annexed to the Straits Settlements in 1907, was constituted a separate settlement in 1912, and went back to North Borneo in 1946.

[2] The history of nineteenth century Sarawak is well told by G. Irwin, *Nineteenth Century Borneo* (The Hague, 1955). See also S. Runciman, *The White Rajahs* (London, 1960).

in China. He insisted on dealing directly with the Viceroy of the Southern Provinces, while the latter insisted that the noble Lord dealt through the *hong* merchants, as befitting his lowly position. Both sides persisted, the one in seeking recognition as an equal, the other in maintaining the pretence that the Englishman was a tribute vassal. Other grievances over opium, the inadequacies and injustices of the cruel and antiquated Chinese law and the restriction of trade to one port brought matters finally to a head. In 1839 two British frigates defeated a fleet of Chinese war junks, and a state of war was created between China and Great Britain.

Although British troops arrived in 1840, the war was fought with extreme caution; one almost might say with indifference. Various desultory attacks upon Canton by the British produced no apparent result. In the spring of 1842, however, the effects of a powerful and sustained naval drive up the Yangtze were instantaneous. Here Britain was cutting a vital artery of the Chinese state. By July the British had taken Chinkiang, where the Grand Canal crosses the river, and by August they had arrived off Nanking. It was an irresistible advance along the Empire's great interior waterway, so China negociated. On 29th August 1842, the Nanking Treaty ended the war. China paid a large indemnity ($21,000,000), permitted foreigners to reside and to trade at Canton, Amoy, Foochow, Ningpo and Shanghai, accepted the suggestion that a regular tariff and customs schedule be drawn up, agreed to treat British officials as the equals of Chinese officials, and finally ceded the uninhabitated and rocky island of Hong Kong to Britain as a base depot for its merchants. So began the economic penetration of China.

At the same time as the interior was penetrated, there radiated out from those ports, but particularly from Hong Kong, an arc of trading contacts with other lands, of which the most important was the direct connection between Hong Kong and Singapore established by Chinese and British shippers and merchants. This artery of trade grew steadily as at each end the hinterland was developed and extended. Both Hong Kong and Singapore mushroomed into great cities as the nineteenth century progressed, flourishing on the steady growth of East-West trade, as well as regional and local developments. Each fed the other, stimulating and being stimulated by their mutual success. It is still the same today.[3]

During this period (1833–1873) Singapore benefited by the growth of trade that followed this British expansion round the South China Sea, to Sarawak, Labuan and Hong Kong. Another external development that affected Singapore considerably was the establishment of trading facilities in Siam. The efforts to promote trade, by Crawfurd (in 1824) and Burney (in 1826), have already been described. Another mission by Raja Brooke in 1850 was also unsuccessful. Siam remained, before and after their efforts, as indifferent to the West as it had been a hundred years before. Of more importance to its inhabitants, it remained also capricious and incompetent, and it existed as a primitive, backward country throughout the first half of the nineteenth century.

In 1851 there came to the throne one of Asia's outstanding men, King Mongkut. His brother had thrust him aside to take the throne, and for thirty years Mongkut had been a Buddhist priest, free of court restrictions, able to mix without restraint and to indulge in his search for knowledge and education. While his brother lived a very isolated life Mongkut learned English, studied mathematics, and read of the many developments that were transforming the western nations. In 1851 when he came to the throne, he decided that the traditional attitude of hostility and indifference would benefit no-one. A strong wind was blowing and he decided to bend with it.

In 1855 Siam signed the Bowring Treaty, as it is usually called, after the able and well-received leader of the delegation that negotiated for Great Britain. By it Siam agreed to limit the duties payable by British merchants to 3%, and laid down an agreed schedule of tariffs. British subjects were permitted to purchase land in Bangkok, and so safely erect godowns and offices; and a British consul was admitted to the country to watch over their interests.

This 1855 treaty opened the country to foreign trade, and

---

[3] For a further study of the growth see G. B. Endacott, *A History of Hong Kong* (Oxford, 1959).

abolished the crippling and capricious levies that had so hamstrung earlier contracts, and against which Crawfurd, Burney and Brooke had argued in vain. Mongkut at the same time took effective steps to make the country safe, so that foreigners would trade without thought of annexation. The chief British trading interests to benefit from this new state of affairs were the Chinese and British merchants in Singapore. Siam was open, but its chief river was so shallow and its coast so lined with mud banks that only small ships could penetrate to its capital. Almost without exception these vessels came from Singapore, already equipped and experienced in entrepôt traffic. By 1870 over three-quarters of Siam's rapidly growing import and export trade was in the holds of the small ships from Singapore, and Britain was looking with increased interest at the primitive and uncontrolled states on the eastern coast of the Malay Peninsula that lay in between. Mongkut (and his son Chulalongkorn who succeeded him in 1868), by modernizing the state, and making it safe both for foreigners and for the indigenous people, preserved it, alone of the countries of South-East Asia, from European domination; while by opening it to trade he assisted in the growth of Singapore. Singapore's trade with Siam has remained an important feature for over one hundred years.

The Siamese trade constituted perhaps 5% of Singapore's imports and exports by the end of this period, as compared with the 18% from various parts of India. China's trade was about 14%, while the direct exchange with the United Kingdom was over 18%. One other country which came to play a most important part in Singapore's growth was Java and its ancillary islands.

Despite the Anglo-Dutch Treaty of 1824, which by Article 2 permitted either country to impose double the tariff on its rival that it imposed on itself, Singapore's trade with Java, and, to a considerably lesser extent with Sumatra, grew steadily in this period.

A substantial portion of this trade was (and is today) in cotton piece goods, imported from India. These were subject to a levy of 25%, while piece goods from Holland were admitted at 12½%. In 1866 a more liberal tariff was introduced, dropping the tax to 16%. In that year exports to Java totalled $7 million, an increase of 113% over 1824.

The Dutch had attempted to capitalise on the appeal of Singapore by establishing their own free ports. In 1829 Rhio was declared a free port, followed in 1834 by Pontianak and Sambas in west Borneo, and in 1847 by Macassar. This, together with the opening to foreign trade of over thirty minor ports in Java, Sumatra, Bali and elsewhere between 1826 and 1858, assisted trade in general and Singapore in particular. So too did the steady consolidation and expansion of Dutch authority, particularly over the island of Java once the Java War had ended in 1830. By degrees between 1830–1870 Java was completely occupied, pacified and made prosperous, and Dutch activity there and their neglect of the other islands alike assisted Singapore. It was the general prosperity of the ever increasing millions of Javanese however, more than anything else, which made this part of Singapore's trade so valuable. In the twentieth century it was to become paramount.

TRADE OF SINGAPORE

	$ million
1823	11½
1833	18
1853	36½
1863	52
1873	88

This regional trade and the distant connections with Europe were affected profoundly during this period by the technological developments in the means of communication occurring in the West. Sail was giving way to steam all over the world. Over large stretches of wild ocean, where winds blew strongly and constantly, the change was late in coming, and there remained a place in world transport for the graceful sailing ship until the First World War; but in Malaysia, an area of light, variable winds and short voyages, steamships became ever more prominent from the 1840's onward.

In 1840 the Peninsular and Oriental Steam Navigation Company introduced a regular service from the Red Sea to South India, and in 1844 extended it to Singapore and Hong Kong. A regular steamer service from Singapore up the coasts of the Malay Peninsula and on to Siam was begun in 1860's. The British India Line was founded in 1856.[4] The Blue Funnel Line, established by the Holts in 1865, became another competitor of the P. & O. The Dutch, with their Rotterdam Lloyd Company founded in 1839, did not change over to steam until 1870, and the big British ships secured most of the traffic, not merely in goods but also in the increasing migration of Chinese into the *Nanyang*, and especially to Singapore, in this period. Nevertheless they too and the Germans participated in this technological transformation. Simultaneously the telegraph cable came, and Singapore was linked by it to London.

Both the innumerable feeder services that flowed into Singapore, and the big ships that headed east or west received a tremendous stimulus to their operations by the opening of the Suez Canal in 1869. It led to a great expansion of steamer services from Europe to the Far East, for, with much lower cost, far more goods could be profitably imported and exported from Singapore and South-East Asia generally. Singapore, partly as a result of British initiative in availing itself of the opportunities given it by the Suez Canal, partly by its own free port services and specialised skills (exemplified by such great shipping firms as Mansfields), became by the 1870's the economic heart of maritime South-East Asia. "The economic life of all the islands, with the exception of Java, was focused upon Singapore."[5]

The Suez Canal produced not merely economic results. The trade route to Europe, instead of moving from Singapore through the Sunda Straits and across to the southern tip of Africa—the Cape of Good Hope—and then up to Europe, as it had done during the era of sail, after 1869 moved up the Straits of Malacca and across to Colombo, Aden and Suez. This brought the Malay States on to the very edge of what was

---

[4] The fascinating history of this Company, with Singapore ever present in it, is told by G. Blake in *B.I. Centenary, 1856–1956* (London, 1956).

[5] G. C. Allen and A. G. Donnithorne, *Western Enterprise in Indonesia and Malaya* (London, 1957), p. 216.

becoming a very important life-line that stretched from London to Canton. Previously to 1869 it scarcely mattered that the Malay States remained backward, warring and uncontrolled. After 1869 the trade route had to be protected, and it is no coincidence that British intervention in the Malay States followed so closely the opening of the Suez Canal. Here in fact is a great dividing line in Malayan history.[6]

The advent of steam permitted Singapore at last to deal effectively with piracy, a curse which had considerably restricted its early trade. The numerous islands that crowd up to Singapore, the shallows and reefs that intersect them, the mangrove lined inlets that flow into seas that are scarcely ruffled by breezes for long stretches of time: all this favoured the pirate and the slaver in the days of sail, and at times early Singapore resembled a besieged town as the pirates prowled offshore.

During the eighteen-twenties and -thirties, as Singapore developed despite them, the pirates became increasingly audacious. The Lanun pirates, from Mindanao and North-east Borneo, were perhaps the most numerous, the best organised and the most feared. Their fleets came up to Singapore with the advent of the southerly monsoon, sometimes in units of one hundred *prahus* or more, their leaders in chain armour, their discipline perfect and their intent obvious. The only consolation was that they appeared only with the monsoon. The Chinese pirates, on the other hand, lurked continually off the east coast of Johore and the prominent islands there, such as Pulo Tioman and Pulo Aur, that have guided South China Sea sailors to the Singapore Straits for millenia, and only a very severe north-east monsoon drove them away. Even then it often merely drove them before the wind closer to Singapore Island. Thirdly, on the island itself, at Changi Point for example, and up all the neighbouring rivers such as the Sungei Johore were Malay pirates, less feared than the others, as they were less ferocious and not as well organised, but they were dangerous enough to the owner of the *prahu* heading for Singapore from Sumatra with a small cargo of coffee, and worthy to be feared even by a small sailing coaster. The

---

[6] The implications of this are examined in the next chapter.

exploits of these and others filled the *Straits Times* and other Singapore papers with accounts of the most brazen and barbaric crimes committed at sea, and caused them to hail with delight the arrival in 1837 of the first steamer, the *Diana,* which secured dramatic successes against the pirates, as it steamed up-wind, or without wind altogether, when they lay becalmed and powerless.

It was a long struggle which continued throughout this period, however, flaring up and then being beaten out like a half extinguished forest fire. Although by the 1870's organised piracy was driven from the waters immediately adjacent to Singapore as the Lanuns, Balagnini and Chinese retreated closer to their home bases, the indigenous Malay pirates, thriving on the chaos of their peninsula, remained and the habit itself was not suppressed until European control was established over the peninsula in the 1870's. As Brooke had demonstrated, the rivers had to be governed for the seas to be safe. But by the 1870's small ships approached Singapore almost as safely as they do today.

During the first fifty years of its existence, Singapore grew up round its river. Here was the heart and here lay the wealth of the port. The river was its first and natural commercial centre. Square rigged vessels from Europe, India or America, junks from China and Siam, *wangkang* and *tope* from Cambodia and the Gulf of Siam, *palari, lambok, golekkan, leteh-leteh* from the islands to the south: all anchored in the shallow bay off the river mouth. Their cargoes were brought to shore (as they are today from the coastal steamers of less than 5,000 tons) by lighter and *tongkong,* and the greater part of the trade of the port was done in the warehouses and the offices of Boat Quay and Raffles Place.

With the advent of steam, and particularly with the cutting of the Suez Canal in 1869, the growth and even the life of all this was threatened. The banks of the river being crowded by fifty years of hectic growth, there was nowhere in the immediate vicinity for the essential coaling facilities. A port without coal had become as useless as a ship without a bottom, and there was every indication that Singapore increasingly would have been bypassed by the big ships, and would have become another Malacca or at best another Madras, but for a most fortunate development.

The geological structure of the Malay Peninsula west of the main range is such that the coastal strata of rocks slope gently downward, almost horizontally out to sea, producing mud banks and shallows stretching right across to Sumatra. Similarly, to the east of the main range the strata there too slope gently down, and again there is a shallow sea. Nowhere on either coast is there deep water close in, with one exception. A few miles from Singapore River, at the southernmost tip of the island, where two offshore islands form a narrow strait, a most untypical geological fault has created a deep fissure, an abrupt drop, hard against the land. Scoured constantly by tides that sweep in and out of either end, this narrow strait saved Singapore from decay and possible extinction. By keeping the channels clear of silt it helped to make it one of the world's greatest ports.

The depth and possible utility of this harbour was discovered as early as 1819 by Farquhar, who wrote a glowing report on it which was ignored.[7] The harbour had been used in preference to the main Straits of Singapore from as early as A.D. 1300, although its use as a means of passing from the Straits of Malacca to the South China Sea had been forgotten by Europeans by the close of the seventeenth century, and its very existence was unknown a century later. Throughout all this time a community of *orang laut* lived there, unchanging in their manners, living in the nineteenth century (and indeed in the twentieth) as Dampier and others had described them centuries before. In 1823 they were joined by the Temenggong, ordered there by Raffles (and where he became immediately a pirate), and in the late 1830's by the first Europeans to move southwards from the town in order to reside on the hills near New Harbour, as it was called; but still it remained unused.

New Harbour began to attract attention only after the advent of steam had made coal bunkering necessary, and docking facilities desirable. Sailing ships can be beached and hauled over on to their beam ends, but steamers with propellers or paddles

[7] For a comprehensive account of the harbour, see C. A. Gibson Hill & G. E. Bogaars, *Singapore Old Strait and New Harbour, 1300–1870;* and *The Tanjong Pagar Dock Company, 1864–1905*, Memoir of the Raffles Museum, No. 3 (Singapore, 1956).

need protection. Shortly after the P. and O. service started in 1845, plans were published in Singapore for a dry dock in the New Harbour area, and although this scheme lapsed, in 1852 the P. & O. Company opened up New Harbour by building their own sheltered pier. This provided ample godown space for bunkering, and its worth led others to follow suit. In 1859 a patent ship and graving dock was built there at the western end by Captain Cloughton. Another dock was built in 1866; but useful though the Strait was for docking purposes, it was as a deep water harbour that it came into its own.

In 1864 a number of local merchants, led by James Guthrie, formed the Tanjong Pagar Dock Company. Intended originally to build a dry dock, the firm was sustained in its early years by the revenue derived from the small wharf it built nearby. Its management was quick to grasp the implications, and it set out to build more. The company's activities coincided with the cutting of the Suez Canal,[8] and as the flow of ships increased, so too did the facilities for them in New Harbour. In 1869, before the Canal shortened the east-west journey, the tonnage of steamers calling at Singapore was only 265,000, a third of the total tonnage of 620,000. By 1874 the steam tonnage stood at 850,000, out of a total tonnage of 1,104,000. Other concerns too participated in this business, but the Tanjong Pagar Dock Company swallowed them all. By 1899 it owned the whole northern side of the Strait, where 15,000 feet of wharfage provided quicker, safer and cheaper service than anything round the corner in Singapore Bay. Singapore had been saved by a geological fault.

While every year hundreds of big ships used New Harbour, renamed Keppel Harbour in 1900,[9] the river continued, however, as the main centre for the small craft and coasters, as the grading, sorting and packing godowns for their Straits Produce remained there. Thus there grew up, particularly from 1869 onwards, from the opening of the Suez Canal, two harbours, one

---

8 For an excellent examination of the impact of this on Singapore, see G. Bogaars, *The Effect of the Opening of the Suez Canal on the Trade and Development of Singapore* (JMBRAS, vol. 28, 1955).

9 In this year nearly 6 million tons of shipping called at the harbour.

for the ocean liners, the other for the coasters. This division still exists today, and together they constitute the heart of Singapore.

2

Throughout this period the population of Singapore steadily increased. In 1833 there was an estimated 20,000; by 1873, forty years later, there were 100,000. Many thousands more had come, made a living and left again. This population showed an equally steady increase in the percentage that was Chinese. In 1833 about 40% of Singapore's population was Chinese; by 1873 it was 60%. This Chinese population presented the British administration with numerous problems of a complexity and gravity so acute as to threaten the very continuation of that administration, but which by the end of this period had been faced and solved. Chief of these were the actual traffic in labour from China and the secret society menace in Singapore itself.

The Chinese migrants to Singapore came very largely from Kwangtung and Fukien, maritime provinces of South China, legendary for their turbulence and clannishness; the traditional home of rebels.[10] Many others came from Kwangsi, another southern province, or from the island of Hainan. They were classified under five categories: the Macaos or Cantonese from the neighbourhood of Canton: the Khehs or Hakkas from the interior of Kwantung, Kiangsi and Fukien; the Teochews from Swatow and its vicinity; the Hailams from Hainan; and the Hokkiens from Amoy and other places in Fukien. The Cantonese, Teochews and in particular the Hokkiens predominated, and gravitated to the urban life of the Straits. The Hailams and Hakkas were (and are) considered by the others as somewhat inferior and primitive, although the Hailams from an early period

[10] The standard work on the Chinese in Malaya is by V. Purcell, *The Chinese in Malaya* (Oxford, 1946). See also his more extensive *Chinese in Southeast Asia* (Oxford, 1949).

excelled in cooking, and their coffee-shops were patronised by all. The Hakkas had two characteristics that set them somewhat apart: they were agriculturalists, whereas throughout the *Nanyang* all the other Chinese left that labour to the local communities; and as the nineteenth century advanced they were converted in China to Christianity in small but significant numbers. Irrespective of their differences, however, they all regarded government, from their Chinese experience, as something objectionable. The law as administered by the Mandarins was associated automatically with arbitrariness, and they brought with them from China an innate prejudice against constituted authority.

They came from China under the most appalling conditions. The majority of migrants in this period were unable to pay their way to Singapore, and they came under agreement with junk masters or brokers to work for anyone at the place of destination who was willing to pay for their passage. As the trade developed and middlemen entered the business, Chinese labour brokers in Singapore (or *coolie brokers* as they were referred to for a hundred years) worked in co-operation with coffee-shop keepers in Swatow, Canton, Macao, Amoy and elsewhere, who packed the junks with poor unfortunate flotsam and jetsam collected for the Straits Settlements and the plantations of the Dutch East Indies.

Throughout this period, when the annual arrivals of *Sinkehs* rose, it is roughly estimated, from 2,000 in 1833 to 23,000 in 1873, the labour trade was under no supervision at all, and the abuses grew steadily worse. These abuses, the inhumanity of what became virtual slavery, began in China in the actual recruitment of the labourer. He represented a saleable commodity, and every known method of impressment and kidnapping was used to fill the waiting junks with their human cargo. The abuses continued on the journey, as the heavy junks, with hatches battened down, staggered south through the north-east monsoon. They were 'hell ships,' for as the master's main interest was to import as many Chinese as possible, it was not uncommon for 1400 men or more to be crowded into 800 ton junks, where they lived or died under appalling conditions. The masters were free of nearly all restrictions, for China could then do nothing to control its shipping or its migrating subjects, and British efforts at amelioration undertaken in Hong Kong from 1853 onwards were easily avoided. Finally in Singapore itself there were further abuses, as in many cases the landed labourers were imprisoned in cramped quarters and 'pig-sty' houses until they were disposed of, underfed and generally ill treated.

It became increasingly obvious that these abuses, particularly those being committed in Singapore itself, demanded the intervention of the government. Its reputation, particularly as the 1860's gave way to the 1870's, suffered sadly as whole scale kidnapping of labour for Javanese estates occurred, and as inflammatory notices were posted accusing the police of conniving at such practices. A government's primary duty is to guarantee to its people a minimum sense of security. As the period now under discussion drew to a close such a sense of security was denied to a large section of the community. But the question of rooting out the malpractices of this labour trade, and of protecting both the labourers and the inhabitants of Singapore bristled with difficulties, not the least of which was its connection with the problem of the secret societies that had come down from South China.

South China was the home of the Heaven and Earth Society, or Hung League, a secret society of great antiquity. Although originally a quasi-religious organisation of lofty aims, it became, after the Manchu conquests of China in 1644, a revolutionary political league, an anti-government organisation that bred on the dislike held by the South Chinese for the injustices and cruelty of Peking. It became steadily more and more a terrorist organisation. Wherever the labourer went, the Triad Society (as it was called by Europeans) went too, to protect those within its folds, to tyrannise and terrorise those without, and to become so powerful that everywhere in the *Nanyang* it proved inimical to order and security. Because in this period the Straits Government was both completely ignorant of the character, customs and language of the people it governed, and indifferent to their welfare, at times the Triad Society acquired such power that it threatened the very State itself.

The Ghee Hin Society (the branch of the Triad that was organised in Singapore) dates from the earliest days of the port. It was probably formed by the colony's earliest Chinese migrants, those who came from Malacca. In about 1840, new migrants coming from China formed another branch, the Ghee Hock Society, and from then on, as these two powerful groups fought for power, there was trouble in Singapore. British law was quite ineffective to quell the growth of this dangerous rival to the government. No witnesses would ever give evidence; it was no crime merely to belong to a secret society; and their tentacles of control crawled over the whole island.

In 1851 the secret societies rose to smash one of their rival groups, the Christian Chinese, who were largely Hakka agriculturalists. They had been unable to extend their control over them, so in a wave of violent rioting among the pepper and gambier plantations some 500 were slashed to death. In 1854 there was another violent, uncontrollable outbreak, this time in the streets of Singapore itself, as the Ghee Hin fought the Ghee Hocks. For ten days the town was given up to the murdering rioters until their fury was spent, and boundaries of territory, the cause of the fighting, agreed upon. In 1857 there were anti-government riots, the typical reaction of the ignorant and uninformed Chinese to new regulations the nature of which they did not understand, and the execution of which inconvenienced them. In 1863, again in 1865, and in Penang in 1867, there were further violent outbreaks.

By this time the existence of the Chinese secret societies was known, their organisation, methods and powers published in book and article, and their leaders, prominent men, had been named.[11] There was a steady denunciation of their activities both by the public and by the Straits Government, which constantly pressed Bengal for legislation to solve this evil. Its pleas were ignored.

The indifference of India to a grave social and administrative problem was one of the main reasons that encouraged the leading

---

[11] The standard work of pioneer scholarship was G. Schlegel, *The Hung League* (Batavia, 1866). Its usefulness can be gauged by the fact that it was reprinted as late as 1959.

members of the Straits Settlements to press for a change in administrative control from India to London, a change that occurred in 1867. The Straits Settlements government, whose previous requests for measures by which the relationship of the administration with the Chinese population might be improved had usually been ignored, was after 1867 empowered to legislate fully for the requirements of the Colony. One of the first acts of the new governor, Sir Harry Ord, was to strengthen the government's hand against the secret societies.

By an 1867 Act he acquired the power of deporting offenders of the peace, and of apprehending headmen of belligerent societies, in many cases to do reluctant patrol duty as special constables in riot torn areas. In 1869 a further Act was passed, which insisted on the registration of all associations of ten or more persons, thus permitting the police to discover their office bearers and their objects. This was ineffective, however, as no Chinese secret society felt it necessary to reveal its presence, and of the three extremely respectable Chinese leaders that the government brought in to check affidavits and statements of those that did register, Messrs. Hoh Ah Kay (Whampao), Tan Kim Cheng and Tan Seng Poh, subsequent research has shown that at least the latter two were in fact leaders of the Ghee Hin and Ghee Hock Societies, which by 1871 were rioting again. By 1872 they were rioting against the government, and were claiming to be the real rulers of Singapore, as in many respects they were, while many of their unfortunate compatriots were petitioning the government for an Immigration Officer to protect the *Sinkeh.*

The two problems, that of Chinese migration and that of secret societies were not solved for some time. Pressure from London, perturbed by Parliamentary criticism of the abuses suffered by labourers *en route,* met with determined resistance from the Singapore shipping fraternity, fearful of its profits. It yielded, however, in 1874, to accept an Ordinance that regulated conditions on steamers. The abuses on land and the secret society stranglehold (demonstrated again by bad riots in 1867), were not tackled effectively until 1877, when the recommendation of a Government Commission, that there should be a Protector of Chinese, was acted upon.

By that time at least 60% of the Chinese community were members of one of ten powerful secret societies. Groups of *Sinkehs* were being kidnapped, and virtually all Chinatown was paying in the form of protection money a rate or levy to an *imperium in imperio,* while clashes on society boundaries constantly imperilled what law and order there was. But from this date, 1877, and the appointment of W. A. Pickering, a brilliantly successful man, as the first Protector of Chinese with the task of watching their interests and of combating the societies, the situaction slowly improved. With the help of the Chinese community, already wearied by the secret Societies' excesses, the government gradually acquired a grip on the colony by this Act. By introducing a direct line between government and governed, it took perhaps the most important administrative measure of a hundred years.[12] Chinese co-operation, no less than British initiative, ensured its success.

3.

The indifference of Bengal towards secret societies had been part of a general indifference throughout this period towards the problems of Singapore and the Straits Settlements generally, and although the Supreme Government was criticised for not concerning itself with the secret societies, it was criticised also for ignoring many other problems as well. Chief among the critics was W. H. Read, perhaps politically the most important Malayan outside official circles in the nineteenth century who fought most actively against Indian control, in which the indifference of Calcutta was matched by the ignorance of the officers sent to administer the Settlements.

In the early days after the abolition of the Presidency of

[12] See E. Thio, *The Singapore Chinese Protectorate 1823–1877,* in Journal of the South Seas Society (vol. xvi, 1960) pp. 40–80. Note that it was not until 1890 however, when the Dangerous Societies Ordinance was passed, that a legal measure of equal importance was passed. This ensured as great a control over the secret societies as was possible.

Penang the old civil servants had stayed on the peninsula. They were reinforced after 1824 by the former Bencoolen officers, who knew the Straits and to some extent the language and customs of the people. Through the 1830's and 1840's therefore there may have been but a few officers in the peninsula but they were experienced in local conditions. As they grew old and retired, however, they were replaced by men direct from India, young men who had no training or experience of the peculiar conditions of the Straits, and who regarded a tour of service here as an unwelcome break in their Indian service. As soon as possible they hurried back to Bengal, back to the much richer prizes of promotion in the Indian Civil Service. So in the 1850's there was a continual growing outcry, led by Read, at the lack of knowledge of local conditions, of the indifference and ignorance of Bengal, and of the need for a specially trained Straits Civil Service.[13]

The criticisms of the Indian administrators at the Straits, their scornful comparison of Penang or Singapore with Calcutta or Madras, touched Read and others on a tender spot. By the 1850's many residents of Singapore were becoming rather proud of their city. It boasted of many fine buildings. Its wealthy classes lived a life with many attractions, provincial no doubt in comparison to Peking or London, but equally as pleasant, so they thought, as Calcutta or Canton. Moreover, with the constant growth of prosperity, rising at a rate that left Calcutta in the doldrums, came an increasing pride in the Straits and growing appreciation of its importance. In 1833 the trade of Singapore was a little over $18 million, itself no mean achievement when it is recollected that Singapore had been established a mere fourteen years earlier. By 1873, forty years later, the figure had risen to over $88 million. Yet this immensely prosperous and proud city was still neglected by India. It dumped its convicts there (over 4,000 by 1857), and that is about all.

Businessmen such as Read felt that this indifference was damaging not merely the internal stability of Singapore but its external trade prospects as well. By the 1850's the problem of

---

13 This is well brought out in L. A. Mills, *British Malaya, 1824–1867* (JMBRAS, 1925).

competition with foreign powers was emerging once more. The Dutch were excluding British goods and extending their control in Sumatra, and elsewhere in the archipelago, and there were fears that there the 1824 Treaty was being infringed. Indeed by the 1871 Agreement, which confirmed the Dutch in their possession of Jambi and Siak in south Sumatra, this was recognized. The French were expanding in South Indo-China, and Singapore's trade was threatened there too. The Germans were becoming active in trade, and the Spanish were moving south from the Philippines. South-East Asia was becoming part of a Europe that was hostile to British trade, but in remote India these possible threats to Singapore were ignored.

Read for long had taken an active interest in the Malay Peninsula. He was a close friend of the ruler of Johore. He felt that in this peninsula there was an obvious market for Singapore. Business connections from the island were extending into the various Malay States during this time, Singapore's trade with them being in the vicinity of $1.5 million in 1866, but the investment of capital and the participation of traders in such enterprises was a dangerous affair. The States were constantly warring, and what was a profitable trade one year, would disappear with great loss the following year on an outbreak of anarchy. The Straits merchants, led by Read, knew full well that if peaceful conditions were established in the peninsula a greatly increased trade with Singapore and Penang would result. As no move to establish those conditions could be made while the East India Company maintained its old policy of non-intervention, the merchants found in this economic pressure yet another reason for urging direct control from London.

The final reason for the transfer, the spark which set off the explosive material was the Indian Mutiny of 1857. The ineptitude of the Indian Government was clearly shown by this tragedy. Coming as it did after the maladroit 1855 Currency Act, and the attempt by India in 1856 to impose port dues on Singapore, this terrible year convinced the merchants of the Straits Settlements that they must disassociate themselves from such a decadent régime.

Singapore had been provided with no representative institution, no Legislative Council (another bone of contention among the British merchants), and the arguments against Indian control and against local bureaucratic blunders had been held most frequently, as a result, in the Press, the *Straits Times* and the *Singapore Free Press* being the most powerful. These papers now supported the storm of protest against the continuation of the Company in India, and they noted with favour the Bengal petition to the British Parliament which requested the reform of the Indian government. Among those reforms, they urged (in a Petition which they were instrumental in despatching to London in 1857), was the separation of the Straits from that government.

Although the numerous points of criticism were well founded, although the neglect and ignorance of India was tacitly admitted, it still took ten years of discussion, largely over financial matters, before the British Government would accept the argument that it should administer the Straits, for it had no desire to inherit the annual deficit that India was still paying. In London John Crawfurd, the former Resident, who was influential behind the scenes, managed to convince the British Government that Singapore could and would pay its way. With this assured, the Treasury removed its objections, and on 1st April 1867 the Colonial Office replaced the India Office (the East India Company having been dissolved in 1858) as the administrative parents of the Straits Settlements.

This, of course, did not solve the problems peculiar to the Straits, and most decidedly it did not alter the official policy of non-intervention in the Malay States. Thus too much emphasis should not be given to this administrative change. Nevertheless, the establishment of a colonial régime was of immediate benefit, for if the problems were not solved, at least they were tackled. With the formation of a Straits Civil Service (begun in 1867), officers became aware of local conditions.[14] A Legislative Council (established in 1867) made available the experience of the business community, and gave adequate administrative power to the

---

[14] A civil service separate from India had been created in 1805, when Penang became a Presidency. It was abolished as a separate body in 1830.

Straits Settlements. By the transfer of 1867 the Straits were permitted to put their home affairs in order, and they devoted themselves to their internal problems with increasing success. At the same time their concern over their peninsula neighbours increased.

7. INTERVENTION

In the previous three chapters we have concentrated on the establishment and development of the Straits Settlements, and on the foundation and growth of the British controlled posts on the flank of the Malay Peninsula. It is now time to turn to a consideration of the peninsula itself, and to narrate the events that led to the intervention of the British in 1874.

For most of the nineteenth century A.D. the Malay Peninsula was much the same as it had been in the nineteenth century B.C., a tangled mass of jungle. Unbroken for thousands of square miles by any clearing, the scattered, primitive kampongs where lived the Malay clung almost invariably to convenient, well concealed reaches of the rivers that alone provided conveyance. The largest of these rivers maintained precariously the political legacy of the centuries, and the Sultanates preserved a traditional framework, but separated by the Anglo-Dutch Treaty of 1824, and the Perak Treaty of 1826, from any outside stimulus, or from the fear of any attack, and thus deprived of any threat to respond to, these river states, as the nineteenth century progressed, turned in upon themselves and sank, into a fratricidal decline.[1]

The Malay State nearest to Singapore was Johore. Here a number of rivers, including the Muar, which flows westwards into the Straits of Malacca, the Mersing, which goes eastwards into the South China Seas, and the Johore, the main stream of the state, which flows south into the Straits of Johore opposite the north-eastern tip of Singapore, were still maintained as one state, under the effective control, in the 1830's, of the Temenggong. Johore was almost uninhabitated. Perhaps 30,000 Malays and aborigines were scattered along the coast and up those streams in 1833, but over most of the State the jungle yielded to no one.

---

[1] For a detailed examination of the structure of these States see Gullick, *Indigenous Political Systems of Western Malaya* (London, 1958).

The same applied to Pahang, its next door neighbour. In size it was another large state, drained by the most powerful of the peninsula streams, the Pahang, together with the Kuantan, yet probably four-fifths of its area was virgin jungle. Nominally part of the Johore Empire, in the 1830's its Bendahara, as with the Johore Temenggong, was in reality an independent ruler. Here some 28,000 Malays were settled along the river, and perhaps 10–12,000 courageous Chinese had infiltrated among them, most of them to work the gold of the interior or to barter sarongs, rice and fish at the squalid villages at the river mouths.

The two other east coast states, Trengganu and Kelantan, each possessed a sizeable river, and retained remnants of an ancient culture. A trickle of jungle produce, a little tin and some gold and pepper were exported. For the most part, however, the Malays here practised, as they still do an agricultural, self-sufficient way of life that did not lend itself to commercial undertakings nor to any other form of economic development; nor was the political stability along the rivers such that they could lead their quiet lives in tranquility, for the ravages of pirates, the internecine feuds of their aristocracy and the intrigues of the Siamese all made their lives precarious and dangerous. Nevertheless the two states between them had a population in the 1830's of nearly 100,000.[2]

Scanty though this seems, the 180,000 people that Johore, Pahang, Kelantan and Trengganu could muster in the 1830's was more than on the west coast, for here the streams were smaller, and the opportunities for the Malay way of life therefore fewer. There were two sizeable units of population in Malacca (40,000) and Penang (80,000), but these were British establishments, epitomising the new Malaya, of Chinese, Indians, Europeans and Eurasians, as well as Malays. Elsewhere on the west coast the old peninsula was almost uninhabitated.

Behind Malacca, on the rivers of the pocket interior states or *negri sembilan* founded by the Minangkabau from Sumatra, a

---

[2] The population figures are taken from a contemporary and extremely interesting account of the Malay Peninsula: T. J. Newbold, *Political and Statistical Account of the British Settlements in the Straits of Malacca*, 2 vols. (London, 1839).

matrilineal society fostered a hardy stock of some 17,000 peasant agriculturalists. Selangor, farther up the coast, although bigger in size (thanks to Bugis strength), than any one of the *negri sembilan,* nevertheless had a mere 12,000. Perak, the ancient state still farther north, had the largest river of the west coast; yet its population was only 35,000. Kedah, the remaining state, and the only one possessing a large area of flat land suitable for padi growing, and where Malay habitation was not necessarily confined to the river bank, did not have a population exceeding 50,000. Excluding the British settlements therefore, the west coast population of the Malay Peninsula in the 1830's hardly exceeded 100,000; and all the states combined barely surpassed 300,000.

The affairs of the peninsula, with only two exceptions, do not warrant close study in a general history of this kind. The north-east states maintained an unobtrusive existence half under the shadow of a Siamese 'umbrella'. Kedah, to the west, was held firmly throughout this period as a Siamese dependency. We can ignore them both. To understand the events of intervention, and of non-intervention, however, we need to look at the history of the tin states of Perak and Selangor, and of Singapore's nearest neighbour, the state of Johore.

Throughout this period Johore was ruled by the greatest Malay of the nineteenth century, Abu Bakar. In many ways he can be compared with King Mongkut of Siam. By the end of the nineteenth century all of South-East Asia had been overrun and occupied by European powers. Two states alone preserved their independence, Siam and Johore. In each case the ruler was largely responsible.

Abu Bakar was the grandson of the Temenggong whom Raffles had met in 1819, and with whom he had signed a treaty. The Temenggong then was the *de facto* ruler of the island, and although Raffles had recognised Hussein, the elder brother of the Sultan of Rhio-Johore, as the legal sultan, and therefore the *de jure* ruler, this was merely for diplomatic reasons. The British did not attempt to impose the Sultan upon the Malays, and the Temenggong kept control of Johore. Hussein, although he came to Singapore and resided there, never had the strength to secure any authority; neither did his son, whereas the Temenggong's son, Ibrahim, became even more powerful, until in 1855, the Straits governor prevailed on the Sultan's son, Ali, to sign a treaty with Ibrahim, ceding the entire state of Johore in full sovereignty, to Ibrahim. Ali was recognised as Sultan, for what it was worth, but he was given merely the small area of Muar.

Abu Bakar succeeded his father Ibrahim in 1862, having inherited from him the authority of an independent ruler. He had inherited other characteristics as well. He was a strong man, gifted with political talents of a high order. He had been brought up in Singapore, and the ways of the West were not unknown to him. The defects of Malay administration at this time were many. Injustice, a lack of security to property or person unless he was of Malay royalty, a lack of endeavour: all these were common place: but not in Johore. "By his exertions, his just rule and his careful preservation of life and property his country has attained a foremost position" as Swettenham puts it.[3]

In 1868, after a visit to England, Abu Bakar dropped his title of Temenggong, and elevated himself to Maharajah. It marked another step. In 1877 Ali died, and after a certain amount of squabbling and disputing, the title of power passed in 1885 to him who obviously had that power, Abu Bakar. An Agreement of 1885 with Britain made him the Sultan of Johore. By this same Agreement Johore surrendered control of its foreign affairs to Britain, but Abu Bakar retained full internal sovereignty. By this time the other states were acquiring British Residents, and their internal affairs were passing into British hands; but not in Johore. If anything the 1885 Agreement strengthened his position, not weakened it. As such it was very different from the arrangements the British had made with the other states, and it illustrates well the quality of Abu Bakar.

Johore during his reign (1862–1895) was a stable, peaceful state. There was no reason whatever for British intervention, as Abu Bakar pursued a competent, independent path. It is not generally realised, however, that his political strength came not merely from his own qualities of mind but from the economic

[3] Swettenham: *Some Account of the Independent Native States of the Malay Peninsula.* (JSBRAS, vol. 6, 1880), p. 199.

development of the territory as well. In 1833 Johore had a population of perhaps 30,000 Malays and *orang laut*. By 1893 there were 300,000 and of these 210,000 were Chinese. Johore was a Malay State with a Chinese population, and it was they who developed the state and provided the revenue that enabled Abu Bakar to remain independent.

The economic activity that was largely responsible for the opening up of Johore in the nineteenth century was the cultivation of gambier and pepper plantations, an extension of an earlier Singapore enterprise. To encourage the Chinese, a unique system of land tenure was evolved, known as the *Kangchu system*.[4] Chinese capitalists were given titles by the ruler (*surat sungei* they were called), which granted them in return for taxes and royalties, exclusive rights to an area up a river. Armed with these documents, the relatives and friends in Singapore would be gathered together, a sampan or two acquired and the *kongsi* would chug off to a new start in Johore. The enterprise would be under the complete and absolute jurisdiction of the *Kangchu* (or headman) who would establish his headquarters at the *kangka*, or village, which served the small clearings. Here he would rule over his domain, the controller of the opium store and the gambling house, head of the only secret society allowed, responsible to remote Johore Bahru (founded in 1855), for the maintenance of law and order and the payment of revenue. Most of the inland towns in Johore began in this way, as a Chinese village by a stream under a headman.

The Chinese under this *Kangchu* system led their own way of life, with no contact whatever with the Sultan or his Malay administration down on the coast. Although this opened up the state, and the influx of Chinese kept Johore going at both ends, their labours creating its prosperity and their taxes its revenue, it was a good custom that went on too long. Admirable though it was in the nineteenth century, the *Kangchu* system continued into the twentieth, with Chinese villages completely isolated from government. The health services, schools, hygiene and other

---

[4] This is described in detail by A. E. Coope, *The Kangchu System in Johore* (JMBRAS, vol. 14, pt. 3. December, 1936).

twentieth century developments all passed them by, as they remained in their squalor. The government rarely visited them, and then only to collect money. As a result, they came to heartily dislike Johore Bahru, which in its turn ignored them. If one added to this the Second World War and the activities in Johore of the underground communist movement, and if it is realised that in some parts of Johore no permanent government officer was established until as late as 1949, then it is not surprising that Johore figured so prominently in the Emergency. It was the custom to explain the communist strength in Johore throughout the Emergency of 1948–59 by its nearness to Singapore. Of even more importance was the neglect of Johore Bahru.

This has taken us a long way from Abu Bakar. Let us return. Without question he was the ablest of the Malay rulers, and he used his influence to interfere in their affairs. In Pahang, long linked to Johore through territorial and marital bonds, he supported a candidate in a civil war that fluttered and flared between 1857 and 1863. Unfortunately it was the wrong candidate. He attempted to interfere again in the 1880's, but strong opposition by Pahang to his vision of a Johore-Pahang empire nullified his efforts. British intervention made impossible any further hopes. He participated too in the disputes and intrigues among the other states. The small territories behind Malacca knew his agents well. In Perak and Selangor he was equally as active. In all these states, however, the whirlwind of anarchy was too strong for him, and in his hopes for an expansion of Johore into another Johore Empire he was quite unsuccessful. Where he did succeed was in Johore, which throughout his reign remained stable and peaceful. It was the only Malay state to benefit from this experience, for elsewhere the narrowly circumscribed outlook of the eighteenth century remained, and the chaos, also inherited from that century, grew worse, as there flowed steadily into the west coast states in particular, throughout this period, thousands of Chinese from Penang, Malacca and Singapore. In Johore they grew gambier, but elsewhere it was a profitable search for tin that sent them in, and the tin states, Perak and Selangor in particular, proved quite unable to master this new element in their composition. It is their changing, worsening condition, especially that of Perak, together with the greatly changed world outside the peninsula, that leads to 1874 and British intervention.

In 1870, on the *Pluto*, one of the first ships to sail through the newly cut Suez Canal, a tall, gangling youth of twenty leaned against the rail. His name was Frank Swettenham, and his career in the Malay peninsula covers almost exactly the eventful years that now follow. All round the world these last three decades of the nineteenth century witness the most far reaching of changes. It is as if Europe had burst its banks, and in a giant movement had flooded the whole globe. Huge expanses of hitherto primitive territory, vast numbers of indigenous peoples in Africa and Asia were caught up and transformed. The world was never the same again. Today the tide sweeps back, but the African and Asian lands once under European control established so dramatically in those thirty years, emerge not as they were before, but stand revealed as new entities, as in many basic respects much that was new had been added to their original shape by the European flood.

This was the period when the West came East, when it came into the peninsula and stayed there, bringing a whole train of results, producing, with what had gone before, the Malaya of today. The most important period of this western flood was the twentieth century, when its influence poured into the whole country; but the most dramatic period was this first tidal wave, this onrush of occupation, in the late nineteenth; and Swettenham was one of the more important of the men who shaped Malaya for the modern world.

Swettenham's route to Malaya through the Suez Canal, and the reasons for his first acquaintance with the Malay States, a trip to Selangor to help recover a British citizen from Singapore, an abducted Chinese girl, are both pointers to the reasons why the British intervened in the peninsula. There was the external or strategic reason. This was the underlying need to protect the British trade route to East Asia, a route that with the opening of the Canal now ran down the Straits of Malacca, close to a shore where anarchy lurked amid the mangroves, and where pirates peered hopefully through the nipah. There was also the internal or commercial reason, the need to protect Chinese interests in the Western Malay States.

There are historians who claim that Britain moved into the various states in order to safeguard British investments in them. They are wrong. There was little if any investment of British capital in the Malay States until after they were Federated in 1896. The British in the United Kingdom were far more concerned with the trade route to China, while those in the Straits were happy with the entrepôt trade, and with selling and buying to the Chinese safely in Singapore. What investment there was, was undertaken by the more adventuresome or more fortunate Chinese merchants of Penang, Malacca and Singapore. They possessed an asset the British lacked; a large number of their countrymen close at hand ready for economic exploitation, and the Chinese labourer was exported to Malaya in his thousands.

Very largely this investment and these labourers were concerned with the financing and the staffing of tin enterprises. It was partly to safeguard these Chinese interests that the British moved. It was essential for the prosperity of Singapore and Penang that the Chinese businesses should be successful, for it was not as if the city was divided by a wall, with British merchants doing their business on one side, and the Chinese merchants the other. The two were (and are) inextricably linked together, like threads in a carpet, in all their enterprises. So if the large scale Chinese investments and undertakings in the Malay States should collapse, the British firms associated with them would suffer too. A depression, like a cold, can rarely be isolated: all suffer the same fate.

Let us see how in 1873 both these reasons were present. Firstly let us examine the external scene, the strategic picture, of more importance to London perhaps than to Singapore. This section of the sea highway was a worry to Great Britain for two reasons. First of all it was uncontrolled. The Malay States on one side and the Sumatran rivers on the other constituted the most uncontrolled section of the route from Europe. Except for Egypt, where Britain also intervened a few years later (and for the same reason), by the 1870's this tremendous artery was safely protected throughout its length. Gibraltar, Malta, Suez, Aden,

India, Burma, Penang, Singapore, Labuan, Hong Kong: the bases were established and the territories between either occupied or in treaty to Great Britain. But with the Malay States there was neither treaty nor occupation. This implied two dangers: one, that another power avid for expansion, the new Germany perhaps, or France, would step in; and secondly, the danger feared by London, was that these anarchic hang-overs from the eighteenth century would secure the strength to menace the trade route themselves.

In 1871 Britain partly removed the first danger by signing a treaty with Holland which gave it a free hand in Sumatra. It was a sad day for this great island and for brave Acheh, when this treaty was signed, but it did ensure that one side of the Straits came under the control of a power allied to Britain, and of whom it had little to fear. There still remained the possibility that the Malay States themselves would fall to another European power.

This fear was coupled to another, that of piracy. In 1871 pirates from Selangor attacked a coastal vessel, a junk flying the Union Jack, and when a British gun-boat was sent to intervene she was fired on by coastal guns. To fire on the Royal Navy was to attack Britain at its most sensitive and proudest point. There was immediate retaliation, the forts were destroyed, and the coastline was regarded henceforth with a new interest, a new awareness by Britain that here lay trouble. The British attitude remained, however, one of non-interference, and despatches couched in language that Light might have heard went out to Singapore, instructing the Governor not to interfere in the Malay States, and to remain aloof at all times. This policy, however, had outlived its usefulness. It was soon to change.

British policy was changed by a combination of two factors, one in Europe and one in the peninsula. In London an infusion of fresh blood into the Colonial Office (the young Lord Kimberley becoming the Minister in 1870, for example), had brought a new approach towards British overseas possessions. The British attitude of non-interference during the first seventy years of the nineteenth century had been characteristic not merely in the Malay Peninsula, but throughout the world. Occasionally, reluctantly, the flag had followed trade, but there was a constant aversion to the acquisition of fresh responsibility that became at times, as when Gladstone was Prime Minister, almost an obsession. By the 1870's this attitude was changing. Young men such as Kimberley, masters of a powerful nation, were not averse to tackling overseas problems, and to accepting increased responsibilities, and to them the cure for troubles on the frontier was to step across and to annex and pacify the neighbouring area. This is a recurrent historic phenomenon, widely recognized as characteristic of imperialism. In such a way did Russia expand, and the U.S.A., to mention but two present day empires, while Rome, of course, and innumerable other Empires of the past have followed the same path.

The European factor that initiated a British imperialistic move into the Malay Peninsula was the fear of foreign intervention, a fear which had been quite absent from any British consideration of the Malay States after the position of the Dutch and Siamese had been stabilised in the eighteen-twenties. In the 1870's, however, a new European power, Germany, had emerged with startling rapidity, and led by Bismark had struck down France in 1870–71 to claim political predominance on the continent.

Although no proof that Germany intended to utilize the disorders of the Malay States as a pretext for intervention has been discovered, British fears for the safety of its trade route to China by 1873 were strong enough for Kimberley in London to consider acting in anticipation; and in his instructions to the new governor, Sir Andrew Clarke, who sailed from London in late 1873, he wrote on 20th September that he was to "report to me whether there are, in your opinion, any steps which can properly be taken by the Colonial Government to promote the restoration of peace and order and to secure protection to trade and commerce with the Native Territories."

He continued, "I would wish you, especially, to consider whether it would be advisable to appoint a British officer to reside in any of the States. Such an appointment could, of course, only be made with the full consent of the Native Government, and the expenses connected with it would have to be defrayed by the government of the Straits Settlements."

He added, in a paragraph that was deleted from the final despatch, "we could not see with indifference interference of foreign powers in the affairs of the peninsula; on the other hand it is difficult to see how we should be justified in objecting to the native states seeking aid elsewhere if we refuse to take any steps to remedy the evils complained of." Here in a nutshell is the reason for intervention.[5]

Kimberley therefore in an effort to anticipate foreign intervention, proposed a forward move by Britain. This however might not have been sufficient had the Governor faced a determined opposition to the suggested new policy. Had the mercantile community taken objection, had the Legislative Council members stood firm the government in London would have been reluctant to override local feeling. But in the Straits he found a unanimous body of opinion whole-heartedly in support of intervention, and he was strengthened in his resolve to act by the petition waiting for him from just on 250 Chinese merchants, who wrote complaining to the British government that the anarchy of the west Malay States was so affecting their interests that there was serious danger of all their tin undertakings being ruined. Britain was asked to provide protection for their trade.

Thus the two factors combined. The fear of a foreign move that might threaten the China trade route induced London to make suggestions to its Governor of the Straits, and the Chinese petition induced Singapore to act on it. Malaya's fate was therefore settled. Sir Andrew Clarke, the typical strong man on the spot, characteristic of the British in Malaya from the days of Light, Raffles and Fullerton, did not hesitate. With the unanimous support of the Chinese, Indian and European traders and merchants of the Straits, and with the supreme self confidence of the Victorian Englishman, convinced that the extension of British control was automatically of benefit to the races thus governed, he moved swiftly but not altogether effectively.

---

[5] See *British Intervention in Malaya* by D. MacIntyre, (Journal, South-East Asian History, vol. 2, no. 3, October 1961, pp. 47–69).

The story begins in Perak,[6] the state with the most tin, and therefore the most Chinese, who as yet had not been incorporated into the political framework. Swettenham has described Perak in a passage of his *British Malaya* (pp. 116–122) that gives a vivid pen picture of the condition of this 8,000 square mile state, with its magnificent river and its isolated, squabbling inhabitants. They had been isolated and squabbling for centuries, but from 1848 onwards, when tin was discovered in Larut, a new element entered the scene, the Chinese tin miners. In Selangor to the south, Yap Ah Loy the great leader of another tin village, Kuala Lumpur, had gained partial control of the Chinese in the interior during the 1860's, but in Perak the important tin area, Larut, its 5,000 Chinese were more or less equally divided in warring factions, representing two rival secret societies. Both they and the Perak Malays were divided, for although the ancient Indian legacy was strong in Perak, and there was a definite organisation of state officers, each with well defined titles and an ancient royal line, law and order was the theory; but in practice there were constant feuds and wars for the Malays found the Chinese uncontrollable.

The Chinese struggle for power on the Larut tin mines which began in 1861 reached Penang, from whence came its provisions, its leaders and its manpower. There was fighting and rioting there too, a particularly violent outbreak occurring between the rival supporters in 1867, many of whom, wounded and starving, had escaped from Larut or other parts of Perak. These Chinese factions had found allies with the Malays amongst whom they lived, for following the death in 1871 of the Sultan of Perak three rival claimants had striven for the vacant throne. By 1873 the state was therefore completely divided.

Sir Andrew Clarke with the support of the Chinese (indeed possibly at their instigation through the representations of their respected community leaders, leaders also of their Secret Society, the Triad), attempted to solve the problem of Perak by calling together a number of the prominent chiefs. They met on his ship at Pangkor Island between Penang and Perak in January

[6] The story is told in vigorous detail by C. N. Parkinson, *British Intervention In Malaya, 1867–1877* (Singapore, 1960).

1874, and they were reluctantly and with suspicion rushed into signing an agreement by which one of them, Abdullah, was recognised as Sultan, and by which he accepted a British Resident to advise him on all matters of importance other than matters affecting the Muslim religion. J.W.W. Birch, the Colonial Secretary in Singapore, was sent in as the first British Resident, an unlikely man named Speedy was made Assistant Resident in Larut, the scene of most of the Chinese disturbances, and a coastal stretch of Perak, the Dindings, was ceded to the Crown.[7]

Nearly all of these steps were very imprudent. Abdullah became increasingly unacceptable to the Perak Malays, the farther the British gunboats steamed south. Birch, by reason of his autocratic behaviour and his inability to deal sympathetically with the Perak Malays, produced a conspiracy of resistance within a year of his appointment, as both the man and his policy came to be resented and resisted. Birch was not a good appointment for this new post. He was 49, set in his narrow and rigid ways, rather stubborn and determined to change everything he found distasteful, but not particularly efficient; and he failed to capture the support of the Malays at all. His assistant in Larut, T.C.C. Speedy, a huge bearded man well over six feet tall was an eccentric character. He had served in Abyssinia, and had been the commander of the army of the Mantri, one of the major participants in the Perak struggle. He was thus heavily committed, and failing in administrative ability, he was quite lacking in the virtues of impartial government.[8]

In October 1875 Jervois, the new Governor, told his Residents not to advise but to rule, to take firm action and to control directly the revenue and policing of the state, together with all official appointments. This brought discontent to a head. There was a rising in November, and Birch was stabbed to death. Swettenham nearby was lucky to escape with his life. There was no general revolt however. Raja Yusoff, the main chief upriver, who had the best claims to the throne but who had never been invited to Pangkor, did not join the revolt. (Indeed it is doubtful

---

[7] It was returned to Perak in 1935.

[8] Speedy is described well by J. M. Gullick, *Captain Speedy of Larut* (JMBRAS, vol. 26, pt. 3, 1953).

if his existence or lineage was known then to the British.) Abdullah himself was too timid to move whole-heartedly in support of the chiefs who had been the main organizers, and something like a period of anarchy followed.

British control was soon established after a flurry of fighting. Abdullah, the Laksamana, the Mantri and the Shahbander were all arrested and exiled for their part in the conspiracy, and Yusoff was established as Regent (eventually becoming the Sultan). However, a new Resident J. G. Davidson, a Singapore lawyer who had been in Selangor as Resident (having been previously the Sultan's adviser, and having considerable financial interests in the State), considered Perak too difficult a post, and resigned rather than go there. Speedy resigned too. They were replaced in February 1877 by two most satisfactory appointments, Hugh Low from Labuan becoming Resident, and W. E. Maxwell his Assistant. Under them and their reorganization and sympathetic administration Perak began to settle down.[9]

British intervention in Perak had been badly handled by an inexperienced Governor and Resident. A rather similar collapse occurred in Selangor. Here as in Perak the disputes of Chinese tin miners coupled with the dynastic squabbles of the Malays had produced most insecure conditions. Between 1866 and 1873 there was open fighting. Part of the conflict was between rival Malay groups, in which Tungku Kudin, the Viceroy, was finally successful, due to considerable help given by Pahang forces in 1873. From 1870 onwards there was also fighting between the Chinese in the interior mining areas, from which Yap Ah Loy, the great Capitan China of Kuala Lumpur, emerged triumphant.[10] Although exhaustion brought peace to the five tin valleys of Selangor, on the coast piracy was sufficiently active for it to offer an excuse to the ambitious and active Clarke, who, in company with the Admiral of the British China Fleet, visited the Sultan

[9] Swettenham participated in much of this as a young man in his early twenties. He was never very modest in his writing, but by the time he came to write his role appears vital. If we ignore this aspect, which is common in most autobiographies, his *Footprints In Malaya* (London, 1941) makes excellent reading.

[10] For his life and the growth of Kuala Lumpur see S. M. Middlebrook, *Yap Ah Loy* (JMBRAS, vol. XXIV, pt. 2, July 1951).

in the *Pluto* immediately after Pangkor.[11] The Sultan promised, for what it was worth, to suppress piracy, the main employment of his coastal relatives and connections. It has been maintained that he was induced to ask (for it was not a written request) for a British officer to advise him. This was not acted upon until December, when J. G. Davidson, Singapore lawyer and an old friend and employee of the Viceroy, was sent with 24 year old Swettenham as Assistant Resident; but when Birch was murdered in November 1875, he resigned rather than go there, and the Resident's post went to Captain Douglas. He so mismanaged Selangor and so antagonised both Malays and Chinese through his arrogance and incompetency that although there was no rising, he was obliged to resign the service in 1882, yielding to the much more efficient and dynamic Swettenham. Only then did the troubles begin to vanish.

Sungei Ujong, the most important of the pocket states near Malacca, also received a British adviser in 1874. Here the internal disputes were affecting the trade of Malacca. Sir Andrew Clarke intervened in these disputes, and the Dato Klana of Sungei Ujong, who came to Singapore seeking support for his case, agreed in April 1874 to keep the peace on the Linggi River, and to accept a British officer. Tin began to flow down to Malacca again. However a rival chief, the Dato Bandar of Sungei Ujong, who was in some ways of equal status (but who had not rushed to Singapore to acquaint the Governor of his position), felt that the free movement of trade on the Linggi clashed with his entitlements, and there was much justification in his claim. As in Perak, part of the trouble caused by British intervention was that the Straits Settlements officials, despite their desire for occupation, were ignorant of the complicated distribution and allocation of Malay power, and as in Perak this ignorance led to war.

Fighting between the Dato Bandar and the Klana broke out in November 1874. British troops supported the Klana, and the Dato Bandar was forced to surrender. He was exiled, un-

[11] A delightful eye witness account of this meeting is given by Parkinson, *British Intervention in Malaya*, p. 146.

complainingly, to Singapore, while in December 1874 an Assistant Resident was appointed. Commander P. J. Murray, who took over in April 1875 was the best of Clarke's appointments, but during that year he did not prevent a serious deterioration in relations between the small states. The Dato Klana, although the head of Sungei Ujong, was merely one of the chiefs of the *negri sembilan*. In 1874 it had not mattered that he was not paramount in the larger, looser organisation, for it had no *Yam Tuan Besar* or head of the confederation since 1869. But in 1875 one was elected, and partly as a result of the Klana's alliance with the British, his jealous rivals elevated Tungku Antah of Sri Menanti, the leader of another of the small states, to be the *Yam Tuan Besar*. Antah refused to recognise the Klana, and vice versa, and in November war broke out.[12] The British troops defending the Dato Klana were forced momentarily on the defensive, but by the end of the year Antah had fled, and most of the confederation was in British hands. The issue here was not complicated by the presence of Chinese, and the chiefs were quite clear that they did not want a Resident. Thus, while a Resident remained in Sungei Ujong, the remaining states turned their backs on him, and for the settlement of any dispute they sought out the ready offices of Abu Bakar of Johore. There matters rested uneasily for some years.

This initial stage of intervention has two cultures clashing together most clumsily and awkwardly. The cautious advice from London was translated in Malaya into something much bolder and more extreme than had been anticipated, and the local officers' ignorance of the affairs of the Malay States, together with the almost complete absence of any experienced administrators, combine to produce the rude impact of 1874–1875. In Perak, although the Chinese riots were settled, a Resident was murdered and two rather hectic years of war and pursuit followed. In Selangor there was confusion and incompetency and more fighting, and in the little states in the south there was still more fighting. Most damaging of all to a Victorian Englishman's self-esteem, there was the frank statement, which Perak and Selangor had been

---

12 For this, see Parkinson, op. cit., pp. 274–293.

unable to express, that he was not wanted, and that the states would settle their disputes by arbitration under the chairmanship of one of their own. When reading the works of Swettenham, one often feels that this latter area was a part of Malaya he did not particularly care for and it is easy to understand why.

2.

This initial phase however is followed by a long steady period where the new world of the West is brought into Malaya to be assimilated by the Malays at their own speed, and without friction. It is a period marked by three big men, men of stature, and a host of others: competent, adventuresome Englishmen, who work with them; men in sympathy with the land, with the people suddenly facing this flood, and who help them breast the flood and save them from needlessly fighting it.

The leader, the man who did more than anyone else to inaugurate the second wave of British expansion, was Sir Frederick Weld, Governor of the Straits Settlements 1880–1887. With this renewed movement of continued intervention, the fears of Britain that rival European powers might secure treaty rights with the uncommitted states played as big if not bigger part, than the desire to protect and extend commercial interests. In addition Weld was suspicious of the designs of Siam in the north and of Johore in the south.

He moved against the influence of Abu Bakar in the small southern states, known as the Sri Menanti Confederation, by calling a conference of the chiefs on the border of Sungei Ujong in 1881. Here he told them that in view of the failure of Abu Bakar to settle their disputes, a failure that was damaging trade and security, he was substituting the highest authority of all, that of the Queen's government in the next few years. All attempts by Johore to meddle were rebuffed. A British collector and magistrate took up his post in Sri Menanti in 1886, and at the request of Yam Tuan Antah he was given the face saving title of Resident in 1889, when Sri Menanti, together with Tampin and Rembau became the Negri Sembilan. Seremban, the capital, owes much of its charm to the first Resident, Lister, one of Weld's young men.

Weld also attempted to interfere on the east coast, in Pahang, but here he was less successful. Although not possessing the ample tin supplies of the western states, Pahang had been the object of Singapore attention for some time as a considerable trade went either to its rivers or along its coast to Trengganu, Kelantan and on to Bangkok. It was a precarious trade but a valuable one, which Singapore had taken great efforts to safeguard once before, in the 1857–1863 Pahang Civil War.

The dispute then had arisen after the death of Bendahara Ali in 1857, when his two sons, Wan Ahmad and Tun Mutahir, had fought in typical fashion for the succession. Ibrahim, the Temenggong of Johore, had wanted to send help to the new Bendahara, Mutahir, but the Straits Government had managed to prevent him from interfering. Nevertheless the revolt could not be localised. The situation became more complicated in 1858 with the arrival in Pahang of the deposed ex-Sultan of Lingga, a direct descendent of the royal line that at the beginning of the century had ruled both Pahang and Johore. He soon moved to Trengganu, where his nephew was ruling, and intrigued with Wan Ahmad from there.

Cavenagh, the Governor in Singapore, feared that the quarrel, which broke out into armed clashes again in 1861, would ruin Singapore's trade with the east coast, and would spread into a general conflagration, as Johore and Trengganu were supporting the rival combatants. He feared too that the ex-Sultan of Lingga, who had moved in 1861 to Bangkok, would be exploited by the Siamese as he searched for a new throne in the Malay States, and that in this way Siamese control would be extended down the peninsula.

In June 1862, while the interior of Pahang was in revolt, Abu Bakar, who had succeeded his father in Johore that year, signed a treaty of friendship with the Bendahara of Pahang, by which he acquired Tioman Island. In August, however, Wan Ahmad returned again to the attack, and supported by the ex-Sultan of Lingga, who had returned to Trengganu, launched another invasion of Pahang. This time he was successful.

Cavenagh was most anxious to localise the struggle, to keep the ring clear so that power in Pahang would pass to the ruler who had the most support in the State. He had refused support to both Wan Ahmad and to Tun Koris, the son of Tun Mutahir who had been nominated Bendahara, and he reacted vigorously at the interference of Trengganu in this quarrel, which he viewed as a veiled move by Siam. After demanding in vain the return to Bangkok of the ex-Sultan of Lingga he sent north a naval force that in November 1862, to substantiate his demand, bombarded Kuala Trengganu. The ex-Sultan took no further part in the Pahang dispute.

This event made no difference to the outcome, although it freed Wan Ahmad from any Siamese hold. Despite the support of Abu Bakar and his Bugis from Johore, the Bendahara lost skirmish after skirmish. Wan Ahmad gained steadily in favour, desertions of leading Pahang chiefs to his side became frequent, and in May 1863 the Bendahara and his father were forced to flee overland to Johore. Here both mysteriously fell ill and died within a few days of one another. Abu Bakar tried to put forward the twelve year old son of Koris as a puppet Bendahara, but in October 1863 Wan Ahmad informed Cavenagh of his own accession to the throne, and his assumption of the title of Bendahara. A tolerable peace then fell over Pahang and both Siam and Johore retired from the scene.

By the time Weld came however in 1880, Abu Bakar, endeavouring to win support away from Ahmad, had regained the favours of the chiefs of Pahang. Perturbed at this, and also at Ahmad's cavalier method of ceding vast stretches of his State to whomsoever paid him, without respect for the rights or concessions granted to resident Chinese or Malays, Weld endeavoured to impose some sort of British control over Pahang.

Here Ahmad's waning popularity and his lack of administrative ability together with Abu Bakar's strong moves plunged him into a critical position. With great difficulty the Straits Government in 1884 prevented Mansur, Ahmad's brother from invading the State and from placing himself at the head of the discontent.

In the same year Ahmad irresponsibly granted two mining concessions of 900 square miles to Europeans which caused further unrest in Pahang and gave Singapore further worry. In 1885 Swettenham was sent overland from Perak to report on the state and to investigate whether the Sultan (for so Ahmad in 1884 had styled himself) would accept a Resident. He found signs of numerous Johore emissaries, particularly at the gold centre of Raub, and a discontented and ill governed population. The Bendahara however (for so Singapore regarded him), was quite unprepared to relinquish his unfettered authority.

Weld persisted. His opportunity came in 1887, when Mansur was invited to return to Pahang. He was reluctant to go back, but Weld promised him the safety of a European officer. Hugh Clifford, his dynamic young nephew, was sent in, and although unable to secure the Treaty that Weld wanted, by which Ahmad would be controlled by a Resident, he did succeed in October 1887 in securing his consent, to the establishment of a British Agent in return for his recognition as Sultan. It was an emasculated post, with little authority or power, but it was a beginning, and Weld had to be content with it.

South Malaya was thus brought into the British fold. Weld had no success with the north, for here his hopes clashed with the foreign policy of Britain, which regarded Siam as a very useful buffer between it in Burma and the French expansion in Indo-China. The Government in London accepted the memoranda of its Consul-General in Bangkok which showed that northern states of the Malay Peninsula—Trengganu, Kelantan and Kedah—were Siamese. To detach them from Siam would weaken that country and would establish a precedent France might follow. In 1873 Britain had initiated a policy of intervention in the peninsula, but that had been inspired by a desire to safeguard the sea route to China. The northern States played no part in this, and consequently were ignored. Weld was thus restrained in his expansionist plans and projects.

Despite this failure, Weld had succeeded in establishing British Residents in almost all the Malay states except those claimed by Siam, and Johore; and even here it had the treaty right to so establish one. Although in theory they were confined to offering advice, in practice the powers of the Sultan were so slight in relation to the new social and economic pressures of the nineteenth century that the Residents were able to assume the major responsibility for putting their advice into action. As the Governor at Singapore was too remote to be referred to, the Residents became rulers. Weld chose wisely: men of vigour, enthusiasm and sense were found to fill the posts established, and by their work they remain a credit to the Britain and to the Malaya they served. Resented by only a few of the aristocrats, who saw their days of uncontrolled tyranny vanishing, and hardly challenged elsewhere, the British Residents were presented with a unique opportunity. Their work brought immeasurable benefit to the people of Malaya.

Outstanding among the Residents under Weld were Hugh Low of Perak and Frank Swettenham of Selangor. Low came to Perak in 1877 at the age of fifty-three, after thirty years of quiet uneventful service on Labuan Island. Here he had observed, and for a time worked under, the humane rule of Rajah Brooke. At an age when most administrators in Malaya must now consider retiring, Low was pulled out of this backwater and thrust into the tidal-race of anarchy in Perak. He found the state terrified, suspicious, undeveloped, and bankrupt. Quietly, sympathetically, firmly, he worked unceasingly to effect a transformation.

Never too busy at his desk to visit all parts of Perak, never too pre-occupied with paper to talk to a Malay, and yet never hurried, he proceeded step by step. One of his most effective measures, whereby he won the active support of the Perak chiefs, was his formation of a State Council on which Malays and Chinese sat to consider the development of the country. This was a statesman-like act, and the State Council, which first met in December 1877, was a powerful, effective body for twenty years, until the Federation of the Malay States in 1896 and the transference of many of its powers to the Federal capital, Kuala Lumpur, sent it into a grievous decline.

Another effective measure of Low's, and again indicative of how he worked, was his transference to the indigenous *Penghulus* of much of the power that Birch had given to the ill-controlled foreign police he had introduced. By making administration at local *mukim* level the responsibility of people trusted in the kampongs, he created a stable State. By having the chiefs involved again in the affairs of Perak, he won their respect and co-operation to such an extent that with little fuss or bother he was able, by steady stages, to secure by 1883 the complete abolition of debt-slavery in Perak, an institution of unknown antiquity.

Low's work is seen most clearly in the economic transformation which occurred during his régime. In February 1879 Land Laws were passed regulating land usage, fixing tenures and registering land titles. A land revenue followed automatically, but the laws had accomplished something more important altogether, in that they had created a climate of confidence among the tin miners. The revenue of Perak, which rose from $388,372 in 1879 to $1,827,176 in 1887, came very largely from tin, and nearly all of Low's economic efforts, as with his Land Laws, were devoted to assisting the production and export of this commodity.

In 1885, for example, after he had built various roads, and had built up a peaceful and competent administration over the State, he had a railway constructed from Taiping, the tin centre, to Port Weld, eight miles away at the coast. In addition, by 1884 he had connected Perak to the outside world by the construction of a telegraph line through the jungle to Province Wellesley and Penang. By 1887 the trade of Perak had reached $19 million, and the development continued. Low, an old, venerated man, resigned that year. He not only had made modern Perak: he had helped the Malay of Perak adapt himself to all the changes with as little friction as possible, indeed with eager co-operation. It was to be the Sultan of Perak who pressed for more of the same policy, with his advocation in 1895 of a Federation.

In Selangor the start was later, for it was not until Weld sent Swettenham there in 1883 that any worthwhile development occurred. The explorer Cameron made a rough survey of the State that year, Land Regulations were introduced, and sago and pepper estates were begun on the coast at Klang. Under the drive of Swettenham the agricultural possibilities of the State received attention. Coffee and tobacco planting was begun by such pioneers from Ceylon as Hill and Rathbone. Nearly 20,000 acres were under estate production by 1885. As in Perak, however, the mainstay of the State's economy was tin, mined almost entirely by a rapidly increasing Chinese population. Swettenham followed Low in his economic developments (if not in his steady consultation with the Malay Chiefs), and replaced the almost useless stream, and the morass of an earth track that bullock wagons loaded with tin had endeavoured to use, by a railway from Kuala Lumpur to Klang, opened in 1890. In 1882 Selangor's total trade was $2 million; five years later it was $11 million.

Weld left his young men well alone, but assisted where he could. In 1881, anticipating a labour shortage among the sprouting estates, for the Chinese were addicted to the individualistic and more rewarding pursuit of tin, while the indigenous Malays were virtually non-capitalistic in the detached regard they had for economic ends, he entered into a correspondence with the Government of India, and obtained in 1883 its full consent to Indian emigration to Perak, Selangor and Sungei Ujong. In addition he encouraged railroad construction and made great efforts to link up the roads that each Resident was busily constructing. In these respects he went to the heart of the matter, for adequate labour and improved communications were essential for any development; and development was the British article of faith, a piece of dogma that all were beginning to accept. Weld toured the States constantly, being far more interested in the tremendous developments he was driving forward there than in Singapore. On one such trip, in 1883, he went from Malacca northwards close to the main mountain range, and near to the headwaters of the various streams, finally crossing from Perak into the sugar estates of Province Wellesley. As a result of this tour he planned the track that linked the states and which is today the main trunk road of the peninsula. This route had never previously been traversed in its entirety by one man, yet whereas before Weld's journey the rivers flowing westwards comprised the axis of movement, increasingly after him they were neglected for the quickly increasing bridle paths and roads that ran north and south.

The economic development of Perak and Selangor, and to a

lesser extent of Sungei Ujong in these years, was amazing. Less obvious, but of even more value, was the work done by the young Residents in establishing law and order. The constant clashes on the tin fields of militant groups of Chinese became a thing of the past. The wanton decrees of the chief and the unchecked whims of the ruler vanished. Even the tyranny of the secret society leader was thwarted, and the functioning of a system of courts, administering a humane and fixed law, saw that a minimum sense of security and a feeling of equality before the law percolated through the states of the peninsula for the first time in its history. British justice, far more than western ideas of development, secured the passive approval and collaboration of the people, and permitted the bloodless occupation of the peninsula.

Weld participated not merely in the expansion of British power in the peninsula, but in Borneo as well. In 1881 a private company had been formed by some British business men to secure grants of land, made by the Sultans of Brunei and Sulu in much the same irresponsible manner as the Sultan of Pahang. In order to establish governmental control over the activities of this company, deemed necessary so that another exposed section of the trade route to China could be barred from foreign acquisition, a Royal Charter was given to the company.

By 1888 the quarrels of this British North Borneo Chartered Company with Sarawak over the rivers of Brunei that both were endeavouring to annex, together with fears that foreign powers would intervene, led not to intervention, as in the Malay States in 1874, but to the establishment of a British Protectorate over the whole region. Sarawak, Brunei and North Borneo were all brought into the British fold in an Agreement negotiated by Weld, and signed in 1888.[13]

It was thought likely that Weld would become the first Governor-General of a federation of the three Borneo states. Although that never occurred, the links between those states and the Malay Peninsula became numerous. Many of the leading administrators, men such as Clifford, Treacher, Lord Milverton,

---

[13] See *Under Chartered Company Rule: North Borneo 1881–1946* by K. G. Tregonning (U.M.P. 1959)

and others went across, taking with them their ideas and ideals of government, while the establishment of peace and order over a large area led to a steady and increasing trade from which Singapore in particular benefited.[14]

Singapore benefited also from the general transformation of South-East Asia that was occurring at this time, for not merely in the Malay Peninsula and in Borneo was the European assuming control. In Indo-China for example, the French established themselves in the south in the early part of the century in much the same manner as the British had established their Straits Settlements. From 1874 onwards they expanded to the north, into Tongking, over which, after much fighting with Chinese and Tongkingese, a Protectorate was established in 1883. In 1887, (nine years before Malaya's Federation), the whole of north and south Indo-China were brought together under French control into a single administrative unit presided over by a Governor-General.

In Burma too there was European expansion. Here Britain had acquired part of the coastline in 1826, and Rangoon and the remainder of the coast in 1855. The northern part, however, isolated from the outside world, resembled pre-Mongkut Siam in its ignorance and insecurity. Thibaw, the Ruler, precipitated a crisis, and in 1885 Mandalay and north Burma were occupied.

Although Siam survived as an independent state, its stability permitting Europeans to trade and saving them from having to consider intervention, the myriad islands of Indonesia felt the Dutch imprint, most of them for the first time, and most of them without resistance. Only in Acheh, in north Sumatra, where a most cruel and bloody war was protracted for over twenty years (1873–1899), did the strength of Islam and the fervour of Achinese patriotism indicate the beginnings of an Indonesian nationalism that was to characterise the following half-century.

Throughout this period, while politically the most marked factor in Malaya, as elsewhere in South-East Asia, was the as-

[14] This continued throughout the period of British control in Malaya. For example, Sir W. Goode, the last Governor of Singapore, and a member of the old Malayan Civil Service, went to North Borneo as Governor in 1960, the last of a long line of similar exchanges.

sumption of European political control which preceded the equally marked economic development of the area, perhaps of more lasting significance was an Asian social development, the rapid growth of the Chinese population. As Harrison has pointed out, "the rapid growth of the Chinese population of Southeast Asia in modern times is directly linked with the expansion of Western rule and economic enterprise."[15] Between them these two factors brought about the great economic and social changes which we will consider in subsequent chapters. In particular, in Malaya, their activities led to the creation of a plural society, which remains in Malaya as a social phenomenon of great complexity long after British political control has been withdrawn.

---

[15] B. Harrison, *Southeast Asia*, p. 202.

8. THE CREATION OF A PLURAL SOCIETY

The progress of our narrative would appear to lead logically from intervention to Federation, from the establishment of British officers in the Malay States to the next British administrative measure, which was the federation of these states and the co-ordination of their activities. While this step will be outlined, to treat this at any length, however, would be to give a false emphasis to the history of Malaya. If we were to concentrate on the establishment of the Federation, and the subsequent acquisition of other states from Siam, and so imply that these were the most important events that occurred at that time, we would be looking at Malaya through European eyes, so that only the aspect of Malayan affairs that seemed of value in London would be stressed. If we avoid this error of looking at Malaya from outside, however, it becomes apparent that the most important event that occurred in the peninsula during this period was not the badly executed political federation and the acquisition of the northern states that followed, but the creation of a plural society. This means that we must reserve our detailed study for the deep rooted and substantial social changes that occurred in the composition of the peninsula at this time. Rather than the activities of the thin crust of Europeans, it was an internal Asian development, the social impact of the new Chinese and the adjustments of the Malays that we must consider, for this far more than the political measures of Federation was to create the Malaya of today.

The idea of a Federation had been considered in official circles, although nowhere else, for some years. By the time Weld departed, in 1887, it was felt that with the rapid development of the Malay States (in Perak and Selangor in particular) more efficiency would result if a centralised control was established.[1]

---

[1] For a most interesting account of Weld's career, see *The Life of Sir Frederick Weld*, by Lady Alice Lovat (London, 1914).

The individual work of each Resident and his small group of assistants was rarely related, although it was broadly similar to the work being done in the other states. While this had scarcely mattered before, as the states had been primitive stretches of river with uninhabitated jungle forbidding contact between them, this was beginning to change as the states developed. The officials thought it was time to co-ordinate their activities.

A similar administrative reason had played some part in the Federation of Canada in 1867, and it was suggesting the same solution to the Australian colonists. But there was also a financial reason. This is best seen by looking again at Pahang, where in 1887 Weld had installed Hugh Clifford as British Agent.

Here Clifford was quite without political power, and had no means of controlling Sultan Ahmad. Sir Cecil Clementi-Smith, who succeeded Weld, was determined to replace the Agent with a Resident.[2] His opportunity came through Ahmad's habit of ceding large tracts of territory. One such imperious grant to a British company seemed to Clementi-Smith to be so dangerous and so contrary to good government, because thousands of inhabitants were involved, that he refused to permit its acceptance. The firm had influential friends, who complained in London at his action. The Colonial Office then tacitly told Clementi-Smith it would welcome support for British enterprise in Pahang, and with this sanction and anxious that the misgovernment of Pahang should cease, he looked for a pretext for intervention. It was not long in coming.

A British subject, a Chinese named Go Hui, was killed in 1888 at Pekan, the capital, and his wife was taken into the Sultan's *istana*, or palace. Clementi-Smith demanded her release, and insisted on the acceptance of a Resident with full powers to ensure that law and order were established. Additional pressure was brought to bear by Abu Bakar of Johore, and Ahmad yielded. In October 1888, J. P. Rodger assumed his duties.

Unlike the other states Pahang did not immediately enter into a dynamic period of development. Year after year its revenue

---

[2] It was Clementi-Smith who was also responsible for dealing with the secret society menace in Singapore, mentioned on pp. 128–131.

scarcely rose, and the costs of administration were borne by the treasury of the Straits Settlements. To make matters worse, there was a damaging revolt in the interior, between 1890–1892, and this too kept the State backward. What it needed then was what it spends now, the surplus revenue of Selangor and Perak. This was fully appreciated, and the financial problem of Pahang was one of the more important immediate factors leading to the proposals to bring together all the states into one financial and administrative unit.

These proposals began officially when in 1893 the Colonial Office in London asked Smith whether he thought that the condition of the peninsula warranted some form of closer grouping.[3] Smith replied with a detailed memorandum, already prepared, in which at considerable length he advocated a Federation, so that his successor, Sir Charles Mitchell, who took over in August 1893, came out from London charged with investigating and implementing that plan. He did neither. Stubbornly opposed to any proposal that incurred expenditure, reluctant ever to spend a cent, he cautiously deferred Federation for two years, until in 1895, obliged by the Colonial Office which was indifferent to public opinion, he commissioned Swettenham, by then the most senior of his Residents, to translate the proposals into practice.

Swettenham acted as swiftly as Sir H. MacMichael, fifty years later, in securing the consent of the rulers, and in 1896 the Federation of Malaya was formed. Hastily conceived, without any close examination of the details involved, it was one of the great tragedies of the peninsula. Entrusted as it was to Swettenham, who became the first Resident General, or chief administrator, of the four states—Perak, Selangor, Negri Sembilan and Pahang—which were brought into this federal unit, it suffered

---

[3] Swettenham maintained (in *British Malaya*, published in 1906, pp. 272), that the Federation idea originated with him, and that Clementi-Smith's memorandum was in fact one he had submitted. Clementi-Smith denied this, and after a long dispute drew up a statement that Swettenham would not, or could not, challenge. However, in 1916, a month or two after Smith had died, Swettenham announced that he had discovered a document that 'proved' that he had thought of Federation first. By that time no one really cared enough to prove the falsehood.

from the defects of this dynamic civil servant. A great administrator, with a very strong will, an almost arrogant determination to drive ahead, he yet lacked the vision of a great man.

The Colonial Office and the High Commissioner, Mitchell, had one of two Federal proposals to accept. Sir William Maxwell, the Chief Secretary in Singapore, had put forward the logical plan, similar to the one which was later adopted in Nigeria, whereby all the various units that were within the British sphere of interest, both Colony and Protected States, were brought together. To this Swettenham was bitterly opposed. Extremely ambitious and autocratic, he could not imagine himself working as the Resident-General of a Federation, directly under the High Commissioner in Singapore. He wanted to be free of control, a super-Resident, and he fought with great eloquence to convince the Colonial Office that the differences between the Straits Settlements and the Malay States were so basic, the gulf dividing them so wide, that any federal link between them was unimaginable. He gained his point. A few years later, in 1901, he was appointed High Commissioner in Singapore. He held all the reins of government, both Federation and Straits, in his hands, and showed quite clearly that these differences were nominal, that Penang was part of Kedah; that Malacca could not be distinguished from the lands beside it; and that even Singapore was an integral part of the peninsula. But this was of no avail: the damage has been done and the disaster brought about.

Except under Swettenham Singapore has never been the London of the Malay Peninsula, but it has been the New York, the great port and the financial and business centre. To separate the two was most unfortunate. In London at this time the Colonial Office had as its head the very influential Mr. (later Sir) Joseph Chamberlain, who was guiding the senior administration of the Empire: in Australasia, in Africa, and the Pacific. He was advising the men on the spot who had the same dynamic urge to develop their territories: Lugard in Nigeria, Milner in South Africa, Deakin in Australia. Chamberlain encouraged imperial ambition. Swettenham, however, did not come up to those standards.

Swettenham, appointed Resident-General, fashioned within a

few years a highly centralised administration which by depriving the states of most of their power, and by centralising that power in his own hands, made the word Federation ridiculous. Among his more important measures was his selection of Kuala Lumpur in Selangor as the Federal capital. Strangely enough, neither in 1896 nor later was the Federal capital ever given any Federal status. Unlike Washington, Canberra, Ottawa, or Delhi, no Federal enclave was created for it, and it remained part of Selangor. Part of Selangor, but neither its Sultan nor any other ruler was created Head of State, and whereas the Residents had worked under the Sultans and had preserved the structure of the Malay State, Swettenham made no attempt to create an object of Federal loyalty under which he could work. As executive head he took full powers into his hands from 1896 onwards. No Malay Ruler was made the symbol of the new state, and as a result Swettenham created not a nation but an amalgamation. Thanks largely to Swettenham, Malaya advanced through the years of the twentieth century merely as a collection of initials, S.S., F.M.S., U.F.M.S., which stood for a divided country. A great opportunity had been lost.

Nevertheless Swettenham saw to it that the Federation immediately received the best possible administrative framework.[4] He organised such fundamentals of government as Justice, Police and Finance on a federal basis, and initiated the Federal Public Works Department, which transformed the Malay Peninsula more in the following forty years than it had changed in the previous 4,000. The roads of Malaya, like the Roman roads of Britain, are a reminder of a great colonising power. In his parochial determination to do without Singapore he had a new port carved out of malarial mangrove, Port Swettenham, while rail transport too was brought into the federal sphere, with a General Manager to co-ordinate state activities. By 1903 a continuous line ran from the coast opposite Penang to Seremban, the route once traversed so laboriously by Weld. Subsequently in 1909 a Federal loan assisted Johore to carry the line to Johore

[4] His work in establishing a Federal administration is dealt with in his *British Malaya*, pp. 275–305.

Bahru, opposite Singapore.

All these improvements in law and order and in communications greatly assisted the material development of the area. Swettenham has described his policy: "In the administration of a Malay State, revenue and prosperity follow the liberal but prudently directed expenditure of public funds, especially when they are invested...in everything likely to encourage trade and private expenditure. I am inclined to carry this principle of the value of liberal expenditure on well considered objects into almost every department of the public service. The money that is spent is only invested, and comes back in increased revenue. . . ."[5]

With this policy, the Federal States began to develop at a great rate.

	Revenue	Expenditure	Imports	Exports
	($ million)		($ million)	
1875	0.4	0.4		
1890	5.0	5.3		
1895	8.5	7.5	23.0	32.0
1898	9.0	11.0	27.0	
1899	13.5	11.5	34.0	55.0
1900	15.0	13.0	38.5	60.0
1901	17.5	17.2	39.5	63.0
1902	20.5	16.0	46.0	71.0

Swettenham was a greater builder than an architect. Although he can claim considerable credit for the growth of the Federated Malay States, he must accept part of the blame for a divided Malay Peninsula, and for the failure to create the framework of a nation. Although he failed in this—or rather, never strived to succeed—he was successful in another important role, and that was the establishment of British control over the northern Malay States of Kedah, Kelantan and Trengganu, and in their severance from Siam. In this he, more than any other single person, effected a reversal in British foreign policy.

---

[5] *British Malaya* pp. 294–5.

Throughout the nineteenth century these northern states had been accepted by Britain as lying within the Siamese sphere of influence. Indeed Kedah, since its conquest in 1821, was controlled firmly from Bangkok, and although the Burney Treaty of 1826 left the status of Trengganu and Kelantan ambiguous, and Siamese control for the most part was negligible, no attempt was made by the British to interfere. It was a cardinal point of foreign policy that Siam must not be weakened. British trade in Bangkok, after the Bowring Treaty of 1855, was considerable, and British interests in Siam were growing steadily. In addition, Siam was useful as a buffer between the British in India-Burma, and the French in Indo-China. Should Siam be weakened, or should it be alienated from the British, so the statesmen in London reasoned, France might seize her opportunity and secure a paramount position on the Menam. Although during the eighties and nineties repeated opportunities for intervention occurred, on the east in particular, they were ignored, and the states were left to languish.

The reversal in British policy towards these states was caused to a large extent by that same factor that had so influenced its reversal of policy towards the western Malay States in 1874: fear of German intervention. This fear became active from 1899 onwards, when a new Germany, determined to rival Britain at sea and to acquire naval bases, began negotiating with the Siamese for such a base on Langkawi Island north of Penang. It combined with other disturbing features. There was the activity of the Duff Development Company, a British firm which had acquired sovereign rights over half of Kelantan in 1900, there to quarrel with and challenge Siamese officers to the embarrassment of Britain; and there were the efforts of Siam from 1895 onwards to impose a real control over Kelantan and Trengganu farther south. All this, but particularly the German activity, produced much new thinking in London.

The thoughts of the Foreign Office in this matter were stimulated by the cogent despatches of Swettenham. He and his colleagues in Malaya cared little for the traditional Foreign Office attitude which insisted that Britain must not weaken Siam in the south for fear of France in the east. He saw badly administered and suffering Malay States, and he received the constant appeals of their rulers, particularly of Patani and Kelantan, who were fearful of the Siamese. Swettenham had been most critical of an unpublished Siamese-British Treaty of 1897 by which, in return for the exclusion of Europeans from the Kra Peninsula, the British had tacitly recognised Siamese claims to the northern states. He was also working determinedly to bring within the British sphere all the Malay speaking Muslims of the Peninsula.

From Singapore he fed the flames of fear in London by reporting each and every account that reached him of foreign activity on the peninsula, particularly that of Germany. He minimised the extent of actual Siamese control in Kelantan and Trengganu, but described the parlous condition of the Malays there. He suggested that British interests should be safeguarded, either by negotiating with the States for the right to conduct their foreign affairs (as with Johore in 1885), or by negotiating with Siam for the right to instal British officers there. Chamberlain supported Swettenham, and the Foreign Office was won over, being convinced that Germany, invited by Siam in 1901 to participate in an international guarantee of its provinces, was anxious to acquire rights, and that Siam was not capable of managing the States itself.[6]

Negotiations between Siam and Great Britain resulted in the Anglo-Siamese Agreement of 1902. This provided for Siamese control of the foreign relations of the two states, and for the appointment of Advisers to attend to the internal administration. In a secret note it was agreed that these Advisers, while servants of Siam, should be of British nationality and appointment. In this strange way Britain took a step forward. Siam saved its face, as it had done with Burney in 1826, by retaining sovereignty, while Britain effectively safeguarded its east coast interests, but only by acting as an executive instrument for Siam.

From the beginning this 1902 Agreement was unsatisfactory. Although the northernmost state, Kelantan, welcomed it, as giving it a British Adviser, W. A. Graham, instead of a Siamese

---

[6] See E. Thio, *British Policy in the Malay Peninsula, 1880–1910* (U.M.P. forthcoming) which I have been privileged to read in manuscript.

Commissioner, yet Siamese troops remained, and in Trengganu, farther south, the Sultan Zainal Abdidin, who had successfully maintained his independence against the Siamese, saw no reason why he should surrender it to the British. Swettenham attempted to secure his acceptance of an Adviser in September 1902, and again in 1903. Each time the brave old warrior entertained him at Kuala Trengganu with shadow plays and kite flying, thrust sarongs and silver work on him, and refused to surrender one iota of his independence. It was difficult and unsatisfactory for the Governor in Singapore to try and implement this Agreement, for he was acting in effect as a Siamese agent, and with the Germans increasing their attempts in Siam to secure concessions of all kinds in the other states, there was considerable pressure for a more logical and more far reaching settlement in the north of the Malay Peninsula. European developments made this possible.

Almost isolated in Europe through the ostracism it had incurred by reason of the Boer War, and faced by the rapidly increasing might of belligerent Germany, Britain was reconsidering its attitude to France. By the 1900's, as part of its search for a possible ally, the Foreign Office had decided that after all no British interests were involved in any French expansion up the Mekong, and that it need not be regarded with apprehension at all. Elsewhere in the world Anglo-French rivalry was muted, and in 1904 in Paris an Entente Cordiale was signed between the two powers. Amongst other results, this gave a new freedom of action to the French in Cambodia. Damrong, the great Siamese Foreign Minister, was quick to seize on the opportunity for a settlement, and in 1907, by ceding Angkor and Battambang Province, he secured in return the elimination of a number of grievances that had long irritated the Siamese. Siam and France then settled down to increasingly amicable relations.

Siam moved too to settle the Malayan frontier problems, not merely on the east coast but on the west as well, where Kedah languished. Siamese since 1821, it was linked economically to Penang, and in 1904 a grave financial crisis, precipitated by the excesses of the Sultan, had induced Siam (after British representations had been made) to send in a financial adviser, G.C. Hart, in 1905. He struggled to control the finances of the State, but as German intrigues for concessions increased the situation became most unsatisfactory.

On the east coast the Kelantan Adviser (locked in argument with the seven uncles of the Sultan, who disputed his efforts to establish the basis of an administration, where savagery and licence had reigned before) was also heavily involved not merely with the Duff Development Company over its assumption of sovereign powers, but also with his superiors in Bangkok over the legal status of British civil servants. In Trengganu the Sultan stubbornly maintained that he was independent, and cursed both Siamese and British with fine impartiality.

Britain was anxious for a settlement of all this, particularly after 1906, when it heard that Germans in the employ of Siam were to build a railway connecting these states to Bangkok. Economically this was a blow to Penang and Singapore, but a far more serious consideration was the thought that this might foreshadow German concessions on the east coast north of Kedah. A German naval base on the Indian Ocean, a British sea throughout the nineteenth century, was a nightmare-thought.

Britain responded immediately then, when Siam, shortly after concluding its 1907 Treaty with France, suggested that all these points might be settled, and after official discussions signed a Treaty in 1909. By this Anglo-Siamese Treaty Siam transferred to Britain all its claims, rights and responsibilities in the States of Kelantan, Trengganu, Kedah and Perlis. It realised, with unquestioned realism, that it was well rid of something it could not control. In return Siam secured the abandonment of British extra-territoriality in Siam—British subjects henceforth could be tried in Siamese courts—and the granting of a large railway loan from the Federation for a line from Bangkok to Alor Star, and connecting then to the Federation network. Both sides were well satisfied with the Treaty, and despite the protests of some who felt that the Malay-Muslim States north of Trengganu also should have been exchanged, they too settled down to increasingly amicable relations. The realism of Damrong, and the drawing together of France and Great Britain, had made possible this move northwards. It had been the persistent Malayan-centred outlook of Swettenham above all that had initiated the move. Not for the first time had the strong man on the spot been the decisive person.

Although by this Treaty of 1909 the Siamese interests were surrendered, it took some time for British control to be established. In Kelantan a British officer, J. S. Mason, took over from Graham in July 1909 without incident and British authority was confirmed by Treaty the following year. In Trengganu, however, all that the Sultan would accept in an Agreement of April 1910, was a British officer with consular powers only, and it was not until October 1919, following revelations of extreme barbarity and near anarchy, that an Adviser was appointed, and the basis of an administration, such as Graham had instituted in Kelantan in 1903, began in Trengganu. In Kedah no Agreement was signed, merely a few British officers led by G. Maxwell moved in and took over in 1910 from the Siamese. Here a civil service was in existence, and unlike the other western states, where intervention in 1874 had found them scarcely governed at all, an organised administration was functioning. On this Maxwell built the basis of his later great reputation.

The same year that witnessed the signing of the Anglo-Siamese Treaty (1909) saw Britain increase its control in the south of the Malay Peninsula as well. Here Johore, ruled competently by Abu Bakar from his comfortable Singapore residence, had developed at a slower pace than the western Malay States, mainly because it had no tin. Although it had surrendered its rights to foreign relations in 1885 Johore was recognised as independent. This was shown clearly by the written constitution which Abu Bakar gave to the State in 1895, shortly before his death that year. Although the possession of a written constitution made the State unique, it merely put in writing the traditional Malay checks to unbridled autocracy. A Council of Ministers was created, corresponding to the customary senior chiefs, together with a larger Council of State.[7]

In the early nineteenth century the rubber boom began, and the

---

[7] These Councils are discussed in R. Emerson's *Malaysia* (New York, 1937), pp. 203–209. This work is an invaluable study of twentieth century Malaya.

Malay States within the Federation experienced an economic stimulus. The impact of this reached the other states later, but by 1909 the complexity both of land administration and of general development induced the Sultan to secure an adviser. Although a British officer, he was merely loaned as an unofficial assistant, and Johore retained its independence as stubbornly as Trengganu. In 1914, however, following an exposure of shocking prison conditions in Johore Bahru, and in view of the need to safeguard British-Malayan interests by then extensive in Johore, a new Treaty with Johore was signed, permitting the establishment of a General Adviser, as he was called (a face-saving title borrowed from independent Siam). As in Kedah, Kelantan and Trengganu, Johore retained considerable initiative and individuality, and European officers were kept to a minimum; nevertheless, by the second decade of the twentieth century, Britain had erected an administrative 'umbrella' over the whole of the Malay Peninsula.

2.

Under this 'umbrella', by the second decade of the twentieth century, a plural society had formed. The Malay Peninsula, especially the tin states, had had a mixed population since long before, but particularly after the intervention of the British in 1874; but a multi-racial population is not necessarily a plural society, where groups of marked difference to the resident community establish and preserve their identity, and resist assimilation. The U.S.A. is multi-racial, but apart from the negro community (and even here assimilation is progressing gradually), there is no plural society. In South Africa on the other hand, force has established and maintained a plural society and a divided state, and its problems are very apparent. The Malay Peninsula in the 1870's was multi-racial, but by the 1910's it had become a plural society. How did this tragedy happen?

As in any great historic phenomenon a number of factors were in operation. Chief of these perhaps was the flow of Chinese into the peninsula, steadily increasing, a never ceasing flow of South Chinese from Kwangtung, Fukien and Kwangsi in particular. The annual arrival of migrants from China increased considerably when the British administration was established in the peninsula, and particularly after the founding of the Federation and the development of the rubber industry. This is illustrated by the following table:

Arrivals of Chinese in Singapore[8]

1840	2,000
1850	10,000
1870	14,000
1875	31,000
1880	50,000
1890	95,000
1895	190,000
1900	200,000
1912	250,000

The number of new arrivals thereafter varied between 150,000 and 250,000 a year, until in 1927 a record arrival of 360,000 Chinese was registered. In the thirty-two years between 1895 and 1927, 6 million Chinese had come in.

Why did this flood occur? The basic cause for most migrations of any length and strength is economic; thus it was with the Chinese. Unsettled conditions in the South China provinces, over-population and unemployment, famines and floods, chronic maladministration and injustice: all this might have been endured, for they had been constant features of South China for centuries. But the people of the provinces, slightly more experienced of foreign countries and of travel than their neighbours, learned through Hong Kong and Cantonese contacts of the new wealth to be won in the western *Nanyang*, in Singapore and

[8] These figures (given in round numbers) are taken from the Annual Reports of the Straits Settlements. It should be noted that they are *not* numbers of migrants to Malaya, but merely to Singapore. Many migrated elsewhere, to Java in particular.

Penang, and in the Malay States in particular, especially after British capital began to be invested there. In the late nineteenth century millions were emigrating from Europe to America. A similar impulse sent the Chinese south to Malaya.

This new population by itself would not necessarily have created a plural society, had not other factors begun to work during this time to make assimilation more and more difficult. Chief of these was the collapse and the resurgence of China herself.

In 1895, the year in which Swettenham collected the signatures of the Sultans for the establishment of a Federation, China suffered a most humiliating defeat at the hands of Japan, and was forced to sign the Treaty of Shimonoseki. Thus far had the Empire fallen from its arrogant height of a hundred years before. Throughout the nineteenth century the incredibly conservative court and administration had blocked reform, had inhibited change and ignored the outside world. Steadily the aged state had slipped towards collapse. Increasingly adventurous foreign Powers had exploited China with impunity and by 1895 even Japan, modernised at breath-taking speed by the Meiji, could participate too. China was ripe for invasion by the great powers.

In this plight, China, although prostrate, was not mute, and a group of young liberal minded scholars, led by Kang Yu Wei, a South Chinese from Kwantung, tried desperately to introduce a number of reforms. By 1898 his movement, benefiting from the growing realisation of national incompetency, had gathered so much weight that the Manchu Emperor, leaning towards reform after the Japanese War, met Kang Yu Wei, and in 'The Hundred Days Reform' attempted to implement his recommendations. It was the last chance of the liberals, and it failed. The Dowager Empress relieved the Emperor of his power, and a fanatical conservative reaction dominated China. This led to the Boxer Risings in 1899, the intervention of European forces in 1900 to rescue their nationals besieged in Peking, and the further humiliation of China.

Kang Yu Wei, who fled the country when the Dowager Empress removed the Emperor, turned to the overseas Chinese for support. In 1899 he established contact with Khoo Seok Wan, a leading Chinese merchant in Singapore, who formed a branch of his Royalist Party, and who collected over 1,000 signatures to a cable demanding the return of the Emperor to the throne. The value of Singapore's initiative, which was followed by cables from the Chinese in Penang and Kuala Lumpur, and then in Hawaii, Panama and Sydney, was recognized by Kang, who came to Singapore in 1900, and through Khoo Seok Wan collected $100,000 to assist in a revolt in Hankow that year.

Neither the cables nor the revolt were successful, but the unprecedented participation of the overseas Chinese in these activities is most important, as being indicative of the growing interest of the migrants in Chinese political affairs. Fifty years previously they had been worthy of the utmost contempt, poverty stricken peasants abandoning their country, which in its turn abandoned them. Indeed, it was not until the late nineteenth century that the edict forbidding migration was replaced. These migrants had made little deliberate effort to resist a gradual assimilation, and slowly they were fitting in to their new environment.

This was most marked in the Malay States, where the sharp edge of contrast between them and the Malay had gradually blunted, and they had become by degrees less Chinese; indeed eventually they forgot their language, and the Malacca *baba* community dressed and spoke in the Malay manner. Even in Singapore almost imperceptibly the climate and environment shaped each overseas-born generation anew. Nearly all were illiterate, and the positive assimilating force of education worked on very few. Those who were educated during the nineteenth century were taught for the most part in the few government or Christian Mission Schools, to become clerks, teachers, business men or (rarely) doctors, versed in English. By 1900 this community of English educated, Straits-born Chinese, was of sufficient size and influence to warrant the formation that year of the Straits British Chinese Association. Even among this Anglicised group however, the troubles of China and the strivings of the reformers stirred many,[9] while some of the illiterate but wealthy merchants also were beginning to look back to China with sadness, humiliation and anger.

[9] Khoo Seok Wan being one of them.

Thus when Kang came to Singapore, and then moved on to reside during 1900–1901 in Penang, he found considerable support. His work and that of his Royalist Party was most successful in education. Most of the policies advocated by the liberals in China had been rejected by the Manchus, but the educational suggestions had been accepted and introduced. The new education was a combination of Confucianist teaching and western science, and Kang vigorously expounded the advantages of this. He found a ready listener not merely in the merchant, Khoo, but also in another even more outstanding leader of the Straits-born, English-educated Chinese, Dr. Lim Boon Keng. In 1899 he had founded the first Chinese girls' school in Singapore, and he and others, spurred on by developments in China, spent a most active decade, initiating Chinese primary education on the new, progressive pattern throughout the western Malay States. The first modern Chinese school was opened in Kuala Lumpur in 1900; in Penang in 1904; in Perak, at Ipoh, in 1906; in Negri Sembilan, at Seremban, in 1910; while in Singapore, the centre of this Chinese colonial renaissance, six big new schools were functioning by 1906. Thus initiated by this political movement in China Chinese education began in Malaya.

Kang came back to Penang and resided there for three years (1908–1910), and although he never acquired again the prestige that was his in 1900, nevertheless he remained most active in his educational work. Many of these primary schools had their constitutions written, their syllabus arranged and their staff secured by him, while in addition, by promoting the formation of Confucianist clubs and Chinese societies, and by assisting in the formation of Chinese newspapers, such as the *T'ien Nan Shing Pao*, established by Khoo in 1899, he endeavoured to publicise his liberal reforms. His intention was to secure through these schools and these clubs strong support for his movement of reform in China. His more lasting, if less intentional, achievement was to make available to the post 1895 flood of Chinese migrants an education which had scarcely existed before, a Chinese education totally different from that acquired by the other communities in Malaya, one which set them apart and which made them increasingly resistant to assimilation. Similarly the Chinese Chamber of Commerce, formed in 1906 indicated their separation.

Kang was a reformer, a gentleman-scholar, and his influence both in Malaya and in China itself was far less than that of his contemporary, Sun Yat Sen. Also from Kwangtung, and trained as a doctor in Hong Kong, Sun was a revolutionary whose first objective was not to reform but to overthrow the Manchu dynasty. He came increasingly to rely on the *Nanyang* Chinese for the financial support needed to make this possible.

The Treaty of Shimonoseki in 1895, which had stirred Kang into decisive action, had stimulated Sun as well. In that year he attempted in Canton the first of his many attempts to stage a successful rising. It failed, and he fled the country to plan another revolt, this time in Hankow. It was the failure of this second rising, due partly, it was thought, to Kang, that first brought him to Singapore in 1900. Here he broke with the moderate party of Kang, and assisted by his follower Yiu Lieh, he established contact, with the poorer, non-educated Chinese. Sun looked for fellow revolutionaries in a most democratic manner, recruiting peasants and *towkays* alike, while associating intimately with secret societies. This gave him greater influence than Kang, a Confucianist scholar. It meant also that through Sun Yat Sen a far greater proportion of the Chinese in Malaya than before became conscious of the struggle in China, and were made aware that they too were participants in that struggle.

In 1906 there was established in Singapore, at a meeting presided over by Sun Yat Sen, a branch of his revolutionary party. Two prominent Chinese who were original members were Teo Eng Hock and Lim Nee Soon. That year Sun toured the Federation, speaking to groups and gatherings. Eight more branches of his party had been formed before he moved on, including one in Penang, whose President, Goh Say Eng, later represented Malayan Chinese in the Republican Government. The interest of the Chinese in events in China, sustained by the publication in 1907 of a revolutionary paper, the *Chung Hsin,* and the formation of Reading Societies, was aroused to a new height.[10]

[10] One of these Reading Societies formed in 1911 by Sun Lat Sen's supporters to cater for illiterate Teochews, the United Chinese Library (or T'un Te Reading Society), is still in existence.

Sun Yat Sen steadily increased his support, and his revolutionary influence spread out from the Reading Societies and branches of his party into the schools that were being founded. He paid repeated visits to Malaya, for the wealth of the migrants became of vital importance to him. His attempted revolts in Hankow and Hueichow in 1900, the rising led by Hung Chuen Fook in 1903, the Changsa revolt in 1904, whose leader also took refuge in Singapore, and the Teochew rising in the same year that sent six of its leaders south to the safety of Singapore, were all financed to an increasing extent by Malayan money.

Despite the failures, the régime in China did little to dampen the ardour of the revolutionaries or to weaken the overseas supporters. Its extreme attitude indeed encouraged the revolutionaries and depressed the dwindling band of reformists. In 1908 there were two more revolts, another in 1910, and another in 1911, all organised by Sun Yat Sen and led by men who had found safety and encouragement in Singapore or Penang. Sun Yat Sen himself in this decade (1900–1910) paid eight visits to the south, in 1908–1909 staying for over a year, travelling extensively, lecturing, appealing, organising, and in 1910 staying in Penang for nearly six months. When he came again it was in December 1911. He paused at Penang only long enough to pick up his family. The Wuchang Rising, financed from Malaya, had been successful, and he was on his way to Shanghai to be the Provisional President of the Republic of China.

His success after this ten year struggle brought intense jubilation to the great mass of the Chinese in Malaya. The hated queue, the sign of Manchu inferiority, was cut off with fervour, if this had not been done before, while another large donation was sent to the republicans to relieve the suffering of those caught in the last revolt.

Still, however, the Chinese poured into Singapore. China remained disunited and the south still had years of struggle ahead before its government controlled all China. It remained a twisted and unhappy land, from which many migrated. These migrants, however, did not abandon their country, nor did their country abandon them. Well aware of the importance to China of the overseas Chinese, the Republican leaders, as soon as the Kuomintang was formed in 1912, devoted a considerable part of their effort to winning and retaining the support of these people, and branches of this monolithic nationalist party were formed immediately in Malaya. Singapore was the first to be registered by a benevolent government in December 1912.[11] Dr. Lim Boon Keng, Lim Nee Soon and Tan Chay Yan were three of the original office bearers. Henceforth a direct, strong, active, Chinese political organisation operated in Malaya, working on the emotions of one community only, and the forces tending towards the creation of a plural society, which separated the peoples of Malaya, were increased accordingly.

The decade 1910–1920 witnessed an intensification of this Chinese education, and by 1920 there were over forty large Chinese schools in Singapore, over thirty in Penang, and at least one or more in every town in the Malay States. To the primary schools had been added the occasional secondary school (Middle School), while in one and all there was bred a Chinese patriotism.

Hitherto the British government had noted with indifference this ferment of the Chinese as they crowded under the British umbrella. Provided that they did not disturb the peace, they were ignored. Occasionally a leader, such as Sun Yat Sen, would be told that possibly it might be advisable if he moved on, but otherwise the administration left this bubbling cauldron alone.

By the end of the decade, however, the situation had deteriorated to the extent where the government felt forced to take belated action. Japan, which had emerged from the First World War immensely more powerful than before through its painless support of the Allied Powers, attempted in 1919 to wrench away another part of China. The Republic of 1919 was not the Empire of 1895, and there was a fierce reaction which spread immediately to the overseas Chinese. Large scale riots led by the students broke out in Singapore, Kuala Lumpur and Penang, while Japanese businesses were boycotted throughout the peninsula. The

---

11 This story is well told by Png Poh Seng, *The KMT in Malaya* (Journal, South-East Asian History, vol. 2, no. 1, March 1961). See also Wang Gungwu, *Sün Yat Sen and Singapore* (Journal of the South Seas Society, vol. xv, 1959).

riots were suppressed with difficulty, for the administration were caught by surprise, and the government decided that some control over the Chinese schools must be established. An Education Bill attempting this was passed in 1920, which put an end to the complete official ignorance of Chinese education with only a nominal supervision. As neither the smaller problem, that of Chinese education, nor the greater, the creation of a plural society, was surveyed effectively, both problems continued to grow.

By 1920 a divided land and a plural society were being created not merely by the uncontrolled activities of the thousands of Chinese educated migrants. There was in addition the influence of the English educated Chinese, as well as the influx of Indians which occurred during this period; and finally there was the growing awareness of the Malays that they too were different.

The English educated Chinese were very largely people born and baptised in the colony of the Straits Settlements. As British subjects, possessing many privileges, they tended to ally themselves, although in no uncritical spirit, with the government. They worked successfully during this period for the extension of English education in Singapore, Penang and Malacca. Mainly due to their financial support a number of big mission schools were established between 1895 and 1910, while their protests in the legislature ensured that the few government English schools were enlarged. In 1905, although their ambitions for a University were squashed by an unsympathetic government, King Edward VII Medical College was founded by Straits Chinese led by Tan Jiak Kim. The government was quite content to leave the initiative to them. In a community of merchants and administrators, liberal sentiments did not flourish. The Legislative Council saw little reason why the government should squander its money unduly on education, and if the efforts of the missions ensured that an adequate number of English educated clerks were available for the merchant houses and the civil service, there seemed little point in going further. By 1914, for example, educational expenditure in the Federation was only 1.1% of the total. Nevertheless, through the functioning of the government and particularly the mission schools, a considerable section of the educated Asian community by 1919 was English educated. In that year there were 25,000 students at 80 big English schools, and 33,000 at 586 small Malay Schools. There are no figures available of the thousands at the Chinese schools; probably they would not be less than 30,000. Thus there were three clear cut divisions.

The multi-racial composition of Malaya was made more complex during this period by the migration of thousands of Tamils from South India. The links between the Malay Peninsula and India stretch back thousands of years, and there had been a few Indians resident in the Malay States from long before the founding of Penang in 1786. With the growth of Penang and Singapore during the nineteenth century a steadily growing Indian merchant community came into existence. Here, as with the Chinese, there was gradual assimilation. They created no problem. Malaya became multi-racial, but as with the Chinese, it was with the development of the Malay States, particularly after the establishment of the rubber industry in the first decade of the twentieth century, that thousands of Tamil labourers flooded in from Madras to assist in the creation of a plural society.

Although from 1910 onwards the sari was a familiar sight, and little Hindu shrines began to appear amid the rubber landscape, and a few Tamil schools received subsidies from the government, this Indian element was assimilated more easily than the Chinese. Intermarriage between the two races was common. Many South Indians shared the same faith, Islam, and if they did not, at least many of their customs and habits were similar, derived from a common origin. Most of them in any case returned to India after a few years' work. Nevertheless the gap was there, deepened in these decades by the intense interest taken by the Indian in the exciting political developments of his home-land, from which he regarded himself as a temporary absentee. India was on the way to democracy and independence, and all these migrants felt themselves part of this movement. The Malay Peninsula was not their home, they felt little necessity to adapt themselves in any way to their temporary environment, and conscious of their difference they kept apart from their fellow inhabitants of the peninsula. Again as with the Chinese, this would not have mattered had they all left Malaya and returned to their homeland, but an increasing number stayed on. As Parkinson says, "the inter-racial problem began, not when people arrived, but from the date when they began to settle."[12] This was becoming clearly evident by 1920.

Three developments characterised both the Chinese and the Indian communities in Malaya during this period. Firstly there was the sudden flood of new migrants; secondly, there was the educational division of each community into those English educated, in each case largely middle class, and those non-English educated, again broadly representing the poorer classes; and thirdly, there was the great impact made on them by the nationalistic fervour of their homeland. These same developments, to some extent muted and weaker, characterised the Malay community as well.

The British 'umbrella' attracted not merely Chinese and Indians, but a gentle flow of migrants from Sumatra (where the Achinese War of 1873–1899 against the Dutch drove many to Kedah and Perak), from Java, and from the other islands: in particular from the Rhio Archipelago, when the Dutch deposed the Sultan and narrowly avoiding another war, ended the sultanate between 1903 and 1910.

All along the west coast these Malaysian people slipped unobtrusively ashore, and merged with little effort into the Malay community. The majority of their children went to the Malay schools which the Federal and Straits Governments were sponsoring; a few however, the more wealthy or the more progressive, went to English schools, the select few being chosen for the Malay College, founded in 1903 to train Malay leaders; but they never broke completely from their mother tongue, as did many Indians and Chinese.

To this Malay community there came faintly but unmistakably the noise of the socio-religious stirring of the Middle East. In Cairo and in the Muslim lands of Western Asia, a fertile crescent which had long languished under the dead hand of the Ottoman Turk, a reformist movement began in the last few decades of the nineteenth century. This movement was aimed at a religious and

---

12 C. N. Parkinson, *A Short History of Malaya* (Singapore, 1954), p. 18.

national revival, and at the elimination of the innumerable social ills of the area.

One of the outstanding leaders in this revival was the Grand Mufti of Cairo, Shaykh Mohammed Abduh. He influenced, amongst many other pilgrims, Sayed Shaykh Al-Haji. Born in 1867, he was a Malaccan Malay who had lived most of his early life in Rhio. Before the Sultanate was overthrown Rhio was the religious and literary centre of the Malays, and there he had become aware of Malay backwardness.

Sayed Shaykh Al-Haji was inspired by the religious revival in Cairo, and he had also been profoundly affected by the defeat of the European giant, Russia, by the Asian pygmy, Japan. He determined to strive against this Malay backwardness. In 1906 he founded in Rhio his magazine *Al-Iman* (The Leader). It was one of the earliest magazines aimed at the Malay community, and it produced the first stirrings of that community. Owing to political events in Rhio the paper closed in 1909, and Sayed Shaykh Al-Haji came to Singapore, but by then it had helped establish the *Kaum Muda* (Modernist Group), young men anxious to bring forward the Malays, and critical of the numerous social ills in their community. Another paper that assisted in the intellectual awakening of the Malays was the *Utusan Melayu,* founded in 1907. Mohamed Eunos, its first editor, became the first Malay member of the Straits Legislative Council.

These newspapers, and the *Al-Ikhwan* (The Brethren) founded in 1926, benefited immensely from the widespread schooling in Malay which the governments were vigorously supporting. Education in the mother tongue was not a feature of British rule in India, nor in Burma, nor in Ceylon. But in none of these countries were the authorities faced with a Chinese problem. Is it permissible to assume that the educational policy in Malaya which supported Malay and Chinese language schools, may well have been influenced by the desire to establish two communities, not one, and that the balance would rest with the administration? Whatever the reason, the marked favour shown for Malay kampong education enabled leaders such as Sayed Shaykh Al-Haji and Mohamed Eunos to reach an ever increasing number of their community. It assisted both of them and the more conservative

Kaum Tua, or Malay officialdom, in demonstrating to that community not merely its backwardness, in comparison with the Europeans or Chinese, but also, and perhaps of even more importance, its separateness. Between 1910–1930 the Malays became increasingly aware of themselves as Malays and as Muslims. There was a similar if stronger awakening in Indonesia. In both countries there was a revival of Islam, a revival now in full flood; while the awakening of Malay consciousness led in 1926 to the formation of the first Malay political party, the Singapore Malay Union (*Kesatuan Melayu Singapora*), led by Mohamed Eunos. The Malays had moved thus far from the Chinese.

Fostered then by migration, itself encouraged by a benevolent and competent British administration, and encouraged both by national developments in China, India and the Islamic world, and also by educational policies in the Malay Peninsula itself, a multi-racial community was changed during these years into a plural society. No other aspect of Malaya's history has been so neglected; no other holds such danger for the future, unless, understanding how the present came to be, we can create again a multi-racial society in this new nation.

Population of Malaya
(The Malay States & the Straits Settlements)

	1921
Malays	1,627,108
Chinese	1,173,354
Indians	471,628

9. TIN AND RUBBER

Tin has been mentioned many times in this book. Tin and also gold were the two commodities which attracted the Indians, Cambodians, Javanese and others, the commodities which led to the Indianised settlements and the diffusion of the resultant culture which is still apparent today. Although tin played a minor role to gold, it was worked throughout the centuries, and it continued to attract migrants for over a thousand years.

For over a thousand years it was worked spasmodically as long as supply and demand were small. Dug mainly by Malays, tin was exported mainly to China, where it was used very largely for religious purposes, as tin foil at altars and shrines. Then in the nineteenth century came two major developments that ushered in the modern economic age for the peninsula. The Chinese replaced the Malays as miners; Europe and the U.S.A. replaced China as the market.

This modern period can be said to begin, if we are searching for a specific date, in 1848, when the rich ore deposits of the Larut region in Perak were discovered. At much the same time, on the other side of the world, British scientific discoveries were leading to the beginning of the modern canning industry in the U.S.A. The packing of meat, begun in 1860 in the U.S.A. stimulated by the demands of the Civil War, and the making of barrels for the oil industry, which began at the same time, provided the major impetus to the search for and production of tin. Beside oil and meat, numerous other commodities were canned, with the American Civil War figuring in most as the incentive. On a double wave of technological improvements and increased uses for tin, the demand for it rose rapidly.[1] To profit from this demand, the Chinese poured into the Malay Peninsula.

By 1870 over 40,000 of them were in Perak, the major tin

---

[1] See W. E. Minchinton, *The British Tinplate Industry (A History)*, particularly Appendix C: 'The Growth of the Canning Industry' (Oxford, 1957), pp. 254–258.

state, financed as we have seen earlier by the Chinese business firms in Penang and Singapore. They participated also in the increased production along the Selangor and Sungei Ujong river valleys which with the establishment of British officers in the three states, occurred at much the same time.

In one way or the other virtually all the administrative measures taken by the Residents assisted in the production and export of tin. Firstly the rivers were cleared. The Malay chiefs along the banks were restrained from levying tolls and from waging wars (as were the Chinese, too), while the physical snags, such as fallen trees, logs and barriers of all kinds, also were removed. Then from the rivers, roads were built, the first ever in the peninsula, and after the roads, railways, tin again being the inducement. In 1884 Taiping, the tin centre of Larut, was joined by rail to Port Weld, eight miles away on a deep water inlet. In 1890 Kuala Lumpur was joined by rail to the coast at Klang. Then in 1895 Ipoh, the powerful new centre of the fabulously wealthy Kinta area, was joined to Teluk Anson at the coast nearby.

Other steps taken by the British administration ensured that the states were surveyed accurately, so that the tin leases could be demarcated with precision. By the 1880's the incessant disputes over property became a thing of the past. Three other administrative measures that kept the peace and encouraged tin production were firstly the reservation of all minerals as the property of the state, thus making a government licence a necessary prerequisite before they could be mined; the reservation also of all streams as the property of the state, so that a stream could not be monopolised by one miner, and an adequate supply of sluicing water could be arranged for all; and thirdly, a regulation on land use, so that only land specifically leased for mining could be so worked. This prevented random and haphazard mutilation, and permitted the state to maintain control.

These regulations made tin development peaceful, while the profits overseas constantly stimulated its export. As a result the revenue of the states grew rapidly. In 1876 the revenue of Perak, Selangor and Sungei Ujong was $500,000; twelve years later, in 1888, it was $3,600,000. By 1899 the duty on the export of tin provided 46% of the total revenue of the Federation. By the turn of the century the Malay States were in the happy position, almost unique among the tropical countries of the world, in that they possessed in tin a staple in great demand, a staple that gave a strong financial base not merely for administrative running costs, but which in addition permitted large scale capital works, such as ports, railways, government buildings and roads. Without doubt tin transformed the peninsula.

This tin was mined and exported almost entirely by Chinese. The European played no part in this development at all, and the mine capital and even more particularly the mine labour remained largely Chinese until the twentieth century. For example, Kinta, in Perak, vastly larger than Larut, was opened up in 1880. British administration kept the peace and provided the railway to the coast, but the Chinese provided the sinews. By 1890 the Chinese population of this Malay State was over 80,000, and nearly all the mines were Chinese. It was similar elsewhere. European capital and western enterprise followed Chinese initiative tardily, and even as late as 1913 the tin production of the peninsula was almost entirely in Chinese hands.

Malayan Tin Production

(In thousand long tons)

1850	6.5
1881	19.6
1891	41.7
1901	46.7
1913	51.4

A few British firms became established by the turn of the century. For example the predecessor of the present Gopeng Consolidated Ltd. was floated in 1892, and Osborn and Chappel, still the most important firm of mining and consulting engineers in Malaya, began in 1902. Nevertheless in 1913 the Chinese remained predominant in this industry. In that year they were still responsible for three-quarters of the total output (74%).

In 1912, however, there had moved into Perak a monstrous machine that was destined to drive out the Chinese from the industry they held, apparently, so firmly. This was the tin dredge, an adaptation of the gold dredge, and its arrival marks the large scale introduction of western capital, management and technical skill.

Previous to this the Chinese had mined the tin with what the twentieth century recognised as "ridiculous and primitive methods," which had changed not in hundreds of years.[2] A drainage sluice built up from rickety bits of bamboo, perhaps a cumbersome wooden water wheel, a stream, a *chunkol* or shovel: these were the essentials to the miner. He added to this primitive gear various western devices that came with the modern age, such as the small steam engine working a pump, while hydraulic sluices and gravel pumps came from the Australian gold fields, where many Chinese had learned to operate them; but these were basically modifications which the Chinese made to their age-old tested procedures and techniques. The dredge was a fundamental change and they could not withstand it.

From the beginning dredge mining was entirely in European hands. Why was this so? For one thing, these dredges brought from Australia or Alaska were very expensive and made heavy demands on capital. The Chinese did not have this capital, and they lacked the organisation and power to collect it. Moreover the dredge comprised pieces of complicated machinery which demanded highly skilled operators, and again this was something the Chinese did not have; neither, should it be noted, did the British: the dredge masters came very largely from Australia. Finally dredge operations called for large scale management qualities, and the illiterate, independent Chinese miner was quite without that too. At this period, therefore, the Chinese in Malaya had little experience of large scale mining enterprise, and lacked both the means of financing it and the technical knowledge to work it.

By 1929 105 dredges were operating in the Malay States, and by 1930 European mines were producing three-fifths of the total output of tin. By 1939 this had become two-thirds. Production rose from 51,600 tons in 1913 to 77,000 in 1937, yet the quantity

---

[2] F. Swettenham, *About Perak* (Singapore, 1893), p. 34.

obtained from the Chinese mines diminished. Even as early as 1912 the near-surface lodes were being worked out, and the dredges, by operating in swampy ground, or in poor quality areas, floating in their artificially created lakes like dirty ducks, were able to work areas denied or worthless to the Chinese. In just over twenty-five years tin mining was transformed from a predominantly Chinese to a predominantly Western industry.

Unlike the rubber companies, which were being formed at much the same time, these Western tin companies shared their skill and finance. It was a much more technical and scientific business than rubber, and for greater efficiency the tin concerns of Malaya gradually came together. From the middle twenties, although there were about eighty separate companies, the links grew stronger. By 1939 over half the European dredge output, which came from twenty big companies, was controlled by Anglo-Oriental (Malaya) Ltd., the subsidiary of London Tin Corporation.

By 1929, the year in which the great world economic depression began, Malaya had become fully aware that its major export commodities were sold on a fluctuating world market. In 1904 it had produced 56% of the world's output of tin, but since then there had been important discoveries of ore in Bolivia and Nigeria, and although in 1929 its export of 70,000 tons was a record, it was only 36% of the world figure of 190,000 tons. This was more than the world demanded. For several years as consumption in the U.S.A. declined there had been a steady growth in surplus stocks, and prices fell in sympathy.

Price of Tin (per ton)

	£
1926	284
1929	200
1931	120

The employers attempted to control this crisis by regulating production. In 1929 the Malayan government accepted no new application for mining land, and in the same year a voluntary effort at limiting production was introduced, in Malaya and elsewhere. It failed, and prices continued to fall. The following year more drastic measures were taken, and a scheme was drawn up by the Tin Producers Council which had been formed in 1929 from representatives of the four great tin countries, Malaya, Nigeria, Netherlands East Indies and Bolivia. The scheme called for a compulsory restriction on output. The London Tin Corporation, which controlled the major output from Malaya, Nigeria and Bolivia, was in a particularly strong position to see that the governments concerned accepted the scheme. It was introduced in March 1931.

At the beginning it made the same mistake as had been committed by the rubber countries of the world with their Stevenson Rubber Plan: it omitted a number of minor producers, amounting to 15% of world production. These countries, Siam, Indo-China and the Congo immediately began to profit from the forced reduction in output from the major producers. They were included in the scheme on very favourable terms in 1931–32.

Tin output was restricted drastically. Malaya had its export allowance reduced in big stages until in 1933 it was permitted only 33 1/3% of its pre-restriction output of 1929. Thereafter its allowance rose slowly, but it never returned to 100%. This restriction scheme ran for three years. It was renewed in 1934, in 1937 and again in late 1941, when most of the Malayan mines were in Japanese hands. Apart from restricting output by fixing an export allowance, the Tin Committee, which regulated the agreement in London, in 1934 formed a buffer stock of tin to check the wild fluctuations in price that year. This stock was sold in 1935. In 1937 there were again violent fluctuations in price, so in 1938 the buffer was revived and maintained. Judicious selling and buying of this stock kept the price between £200 and £230 per ton.

Restriction favours the inefficient; it keeps prices high, and permits the inefficient to survive. Malayan tin, particularly dredge tin, was produced at a low cost. Bolivia and Nigeria were high cost producers. Instead of Malaya driving them out of business, thousands of Malayans went unemployed, and by 1938 Malaya accounted for only 26% of the world output, as compared to the 36% of 1929. "On the whole it seems probably that the interests of Malaya as a low cost producer gained little if anything from the scheme, and that its adoption and renewal were mainly the result of pressure from one large group of Companies that has extensive high cost holdings in Bolivia and Nigeria, in addition to its Malayan holdings."[3]

Through the mining of tin Malaya's greatest industry was established: tin smelting. The Chinese and before them, the Malays, had been smelting in a very primitive manner indeed. Almost every mine would do its own smelting. A typical smelter would be perhaps six feet high, made of bricks and lined with clay. At the bottom it would narrow down to a small tap-hole, a foot or so above the ground, and it was operated by the throwing of burning charcoal into the open top of the furnace or smelter, following it with a layer of ore, and then more charcoal, and so on. The molten tin thus produced would trickle down through the tap-hole, and be ladled into sand moulds.

This primitive furnace was inefficient and costly. Very large quantities of timber were used, and perhaps only 50–60% of the possible tin obtained. It became increasingly clear that if the great coal operated furnaces of the industrial West could be adapted to this industry, there would be great benefits to all concerned.

In 1879 Mr. Gilfillan, of Gilfillan Wood and Company of Singapore, went on a holiday to Australia. Here the idea was put to him by Mr. J. H. Kelly of Sydney, the owner of a large smelting works there, that tin could be smelted by Western methods. Gilfillan was impressed, but on returning to Singapore he encountered a deadlock. Neither Selangor nor Perak would permit their ore to be exported, and insisted that it had to be smelted in the state first, and no European businessman had the courage to establish such a smelter in any of the Malay States.

In 1885, however, the deadlock was broken, H. Muhlinghaus, a friend of Gilfillan, secured the financial capital necessary from another pioneer, J. Sword, and in partnership with him he opened in 1886 a small smelter at Telok Anson, near the mouth of the Perak River, and thus in contact with both the Larut and

[3] T. H. Silcock, *The Economy of Malaya* (Singapore, 1954), p. 14.

Kinta fields. The partners also secured the permission of Sungei Ujong, Selangor and Perak, by then alarmed at the forest denudation caused by the Chinese smelters, to export ore.

Sword and Muhlinghaus had two great attractions in their business. Firstly, they paid cash for the tin ore sold them by the miners, whereas the Chinese smelters merely gave credit at a store. This produced all the ore they needed. In addition they had the technical ability to smelt efficiently. This produced the profit. In 1887 their partnership expanded into the Straits Trading Company Ltd. with a capital of $150,000 in Kuala Lumpur. It opened branches in Sungei Ujong (1887) and in Perak (1889). In 1890 it moved to Singapore. By 1898 the company's capital was $1,250,000.[4]

As business mounted, the Teluk Anson smelter became too small, and was in any case too isolated. In 1890 a much bigger smelter was built at Pulo Brani, off Keppel Harbour in Singapore. By 1895 twelve large coal-operated furnaces were producing 14,000 tons of refined tin annually, a third of Malaya's production. In 1902 it opened another large smelting works at Butterworth (where oil replaced coal), and in 1937 it established a further one in the United Kingdom near the port of Liverpool.

By this time the Straits Trading Company had revolutionised the tin industry of South-East Asia, for not only did most of Malaya's tin come to these smelters, but also the ore from Banka and Billiton, until a Dutch-British concern, the Consolidated Tin Smelters, built a smelter in 1933 at Arnhem, in Holland. Ore also came from the Siamese deposits in the Kra Peninsula, from Indo-China, Burma and from as far away as Yunnan, in China. Only one Malayan competitor emerged, the Eastern Smelting Company, established in Penang in 1907 from the smelter formed in 1897 by Lee Chin Ho. Chinese-owned until 1911, it was then bought out by British capital, and in 1922 it became part of Consolidated Tin Smelters. Possibly this competition kept the Straits Trading Company to the fore because it never declined

---

[4] Its paid up capital in 1961 was $12 million. See K. G. Tregonning's *Straits Tin: A History of the Straits Trading Company, Limited. 1887–1962* (Singapore, 1962).

with age and today, when it is the greatest tin smelting concern in the world, it is noted as in 1887 for two characteristics: a quickness in appreciating and utilising the latest technical developments in its industry, and a highly efficient business management.

Tin is today Malaya's second most important export industry. Its great days, before it was superseded as the greatest single money earner of the Malay States, were in the late nineteenth century. Even then, as Sword and Muhlinghaus went about establishing their furnaces, and as Residents and High Commissioners spent freely on railways and ports the revenue derived from the exports, another development was occurring of even greater importance to the peninsula: the introduction of rubber.

Prior to the advent of rubber the agriculture of the Malay Peninsula had changed but little in all its history. In a word, it was undeveloped. With the occupation of the islands of Penang and Singapore attempts were made to grow spices and sugar on the one, and gambier and pepper on the other. Both enterprises failed.[5] Johore, as mentioned earlier,[6] was opened by gambier and pepper planters from Singapore, but elsewhere in the peninsula it was not until the advent of coffee planting in the 1870's that any other worthwhile crop was produced. The Malay landscape of A.D. 1870 was almost identical to that of 1870 B.C.

In the last quarter of the nineteenth century however, in keeping with the political and social changes of the country, the landscape began to change too, in Malaya as elsewhere in South-East Asia. Following the establishment of British advisers in the States, and attracted by the large areas of land available, coffee planters came across from Ceylon, where their estates had been ruined by a devastating bug. They negotiated for land, and began small estates in Perak, Selangor and Negri Sembilan; but particularly in Selangor. Their enterprise played a part both in increasing the revenue of the state, and more particularly in opening it up. Coffee flourished for a decade or more. In Selangor,

---

[5] Sugar, however, flourished in a small area on the mainland for over sixty years, in Province Wellesley and Malacca, from 1840–1913.

[6] See p. 140.

for instance, T. H. Hill from Ceylon opened the first estate in 1882, and this was followed by many others particularly during the 1890's. The crop reached its peak in Malaya in 1897; but by the turn of the century most planters had been ruined, partly by the same insect which had attacked them in Ceylon, but very largely by a continuous flood of Brazilian coffee that forced world prices to collapse completely. Coffee was virtually abandoned by the beginning of the twentieth century.

The planters who escaped from ruin were saved by the arrival of rubber,[7] introduced through the initiative of the West and established in the Malay Peninsula largely through the persistency of one man, H. N. Ridley. A man of imagination and great firmness of mind, Ridley had been appointed director of the Botanical Gardens at Singapore in 1888. The Gardens themselves had been an imaginative step, founded in 1858. Had they not existed, Malaya might never have seen a rubber tree. At that time the tree grew wild in South America. It was not a plantation crop anywhere in the world. British botanists thought that rubber trees might grow in India and perhaps elsewhere, and in 1876, Henry Wickham managed to bring to London, from the Amazon regions of South America, some 70,000 seeds. Only a few (4%) germinated, of which a handful were sent in 1877 to Singapore. Five seeds were alive when the case was received and these were planted out immediately. From those five seeds came the mainstay of Malaya today.

For some years this new crop was ignored. Coffee was flourishing, the motor car age had not begun, and although Hugh Low planted several rubber trees behind his Perak Residency in Kuala Kangsar, and they and the Singapore trees grew well, there was little demand for them. Then came Ridley. He was both a propagandist and a scientific investigator. He came to Singapore convinced by Sir Joseph Hooker, Director of the famous Kew Gardens, that rubber was an excellent tropical crop. He was an outstanding public-relations man, constantly on the look-out for ways of persuading planters to grow it. It was his practice to

[7] Some ruined coffee planters took service with the government. One of them was Lister, who founded Seremban.

stuff seeds into their pockets, urging them to give rubber a trial. He was soon given the title of 'mad Ridley', or 'Rubber Ridley'. It was not easy to convince the planters or the government, but tirelessly he continued. In the 1890's the governor reprimanded him for his persistency. His Excellency had sent some Malays to the top of the trees in the Botanical Gardens to see if there was any rubber there; and when they slid down and said none was to be seen he had angrily ordered them to destroy the trees.

Fortunately there were a few who were prepared to experiment and gamble on Ridley's conviction. In Selangor, which became the outstanding rubber state, the brothers Kindersley, who had opened a coffee estate in 1894, two years later planted five acres with rubber, near Kajang the seedlings coming from Ridley. This was the first recorded planting of a separate field of rubber in Malaya.[8] W. S. Bennett, another pioneer, interplanted 40,000 rubber trees among his coffee in Selangor between 1897 and 1900. T. H. Hill quickly abandoned coffee altogether, and from 1898 onwards turned exclusively to rubber. He retired with half a million pounds shortly before the First World War. In Perak the first rubber estate was formed by two more coffee planters, Stephens and McGillivray, in 1897.

By the time their trees were ready for tapping, all these pioneers were able to benefit from Ridley's investigations into the most advantageous way of securing the sap. Ridley experimented for several years with different methods of tapping. In 1897 he discovered the system of 'ibidem' tapping which, when its virtues were recognised, was accepted gradually by all estates. There had been many techniques of tapping, of cutting the tree to secure the latex or sap, but many of these, while producing a large quantity of sap, ruined the tree in a short time. Ridley's method was to cut a single strip from the bark, inducing the sap to trickle into a small cup. He found that this wound healed quickly, and could be cut again and again, with as much latex flowing each time as on the earlier occasion.

---

[8] This was on the Inch-Kenneth Estate, near Kajang. The estate still exists today.

This system made it possible to tap the tree daily for many years. Indeed there are now accounts of trees being tapped that are over forty years old.[9]

By 1900, although the foundations for a great plantation industry had been laid, and the major technical problems had been solved, the slow growth of the tree, seven years from planting to tapping, made a sudden increase of supply impossible. But from 1900 the motor car age was beginning, the demand for rubber was increasing tremendously, and supply fell further and further behind demand. As with tin, it was as much the technological discoveries in the West—vulcanisation of rubber in 1855, the pneumatic tyre in 1889, the motor car in the late 1890's, and its mass production in the 1900's—as the primary developments in the East, that led to this transformation. Far more than tin, prices rose astronomically, and as labour costs could be kept low an extremely profitable field of investment was opened up.

In this field the pioneers, the individual planters with their small 100 acre estates, were thrust aside or absorbed by the big companies formed in London to grow large quantities of rubber in Malaya. One of the earliest was the Pataling Rubber Company, formed in 1903 by Harrisons and Crosfield of London, which had long been interested in trading with the East. It acquired land outside Kuala Lumpur (where the University of Malaya now stands) part of which had been the coffee estate since 1895 of W. W. Bailey, a well known pioneer, who had bought it from T. H. Hill. Harrisons and Crosfield, acting under the drive of A. Lampard, its Chairman, floated the company with difficulty. Agriculture as distinct from trade, was a new venture, and rubber was a very new crop. People were reluctant to invest.[10] Nevertheless Bailey, retained as manager, went

[9] Another discovery of Ridley's that was of great use was in the transport of seeds. Previously nearly all rubber seeds died when being distributed. By constant experimentation he found that if they were packed in moist charcoal their life would be preserved, and they could be sent on long tropical journeys.

[10] For this venture, the reader should refer to a summary of the activities of Harrisons and Crosfield given in K. G. Tregonning, *North Borneo* (HMSO, 1960), pp. 194–197.

ahead planting rubber. Each year a handsome profit was made on the increasing number of trees that could be tapped, and a healthy divided was declared. Seven years later in 1910, when for the first time most of the rubber at last could be tapped, 325,000 pounds of rubber were exported, and a profit of £81,000 was made. Three dividends were declared that year, returning to the original investors in one year a sum equal to 200%. As can be imagined, Harrisons and Crosfield thereafter had little difficulty in floating other rubber companies. So profitable was rubber that although in 1895 there was not a single estate in Selangor (the rubber State *par excellence*) registered under a company name, by 1910 out of a total of 142 estates in Selangor, 122 were owned by companies.

These companies which had succeeded in creating a great new industry down the west coast of Malaya—for the rubber estates, very largely, were in the Federated States of Selangor, Perak and Negri Sembilan and later in Kedah and in Johore—consisted either of Agency Houses, such as Harrisons and Crosfield, Guthrie's, or Sime Darby and Company, firms with their head offices in London but with their Malayan interests managed mainly from Singapore; or the rubber manufacturing concerns themselves, such as Dunlop, which acquired big estates in Selangor; or other companies floated locally in Malaya, such as the Malacca Rubber Plantations Ltd. controlled by Tan Chay Yan, a friend of Ridley's and the first man to grow rubber in Malacca. It was in these Chinese financed firms for example that Tan Cheng Lock, the Straits Chinese leader, made his fortune. Between them all they exported to Europe and America 33,000 tons by 1913. A year later over half the world's supply of rubber came from Malaya.

It is not difficult to grow rubber, and once the technical problems of producing latex rubber sheet had been solved the main worry that occupied the estates was the supply of labour.[11] The

---

[11] Although rubber grows easily, this is not to say that improvements cannot be made, nor that experimentation in various ways may not be profitable. Research is essential in tropical agriculture as in everything else. This was tardily recognised by the formation in 1926 of a Rubber Research Institute.

Malay Peninsula was still very thinly inhabited at the beginning of the century and apart from the Chinese happily working tin, it was still predominantly Malay. The Malay found estate labour distasteful. He had come to terms with his environment, terms which to the great majority were very satisfactory. There was peace in the land, and there was contentment in the kampongs. There was little wealth, but there was enough land and food for everyone, and there was an ordered regular pattern of life, a culture, that did not include the regimented labour of an estate. As a result the Malay played no part in the formation, expansion or cultivation of the big rubber estates, which oddly enough came to resemble internally, in their almost feudal arrangement of devolving powers and responsibilities, the Malay political structure outside. This is not to say that the Malay did not play a part in growing rubber. On the contrary; as a smallholder he came to contribute nearly half of the annual export crop, but that was later. As far as the estates were concerned, he remained aloof and uninterested, and they had to rely on a supply of immigrant labour. This came largely from South India.

The early plantations secured their labour in the same manner as the coffee estates they were superseding, that is by indenture. Indentured labourers signed a certificate or contract before leaving Madras by which they pledged themselves to work for three or five years for a particular estate. This infringement on a person's liberty was justified by the planters, who claimed that they were liable to lose all the money they spent on fares, provisions etc. unless the labourer worked for them in return. But as elsewhere the system was found mutually unsatisfactory. The labourer would often be kept in debt at the estate store, so that he would be forced to sign on for further service, and other injustices too were perpetuated. The employer eventually found that unwilling labour was inefficient labour, and began to seek alternative systems of recruitment.

For a time, as indentured labour diminished in importance (it was abolished in British territories in 1910), it was replaced by the *kangany* system, whereby a foreman or senior labourer from the estate was sent back to India, empowered to recruit in his old village. The labourers so acquired received a free passage to Malaya, usually to Port Swettenham, and then were employed not on a three year contract but on a month to month basis, both parties being entitled to give notice if dissatisfied.[12]

As the big companies moved in, however, and as the need for labour increased tremendously when the estates came to be measured in thousands of acres rather than in hundreds, the *kangany* system, operated by individual planters, could not meet requirements, and the Government itself stepped in. In 1907 it established the Indian Immigration Fund, a levy exacted from all estates for the purpose of financing labour to migrate, and henceforth it operated a highly efficient service of great value to the rubber industry. It established camps in South India (at Negapatam and Avadi), where Indians interested in migrating could obtain a free ticket to Penang or Port Swettenham. On reaching Malaya, after a week's quarantine and medical check, these voluntary labourers were free to go when they liked, being given a $2 hand-out and a free rail ticket to their destination. This government scheme, together with unassisted immigration, formed the backbone of the rubber industry in Malaya by stabilising the labour supply.[13]

The Malayan Government not merely controlled the flow of labour to these estates, but established a legal basis for land holding very quickly after the estate boom began. This modern system of land tenure was the Torrens system, introduced to Selangor from Australia by William Maxwell in 1891, and subsequently extended to the Federation. In 1913 an important

---

[12] The *kangany* system was abolished in 1938; it had been of minor importance for at least a decade.

[13] The Indian Immigration Fund was most active from 1907 until the world depression of 1929–32. From 1922 the Indian Government controlled the flow from its end by the Indian Emigration Act, which appointed Agents to watch its interests. In 1938 it banned the migration of unskilled labour from India, as the number of Indians in Malaya seemed surplus to the requirements of the industry. In 1939, on the outbreak of war the labour position in Malaya was this:

No. of Estates	*Indians*	*Chinese*	*Malays*
4,577	218,548	76,376	40,295

addition to land regulations empowered the States to reserve land exclusively for Malays, thus protecting their kampongs from the rapidly spreading estates.

Together with land tenure, which protected the employer, the Federation Government regulated conditions of employment, which safeguarded the employee. Originally there were separate ordinances for the protection of Indian, Chinese and Japanese labourers, but they were consolidated into one by the Labour Code of 1912. This was constantly under scrutiny. Within ten years it had been amplified and amended a dozen times. In 1923 it was completely revised, in collaboration with the Government of India, which in 1936–37 conducted another searching survey into the conditions of its nationals in Malaya. Its representative, Mr. Srinivasa Sastri, wrote a strong testimonial to the system, and in fact the handling of migrant labour between India and Malaya was one of the outstanding administrative achievements of British rule in the peninsula.[14]

The early boom years of the rubber industry came to an abrupt halt after the First World War. Thousands of trees had become productive between 1914 and 1918, and the rubber had piled up in the godowns of Singapore and Penang waiting for ships to take it to America and Europe. The same thing happened in the other ports of South-East Asia, for rubber growing had spread to Ceylon, Indonesia and Indo-China in particular. When the war was over this mass of rubber reached the market at a time when peacetime reconversion had hardly begun, and a minor economic depression was being experienced.

It created a glut, and prices, which in 1910 had been a little below $5 a pound, fell during 1920–22 to as low as 30 cents. As rubber then cost approximately 40–50 cents a pound to produce, the estates were faced with a crisis.

The remedy they demanded was government restriction of production, not merely on themselves but upon the non-estate producers as well, the smallholders as they were called—Malays and Chinese who after the boom of 1910–1913 had come to see

---

[14] This is dealt with in Norman Parmer, *Colonial Labor Policy and Administration* (New York, 1960).

the attraction of rubber, and who had planted some trees, as many as possible, on their five or so acres of land. These smallholders hardly felt this crisis at all. They carried few if any of the expensive overhead costs of the European estates, where Directors, Visiting Agents, Secretaries and Accountants competed with numerous well paid European managers and a shareholding community for the profits. It is highly probable that the lower costs of the smallholdings and high output would have ensured their survival and would have eliminated the estates, had not the political power of the latter pulled them through.

By the beginning of 1921 their powerful representations had secured governmental response. In February of that year a draft Bill enforcing restriction was submitted to the Legislative Council. The British Government commented initially that it was folly to apply restrictions unilaterally, in one country alone; that there would be no advantage at all, no reduction of world stocks or any improvement in price, unless Ceylon and Indonesia participated too. By 1922, however, a Commission of Enquiry, the Stevenson Commission, had recommended that if restriction of export was adopted by Ceylon and Malaya (which together accounted for 70% of the world production), the results would be favourable and the world supply would decrease. So restriction began.

It was enforced for six years, being finally abolished in November 1928, when its stupidity was patently obvious to all concerned, even at last to the government. The only achievement that can perhaps be claimed for it was that it assisted the estates to survive. Mills says, "It can be put to the credit of the Stevenson plan that it saved many of the rubber companies from bankruptcy, although it is equally true that in considerable measure their predicament was of their own making."[15]

While the latter part of this statement is correct, it is more open to question whether Stevenson saved the estates. It seems more likely that it was a reviving world demand, which took the price from 70 cents in 1922 to nearly 2 dollars by 1925,

---

[15] L. A. Mills, *British Rule In Eastern Asia* (London, 1942), p. 192.

coupled with some drastic administrative pruning, that saved them. What is more clear is that it hit the smallholder. In Malaya a committee allocated an export quota to each grower. Although by 1922 smallholders accounted for 34% of the country's production, they were not represented on the committee, and, as a solitary speaker from the unofficial benches of the Legislative Assembly said, they were the forgotten men of the Stevenson scheme.[16]

Also forgotten was the smallholder in Indonesia, where the government actively encouraged Asian planting. The rapid, uncontrolled growth of Indonesia's rubber exports, largely that of low cost smallholders, and the restricted export of Malaya's estate rubber, is shown in the following table.

Export of Rubber

	Indonesia	Malaya
1913	7 (thousand tons)	33
1919	88	200
1927	232	232

This rapidly increasing flood of rubber on to the world market was more than it could carry at the 1925 prices, and the restraint in Malayan exports was to no avail. The price dropped rapidly until in 1928, when the Stevenson scheme was abolished, the price had fallen to 30 cents. The major result of the Stevenson scheme had been to stimulate rubber growing in Indonesia, particularly by the smallholders, so that Indonesia, which in 1922 accounted for merely 25% of world production, had acquired 40% by 1927.

The moment when the Stevenson scheme was abandoned was also the time when most of the trees on the Indonesian smallholdings, which had risen from 459,000 acres in 1922 to an estimated 1,500,000 acres in 1927, were ready for tapping. An unprecedented volume of exports began pouring out of Malaya

[16] Mills, op. cit., p. 193. It should be noted that this solitary defence of the Asian rubber grower was voiced by a European. He received little support from other members, irrespective of their race.

and Indonesia to reach America as the great Depression began. By 1932 the price of rubber had dropped to 5 cents a pound, nearly 600,000 tons of surplus rubber was on the market, and it was cheaper to buy it than to produce it.

This catastrophic fall in prices[17] produced a chastened Dutch colonial government as anxious as the British in Malaya to save the estate industry. Both were quite convinced that the doctrine of the survival of the fittest meant ruin for all estates. The Dutch however, unlike the British, were reluctant to limit smallholding rubber, and discussions on restriction dragged on until 1934. In May that year the Governments of Great Britain (representing Malaya, Ceylon, India, Burma, Sarawak and North Borneo), Holland (representing its East Indies), France (representing Indo-China) and Siam signed a rubber restriction agreement. The signatory governments controlled 98% of the world's rubber. The main conditions of the agreement prohibited the allocation of land for new planting, and limited exports until 1938. Subsequently this agreement was extended to 1944.

The administration of this International Rubber Regulation Agreement proved difficult, the main initial problem being the sharp difference of opinion between the Dutch and the remainder of the regulating committee in London over the measures to be taken to control the export of smallholders' rubber from the ports of Indonesia. A flood of rubber, sufficient to keep the world price very low, continued to pour out of Indonesia, despite a very high export tax. The low return was adequate for the smallholder, giving him a reasonable return, and the Dutch supported him, while the committee in London, viewing the situation through the eyes of European estates, pressed for an ever higher export tax.

Thus the price of rubber during the 1930's continued to remain low, keeping very close to the costs of estate production. This forced the estates to become and remain efficient and economical

---

[17] Catastrophic that is for the estates. In 1932 the Malayan smallholder was producing good rubber at a cost of ½ cent a pound. Few estates could then cut costs to below 12 cents a pound.

in administration. Large numbers of labourers had already been declared redundant, and had been repatriated to India.[18] Many Europeans were also relieved of their duties, and those remaining received salary cuts and increased responsibilities. Numerous small estates were merged into one, and their rubber growing made more efficient, often by an imitation of the hitherto scorned methods of the smallholder. Work at the Rubber Research Institute tardily followed Dutch pioneer experimentation into higher yielding rubber, so that in selected areas an acre would yield not the average 500 lbs. per acre but 1,000. By 1940 the industry, tempered in the fire of adversity, was decidedly stronger than in the profitable easy-going days of 1910.

In this respect therefore the low prices of the 1930's were a long term asset. There were, however, unpleasant aspects of the restriction that accompanied those low prices, particularly in the treatment accorded in Malaya to the smallholder, against whom, it seems clear, ignorant if not vicious discrimination was practised.

The detailed administration of the restriction scheme in Malaya was carried out by a Controller of Rubber who was a senior British officer in the Malayan Civil Service. He was assisted by a committee of eight, all of whom, except one Malay, were representatives of estates or the government. The solitary smallholders' representative had little say, and the Controller and his committee continued to identify the rubber industry with the estates, even though, by 1934, smallholding production was approximately 217,000 tons, compared to the estates' narrow lead with 260,000 tons.[19] By 1940 the Controller and the committee had seen to it that this smallholding production had dropped to 213,000 tons, while that of the estates had risen to 334,000 tons. Two years previously, at the end of the first period of the restriction agreement, the production of smallholders had been as low as 113,000 tons, almost half of what

---

[18] Between 1930 and 1933, while 127,000 Indians migrated from India, 370,000 went the other way.

[19] These figures, taken from the *Malaya Rubber Statistics Handbook, 1957* (Kuala Lumpur, 1958) are not considered to be particularly sympathetic to the smallholder, and his actual tonnage may well have been higher.

it had been four years before, in 1934, whereas the estate production had scarcely been cut, standing at 246,000 tons.

These figures indicate a story that has been little investigated,[20] of favouritism to the large European owned estates, of inequitable treatment between smallholder and estate, and of a burden of restriction that fell clearly on the indigenous grower.[21] In 1934 the estates produced 52% of Malaya's rubber; by 1938 it had risen to 68%, and by 1940 it was 61%. The smallholder, who in 1934 produced 48%, had been restricted to 32% by 1938, rising merely to 39% by 1940. This is a further illustration of the conclusion drawn from tin production, that restriction favours the inefficient. It also bears out another axiom: that political power ensures economic power.

This later fact is indicated by another aspect of the rubber industry which is often overlooked, and that is the wages of employees. Smallholders who found it difficult to secure licences for rubber export nevertheless could turn to other occupations, and put their land to other uses; indeed the government constantly endeavoured to move them from rubber to padi growing, although more rice could be secured with the cash secured from rubber than by growing it oneself. Despite this, the smallholder did have alternate occupations, denied to the tapper. In comparison the estate labourer was in a most difficult position, as although his wages were scarcely affected by the earlier booms (for he lacked the means of making his representations effective), when the depression came his political and economic masters saw to it that his miserable pittance dropped even lower. He survived, but it can hardly be said that he lived. This is indicated by the table on the following page.[22]

Ignorance of the smallholders' capabilities, rejection of any standard of efficiency other than that of the estates, and

---

[20] A well documented exception is P. T. Bauer, *The Rubber Industry* (London, 1948), also Norman Parmer's *Colonial Labor Policy and Administration.*

[21] Bauer, ibid., estimates a loss to smallholders of $360 million through their excessive restriction (p. 100).

[22] For recent developments see Charles Gamba, *The National Union of Plantation Workers* (Singapore, 1962).

indifference to the estate workers characterised the rubber industry. This outlook, by and large, was that too of the government.

WAGES ON ESTATES

	Average Price of Rubber	Wage Rates
1922	20 cents a lb.	40 cents a day
1925	120	45
1930	20	40
1933	10	32
1937	32	50

Without rubber as a basis, the government would not have been able to build the superstructure of a modern state. Without the revenue it gained from rubber in particular, as well as, to a lesser extent, from tin, none of the services and advantages for which it became famous, and of which it was justly proud, would have been possible. This superstructure excites our admiration even today; but let us also keep in mind the foundations, for unless they are checked and constantly reviewed for improvement and repair, the whole edifice may one day collapse.

10. ADMINISTRATION

During the first half of the twentieth century the influence of the West spread over the Malay Peninsula, and affected many aspects of life. Expressed particularly through the endeavours and activities of the administration, this influence has remained to some extent after the political control of the West has been removed.

What was that influence? What made a lasting impression? In describing the British administration it is easy to point to developments during this period, to facts such as the building of roads or the establishment of schools, and to claim that those facts represent an account of that administration. It is easy to do this, but it is insufficient and almost inaccurate, for a chronicle of history must always be more than a mere catalogue of events, and there is little use in recording merely that an event has occurred, or even when it occurred, unless in addition the reason is given. It is always more important to know not when but why; to answer that question should be the paramount aim of history. Before recording the successes and failures of the twentieth century administration in Malaya, a brief glance seems desirable at the thought behind that administration, at the ideas and philosophy, which, however unconsciously, animated the action of that government; and which, to some extent, still remain.

This can best be done, perhaps, if we attempt to discover the ideas, the dominant forces, which struggled to shape the Britain that was emerging into the twentieth century, ideas which spread out from Great Britain to its overseas territories and to wherever its people migrated. Indonesia (or the Dutch East Indies as they were called then), came to reflect many of the beliefs of the Dutch translated into colonial action, while in Indo-China we can perceive certain strands of French thought. The same connection can be seen between Great Britain and Malaya.

A deep rooted, human attitude, evident since history was

first recorded, has been a belief that existing customs and ways of life are preferable to all others. Man is by nature conservative, and reformers have always had to struggle against a mass of firmly fixed opinion that attempts to alter the *status quo* should be resisted. Britain has long been a country conservative in belief, quiet in manner and slow to change; in this it is akin to the immemorial attitudes of the Malay States. During the nineteenth century both revealed among a great number of their inhabitants this comfortable age-old attitude of inertia.

During the nineteenth century, however, the paralysing influence of this inertia was countered in the United Kingdom, by the effects of two great reforming movements which inspired the thought, and the mental attitude, of those who fought actively to create a new Great Britain. These reformers were inspired by humanitarianism and radicalism.

Humanitarianism was a way of thought which had its origin partly in an earlier Evangelical Movement. This was a religious revival which began in the 1740's, led by John Wesley. He was one of the few Anglican clergymen of his time who was sincerely religious. He preached an urgent message that put spirit into the moribund attitude towards religion. He and Whitefield, the great orator, spoke eloquently and passionately to vast concourses of people who had gathered together in the open air, because the Churches would not permit them to preach inside. They were people who, unlike the ordinary churchgoers, realised that they had wandered away from the tenets of behaviour laid down in the Ten Commandments of the Bible and by the teaching of Jesus. At church they heard merely the conventional platitudes preached by a minister who was a pillar of a conservative society. The Church had no religious or reforming significance, attendance was merely a convention, and the Church had no motivating force of any kind.

Although John Wesley aimed at revitalising the Church, his methods so horrified the Bishops and so shocked conservative thought that he was forced to form a new organisation, the Methodist Church, which captured the imagination and won the support of thousands of the ordinary people, who were filled with a new desire to live a Christian life. Their example became too conspicuous to ignore, and more and more people turned to a study of the Bible and to a practical application of the teachings there. Wesley did not merely revitalise the Church of England: he revived Christianity in England.

To this was added another reforming movement, which was inspired by the French Revolution. National histories paint the enemies of the state in as unfavourable a colour as possible. Revolutionary and Napoleonic France appear on the Malayan scene only as enemies of Britain in the Bay of Bengal, and elsewhere. We tend to forget that the revolt of the French people in 1779 was against injustices and cruelties which were not confined to France alone, and that the philosophical foundation for the many revolutionary reforms found warm support in Great Britain, while it carried a message of hope to the common people everywhere.

The French Revolution in the long run did more good than harm to the development of Britain for while the political aspirations of Napoleon were combated on many a bloody field, the ideas of the Revolution crept in, merging with the Evangelical movement to produce the broad humanitarian attitude that became the major, active factor in British efforts to improve the condition of mankind.

Most notable perhaps of all the early nineteenth century manifestations of this practical Christianity was the Anti-Slavery Society, led by William Wilberforce (1759–1833). The strong vested interest of ship-owners, who carried thousands of slaves from Africa to the cotton fields of North America and the sugar-fields of the West Indies, as well as the powerful influence in Parliament of the 'sugar lords', together with the indifference of the rest of the community which accepted slavery without question as an immemorial institution, made Wilberforce's humanitarian task seem impossible. Yet in 1807, in the midst of the war against France, he saw Pitt pass the Abolition of the Slave Trade Act, and in 1833, the year he died, humanitarian pressure, despite the efforts of the West Indies, brought about the abolition of slavery in all British territory.[1]

[1] This had been anticipated by Raffles in Singapore, for from the foundation of the city in 1819 he had forbidden slavery.

Together with this grant of freedom to all former slaves, numerous other humanitarian acts were transforming Britain. We need only mention a few. John Howard and Elizabeth Fry were two early social workers who devoted their lives to initiating reforms in the terrible jails of the period, and their efforts led to a critical re-assessment of the archaic laws that had sent thousands to death or to transportation overseas; the penalty for over 200 offences. These laws did little to repress or reduce crime, and in the 1820's Sir Robert Peel began a revision of the law that has continued to the present day, when the humanitarian movement still fights conservative opposition or inertia. Peel also introduced in 1829 a Police Force, trained, disciplined and unarmed, a great innovation that was the fore-runner of the Police Forces of the world.

The humanitarians and evangelists caused a stirring of the public conscience in virtually every field of human activity. The ugliness and brutality of the Industrial Revolution (which brought overcrowding in the towns and appalling working conditions), was caused primarily by the government's attitude of *laissez-faire* or non-interference. There were glaring, terrible examples of 'man's inhumanity to man'. The public conscience was aroused, and with the lead given by Lord Shaftesbury, a still-continuing, humanitarian endeavour to secure better conditions for the workers began with the First Factory Act in 1833.

Similarly, it was this same humanitarian attitude that led to schools being founded by a revitalised Church, with the government entering the scene in 1833 by making grants to them. Forty years later this was clearly insufficient, and in 1870 nation-wide elementary education was introduced by the government. In 1880 school attendance was made compulsory.

It will be seen that the humanitarians constantly enlisted the aid of the state in securing social and economic reforms, and it was in Parliament itself that many would say that the greatest reform of all was carried out.

In Parliament the agents for change were known as the Radicals. They turned for their ideas not to Wesley or the practical humanitarians, but to the English political philosopher of the eighteenth century, John Locke, as well as imbibing deeply of the heady draughts of the French Revolution. To them the greatest reform needed was not to check specific economic or social injustices, but to abolish or reform the corrupt eighteenth century Parliament itself, in which seats could be bought and sold, leaving millions unrepresented. With Parliament reformed, with clear water at the fountain head, the whole river would be clear. To leave Parliament corrupt so they argued, was to corrupt the whole nation.

A redistribution of seats and a re-organisation of Parliament was long overdue. It no longer represented politically the social and economic Britain it governed. To introduce reform, however, to secure representation for the new industrial towns, and to devise more democratic and less corrupt methods of election, against the vested interest and the conservative inertia of the upper and landed middle class of Britain, seemed impossible; or impossible without a revolution, as in France in 1789. Yet it was achieved. After a tremendous struggle, and not before the island was brought close to revolt, the Radicals secured the passing of the 1832 Reform Act, which abolished pocket boroughs and re-allocated seats. This was followed about thirty years later by another radical measure, the Reform Act of 1867, which gave the vote to millions of the working class, and began to establish democracy as a parliamentary system. A third great measure occurred in 1884, when the vote was given to nearly every adult male. The secret ballot had been secured in 1872, and payment of Members of Parliament followed in 1911. One final step remained: to give the vote to women. This was done as recently as 1918, in response to great pressure brought to bear upon the government. In such a way was the twentieth century Parliament of Great Britain fashioned, to become an example to the world, not least to its overseas territories.

The influence of the parliamentary Radicals reached out from Britain long before a democratic Parliament emerged. Of immense importance to the overseas territories, although for the most part quite ignored by insular British historians, was the transformation from Empire to Commonwealth, from controlled colonies to independent states, initiated by Lord Durham.

'Radical Jack', as he was called, has received little notice in British histories, for he was not a prominent politician. Nevertheless he is an important figure. He was sent to the Canadian colony to investigate disorders. In his famous Report (1839) he advocated a most radical measure: Responsible Government. To let the Canadians govern themselves and without control from London was the crux of his recommendation; that those most interested and most informed should have the responsibility. This change was introduced into Canada by Lord Durham's son-in-law, Lord Elgin, who instead of ruling as Governor-General (1847–1854) entrusted power to the Canadians. It was a great success, and responsible colonial government was adopted elsewhere. It permitted the growth to independent nationhood of the three European colonies, Canada, Australia and South Africa; but not, until after the Second World War, of the rest. What was the reason for this?

The political philosophy that together with Locke's writings inspired the actions of Durham and the other Radicals of the first half of the nineteenth century came very largely from a school of thinkers known as the Utilitarians. Most influential of these were James Mill, his son John Stuart Mill, and Lord Macaulay. Of these, John Stuart Mill was perhaps the most influential. The war cry of them all was liberty. J. S. Mill enunciated this most clearly in his long essay, *On Liberty* (1859). This became almost the bible of the political radicals. Its basic premise was that intellectual and political freedom were in general of benefit to the society that permitted them and to the individual who enjoyed them. It was essential for the well-being of any community or state for individualism and private judgment to flourish. Without private initiative, without liberty of action, the well-being of the state, being the well-being of its inhabitants, would wither away. Mill held that liberty was the essential core of civilization itself. It was for that reason that he defended democracy, not that he thought that a democratic government would be more efficient than any other—he doubted that very much—but because it would give political liberty, it would permit individual choice, and so give scope to the advancement of civilization.

This doctrine of liberty animated the radicals in their economic measures. They fought for free trade, and for a lifting of trade restrictions. It encouraged them too in their political measures, at home and overseas, and the idea of liberty, a British ideal since the mists of time, received a most powerful philosophical backing.

In Canada and Australia the political application of this idea went unchallenged during the nineteenth century, but in Africa and particularly in India, it came into increasing conflict with the diametrically opposed ideas of another philosopher, long dead, but whose views came to be accepted as far more suitable for the occasion than those of Mill. Hobbes had written his *Leviathan* in 1651, yet his authoritarian attitude seemed most appropriate in India, tropical Africa and Malaya, areas where, so it was argued, the liberty of Mills would generate rapidly into licence. In each of these areas there was a plural society, groups of mutually hostile peoples, uneducated in the complexities and refinements of modern western government. In such a situation, it seemed best, in practice and in theory, for these countries to be governed by the occupying power. To relinquish that control would be to remove the keystone from the structure, and to allow the country to fall into anarchy.

Hobbes had argued that governments were divided into good governments and bad governments. Where was the difference? Hobbes said that man's basic desire on this earth was to survive and prosper. A good government was one that gave him the security to do this. If he could live a safe, secure life, then he was under a good government. It did not matter how it was composed, democratic or autocratic, the composition and structure of the government was quite irrelevant, the important issue being whether the ideals of government were achieved. The aim of a train is to run on time; it is irrelevant whether it is driven by steam or diesel oil; similarly, the aim of a government is to provide its people with security. It is immaterial whether it is democratic or totalitarian. The self-survival of the community, not its liberty, is the prime concern of the government, argued Hobbes, and self-government was no substitute for good government.

When the British Conservative leader, Disraeli, said in 1870 that his policy was to maintain English institutions, to preserve the Empire and to introduce social reforms,[2] he was in effect accepting both the attitude of Hobbes, which would see that the people were governed firmly, and that of the Evangelicals, which would see that they were governed kindly. It was this attitude that came to Malaya.

By the late half of the nineteenth century the popular conception of a state was changing, and it was seen as having far more duties and responsibilities than previously, when it had been considered merely as an administrative unit. This new state, far more active, requiring far more from the government, demanded a much greater civil service; and in tropical Africa, the Malay States and wherever else late nineteenth century imperialism had carried the flag, there was no civil service, and there were few who sought effectively for liberty. The philosophy of Hobbes as expressed by Disraeli then went unchallenged. In India, however, it was resented and resisted. A civil service of trained and experienced Indians and Europeans was well established, the philosophy of Mill and Macaulay, both of whom had worked for India, was felt keenly by many members of the administration as well as by influential sections of this Indian middle class and aristocratic community, and the attractions of the opposite poles of authority and liberty produced a pull and counter pull in Indian affairs that was not felt elsewhere. While in India the country moved slowly towards independence and democracy (for Mill won this tug-of-war)[3], in Malaya a strong government enforced a humane law which protected the individual, particularly if he was a European, and assisted the country to prosper. This was Hobbes' ideal. Nevertheless, in the long run it was the Indian development which was of paramount importance. The victory won there was an example to the rest of European-occupied Asia. All South-East Asia saw an in-

---

[2] For a comment on this, see C. A. Bodelsen, *Studies in Mid-Victorian Imperialism* (Denmark, 1924), p. 120.

[3] This is well brought out in the brilliant analysis by E. Stokes, *The English Utilitarians and India* (Oxford, 1959).

dependent, democratic nation emerging, a tidal flow that affected every backwater, and which could not be resisted. Hobbes never replaced Mill and Locke as the philosopher of the Asian nationalist, although without doubt, between 1874 and 1941 he ruled supreme in Malaya.

The *Leviathan* on one hand, and the New Testament on the other, influenced the British administrator. His entry into Malaya was unresisted, for both Malays and Chinese were accustomed to and indeed accepted without question, authoritarian government. Apart from a small, English-educated minority of Chinese, organized into a Straits Chinese British Association, and an equally small if more influential minority of aristocratic Malays, neither community wanted to participate in the government at that stage. They merely wanted what was given them: security. So the British administrator's progress was unchecked. Behind him, but already retreating into the shadows of the past, was the great builder of the Federation, Frank Swettenham, and much of the trouble of his successors was caused by their efforts to rebuild or redesign the edifice he had left them.

2

The immediate successor of Swettenham was Sir John Anderson, who came to the peninsula in 1904 after a successful career in London, where at the Colonial Office he had been secretary to the powerful Meade, the Permanent Under-Secretary, and then to the Minister, Chamberlain. Anderson was High Commissioner (1904–1911) during a most eventful period, in which a major external development was the acquisition of the northern states, while the newly introduced rubber tree brought rapid internal changes as well.

The rise of rubber, and the increasing influence of the planters had repercussions on the political development of the peninsula. Before 1900 the planters had been few, and their economic contribution insignificant compared to the Chinese tin miners. Between 1904 however, and 1911, the revenue of the Federated Malay States rose from $22 million to $35 million, the increase being largely a result of the levy on the export of rubber. Increasingly there was pressure from the planters and the powerful companies they represented for a voice in the government. "No taxation without representation", the cry of the British since Magna Carta, was heard as early as 1904, when A. V. Carey, a leading planter in Selangor, asserted that the rubber interests should be consulted, while in 1908, after the various State Planting Associations had formed a Planters' Association of Malaya, a more powerful request was made, seeking representation on the Straits Settlements Legislative Council.

Anderson, although sympathetic, deferred this request, for he was preparing to establish what could well have been constituted in 1896, a Federated Malay States Legislative Council. Swettenham had been too much of an individualist to even consider forming a consultative body which might restrain or restrict the rapid execution of his eager mind. Anderson, however, had been most perturbed to find that the Federated States had no control whatever over the central authority, which quickly had taken much power and prestige from the individual rulers and Residents. Malay criticism too had begun, and in 1903 at the second Durbar, or Conference of Rulers, Sultan Idris of Perak, the outstanding Malay leader, had voiced disquiet at this.[4] The Federation had become, most disconcertingly to many, an amalgamation.

One result of these criticisms by Malays, officials and planters was the establishment in 1909 of a Federal Council. It consisted of the High Commissioner, the Resident General, the Rulers and Residents of the four states, and four unofficial members. It was to consider all measures affecting the Federation, including all

---

[4] Idris, who played a slightly suspect part in the murder of Birch, became the mainstay of the Malay administration in Perak during the Residency of Low. He became Sultan in 1887, at the age of 38, shortly before Low left. He led his fellow Sultans into the Federation Agreement of 1895, but soon became critical of it. He deplored the lack of Malays in the growing Civil Service, and was perturbed at the acquisition of control over the state by the central secretariat. He was eager to see Malays being trained and employed in government service. This same active attitude was adopted by his successor.

proposals regarding its expenditure and revenue. This was a much needed body, and by satisfying the planters it quietened some of the more vocal opponents of officialdom. But by making the Federal administration more efficient, by centralising in Kuala Lumpur even more than before and by taking nearly all Legislative power away from the States, posts in the State Councils became virtual sinecures. This assumption of supreme Legislative power by the Federal Council was illegal, in that the British were in the peninsula, in law, by treaty with the rulers. They had not conquered the land as they had done in Burma. They had not, as again they had done in Burma, dethroned the ruler and abolished the state religion. On the contrary, by treaty the rulers and the ancient faith were maintained and protected. It did not matter. Efficient government, it was assumed, needed a central legislature and an executive administered exclusively by Europeans, while the Malay Sultans and the authority of the States were pushed quietly aside, and as quietly resented.

Gradually this lack of support on the part of the governed was noticed. There was a growing feeling, as Mills noted, "that the Sultans and the Malays had been overlooked in the rush of economic development,"[5] and in the early twenties, as the newly acquired Malay States in the north, and Johore in the south sat firmly outside the Federation, there was a growing awareness that the much vaunted efficiency of the administration was nevertheless distasteful to the Malays. A decade before, this would not have perturbed the government unduly. The collection of initials that by about 1910 divided Malaya into the SS (Straits Settlements), FMS (Federated Malay States), and UFMS (Unfederated Malay States), might seem peculiar to an outsider, and might reflect a political weakness, but as the influential *Straits Times* commented, "It really does not matter to business men what the political status of different territories may be...we can in fact leave the political elements to take care of themselves."[6]

---

[5] L. A. Mills, *British Rule in Eastern Asia* (London, 1942) p. 50.
[6] *Straits Times*, 4th December 1913.

But that was in 1913, when business was booming and the government was passively accepted by all. By 1923 there was a depression, among the Malays there was a marked lack of interest in the Federation, and the Chinese, previously dormant, had become violently active. The growth of the Kuomintang, the riots in the Chinese schools and in the Chinese streets, and the fierce Chinese nationalist movement in the Peninsula were all part and parcel of an anti-European, anti-government feeling that became increasingly ominous. Britain's colonial governments have always ruled by securing the passive consent of most of the population, together with the active assistance of a minority. By the 1920's, with the Malays indifferent and with many Chinese in opposition, this axiom was in danger of disappearing from the peninsula.

Sir Lawrence Guillemard came out as High Commissioner in 1920. He had been chosen by his friend Lord Milner, the Colonial Minister, who by linking together the Boer States with those of the British after the South African War had won fame as the constructor of a united South Africa. Guillemard set out to transform the passive acceptance of the Malays into an active support, and to create with that support a single state of Malaya.

The way in which he considered that both Malay support could be won, to balance against the opposition of the KMT Chinese, and a single unit could be constructed, to govern what geographically and economically was one unit, was by a policy of decentralisation. The Malay States which were not in the Federation would not join that Federation because all power was in the hands of the European secretariat in Kuala Lumpur. It was not that it was inefficient, but that it was alien, remote from them: this was their basic objection. Not merely in the Unfederated States was this attitude held. Guillemard, when he began to consider the possibility of decentralising authority, of giving more to the States, won much support also from the Malay governments of the States already federated; and some official support as well.

Sir George Maxwell, his Chief Secretary (for so the Resident-General had been re-named in 1911), appointed in 1923 a committee to investigate how the States could be given a fuller control over their affairs, while maintaining at the same time the financial stability of the Federation. He approached his task sympathetically, for he had been the first British Adviser in Kedah, and he had seen how a Malay State could be developed and yet retain its internal, indigenous strength. In addition he was perturbed, as an administrator, at the bottle-neck his post had become. It seemed that everything required the consent of the Chief Secretary. He was most anxious that more authority and power should be let out, that the tight restricting Federation should be loosened both for increased efficiency and so that others would be attracted to enter. In his efforts to implement this, however, both he and Guillemard, who acted somewhat independently of him on this matter, and Malay opinion generally, encountered increasing opposition.

The situation became confused in 1925 when Guillemard, returning from London, announced in the Legislative Council a scheme of decentralisation that was at variance with that produced by the Maxwell Committee in 1924 and already under way; particularly, Guillemard intended to abolish the Federal Chief Secretaryship, the post Maxwell occupied. Although the Sultan of Perak, who spoke immediately after Guillemard in the Council, welcomed these proposals (in 1924 he had urged in London the need to give the States more power), the Chief Secretaryship was not abolished, and although Maxwell went into retirement, partly it would appear because his own cautiously executed steps towards decentralisation had been judged insufficient, Guillemard was unable to do much more than that done already by his Chief Secretary.

Decentralisation as a means of winning Malay support and of creating a single Malaya became unacceptable to the thousands of European and Chinese merchants, miners and planters, to the people who controlled the wealth of the country. They considered that it meant inefficiency. An inefficient government, or worse, a number of inefficient governments, was to them a step back into the nineteenth century, both unnecessary and most unwelcome. In the face of their opposition expressed in the Press, on the platform and in the Legislative Council (where a solid block of seven unofficials voted in favour of a motion condemning decentralization), Guillemard was only able to give the States a slight increase in financial independence, but could not increase their legislative powers.

Perhaps the most important measure resulting from the British effort to win over the Malays was a constitutional one. By an Agreement signed with the four rulers in 1927 the Federal Legislative Council was altered in two ways. Firstly, the four rulers withdrew from it. This move was long overdue, because their position had become an anachronism. It was undignified to expect them as rulers either to defend measures introduced into the Council, or to attack these measures, and it seems unfortunate that they had waited for so long before withdrawing. To permit the rulers to discuss affairs of State amongst themselves, the Durbar, a ceremony borrowed from India and first instituted by Swettenham in 1896, was revived. The Legislative Council was re-created, adding five new official and three unofficial members, to consist of thirteen official and eleven unofficial, the latter being nominated by the High Commissioner. The three new unofficial members were all Malays. Until they took their seats (in 1927) the premier state, Perak, had had a lone Malay unofficial member, Raja Chulan. In the reconstructed Council the other three States were also represented.[7] They were all government servants but by speaking critically on Malay matters rather than by acting as official nominees, they won much respect among their community.

Undoubtedly Malay support was secured by these moves towards decentralisation, particularly as it was felt that they marked the beginning. Guillemard was followed however by Hugh Clifford, already suffering from an illness that forced him to end his days in a private hospital, and his High Commissionership was the tragic anti-climax to a brilliant career that had begun in the jungles of Pahang in the 1880's. A lover of the Malay, a brilliant writer, swift and determined in act and thought, this giant of a man showed such unmistakable signs of

[7] These four were Raja Chulan bin Abdullah (Rajah di Hilir) of Perak, Raja Udin bin Sultan Alaidin Suleiman Shah of Selangor, Inche Abdullah bin Haji Dahan of Negri Sembilan, and Tengku Suleiman Ibris Almechum Al Sultan Ahmad Al Maagam Shah of Pahang.

mental instability that his tenure of office was not continued and it was left to Sir Cecil Clementi, the nephew of Clementi-Smith to revive the whole issue. Clementi, governor of Hong Kong, was appointed to Malaya in 1929. He accompanied Malaya as it slid helplessly into the depression, an economic factor of considerable importance in thwarting his attempts at decentralisation. The need to win Malay support was still necessary, for Chinese anti-European nationalist fervour in the peninsula had reached new heights, and in the face of a unified and newly established China under Chiang Kai Shek Clementi necessarily incurred much ill-will by acting vigorously in banning the KMT party in Malaya. Since the administration was increasingly out of touch with the Chinese-educated people, there was need to strengthen its ties with the Malays, and following a 1930 Conference in London with Foreign Office and Colonial office representatives, Clementi announced at the 1931 Durbar of rulers, at Sri Menanti, further plans for extending power to the States.

He proposed to break all the Federal Departments of Government into four parts. With the exception of the railways and the postal services, which were to be removed from direct government administration by their creation as semi-autonomous Boards, all other Departments were to be state controlled, and the Federal head was to assume a supervisory and advisory role only. This adviser was to be the Director of the equivalent Straits Settlement Department in order to ensure co-ordination between the Federation and the Straits Settlements.

Clementi also proposed to abolish the post of Chief Secretary. This post had become the administrative head of the Federation. Clementi felt that it stood unneccessarily between the High Commissioner and the various State Governments, and that it was one of the main reasons why power had become centralised at Kuala Lumpur.

Thirdly, he envisaged a Customs Union in which all the various units within the British sphere of influence in the Malay Peninsula—the Straits Settlements, the Federated Malay States and the various Unfederated Malay States—would be joined. This move, of immediate economic significance, had a political importance as well, and because it would help to create one unit, it was the essential pre-requisite to the formation of one state.

Clementi's far reaching proposals aroused the quiet support of the Malays and the very vocal opposition of the Chinese and Europeans. In 1932 a committee formed of five Straits Settlements business men and two government officers, found the Customs Union to be detrimental to the best interests of the free port status of the ports of Penang, Malacca and Singapore, and the scheme was abandoned. If seems that there was little pressure from the Federation for the Straits Settlements to lose their identity by integration with the Malay States.

Meanwhile the proposals of Clementi had created a furore. Many attacked his proposals to abolish the Federal posts and to give control to each State Council. The State Councils were notoriously corrupt and represented no one except the relatives of the ruler, and financial chaos was seen as the price for political devolution. Not many business men were prepared to pay this price.

Others attacked Clementi on another issue. From the time of the establishment of Kuala Lumpur as a Federal centre to this present day, there has been rivalry between it and Singapore as capital cities. In the first half of the twentieth century Kuala Lumpur was constantly suspicious of control by Singapore. Kuala Lumpur was ever on the watch for slights, and a parochial loyalty to the Federated Malay States, and a resentment of the bland assurance of Singapore, was one of the reasons why a united Malaya did not emerge in this period. Another reason as mentioned above was an obsession in the Straits Settlements for free trade, and an indifference to Federation problems and prospects. This parochial loyalty showed itself in Clementi's time by fierce attacks in the Federation not merely on his proposals to make the heads of departments of the Straits Settlements the advisers of the decentralised departments in the Federation, but also on his intention to abolish the post of Chief Secretary, (who resided in Kuala Lumpur), and to assume power himself in Singapore. Both suggestions were seen as part of a general plot to transfer power to Singapore. As Sir G. Maxwell said, "the public cannot be blamed if it imagines that centralisation at Singapore can be the only result, if indeed it is not the aim, of the present policy".[8]

This clamour reached London. In 1932 the British Government, after facing awkwardly some questions in Parliament, appointed the Permanent Under-Secretary at the Colonial Office, Sir Samuel Wilson, to enquire into the whole affair. He was subjected to intense anti-Clementi lobbying and pressure throughout Malaya; nevertheless, when he submitted his report in 1933 he gave full support to Clementi, stating that there was a paramount political argument for decentralisation. The Malays were discontented, and he said, not merely would decentralisation "probably prove the greatest safeguard against the political submersion of the Malays"[9] by the Chinese, but also it was essential if the other Malay States were to be attracted into a Malayan League or Federation.

Amid loud protests from Europeans and Chinese who saw a danger to their economic interests, attempts were then made to implement these decentralisation proposals. Wilson recommended that nine federal government departments be transferred to state control, although the financial position was to be guarded by keeping revenue collection and disbursement under federal control. In the outcome, by 1939 six departments had been decentralised, although in each case the Straits Settlements executive head who had been appointed as an advisory superior was performing, with varying degrees of success, similar executive powers in the Federation.

In 1935 the Chief Secretaryship was abolished, as Clementi had recommended, and a relatively minor office, the Federal Secretaryship, was substituted. Again it grew in importance, but not before the High Commissioner had been drawn into the affairs of the Federated States to a far greater extent than since the days of Swettenham in Singapore.

The State Councils were enlarged and given increased financial and administrative responsibilities. This was an essential part in any scheme aimed at giving power to the Malays. It was a

---

[8] *Malay Tribune*, 25th July 1932.

[9] Quoted by Mills, *British Rule in Eastern Asia*. p. 60. The Report of Sir Samuel Wilson is Cmd. 4276 (1933).

move which had been regarded with foreboding, as the Malay Chiefs who formed the overwhelming majority of the Councils virtually never spoke or voted against their lord and master, the Sultan, except in the more democratic Negri Sembilan, and nowhere was there competency. For them the step into the twentieth century had been too rapid and too great. Nevertheless, the changes made in the composition of each State Council by the introduction of European, Indian and Chinese unofficial members, together with the transference to these Councils of some real authority, marked the beginning of a new era.

Decentralisation had been supported by the government as a political measure. The Federation had been successful administratively, but it had not captured the hearts of the people. Did decentralisation appeal to them? The measures mentioned above were no doubt regarded with interest by the Unfederated Malay States, but nowhere was there the slightest suggestion from any of them that an entry into the Federation would be considered. Although much Malay support or tacit approval of government was won by these measures, the overall political aim of this policy was not achieved. In this respect then, decentralisation was a failure.

3

Decentralisation had been a means to an end. By giving more power to the States it was hoped that more Malay support would be won, and a single Malaya might be created. When this end was not achieved, no other means were adopted. In particular, little attempt was made to create an indigenous civil service. The Unfederated States enjoyed the services of British specialists, but the district administration was Malay. In the Federated States on the other hand, despite the example of India, which had embarked on the steady Indianisation of its Indian Civil Service since 1858, nearly every officer was a European; as also in the Straits Settlements.

In most cases each officer was an efficient European, recruited between 1896 and 1932 by the open competitive examination of

University graduates which simultaneously secured civil servants for the United Kingdom, India and Hong Kong. After 1932, when Colonial service enlistment was unified, Civil servants were secured by a more flexible selection system. Each officer served in any part of the Malay peninsula, rapidly learning Malay or more rarely, Chinese.

The most characteristic post he occupied was that of District Officer. Here he was the lynch pin that held together what most would have said was a fissiparous community; a plural society of Malays, Chinese and Indians which had come into being because of him, and which would disintegrate if his impartial administration was removed. He was responsible for the general health, wealth and peace of his district, and if he did well, he then became, as Resident, responsible for the condition of his State. If he did badly, he was probably transferred to the Secretariats that by the circulation of ever increasing quantities of paper, swamped those fortunate enough to remain in the field.

These men served well the Malaya they knew, and in those peaceful inter-war years they established with the country bonds of affection that survived all. A few, by reason of their enthusiastic part-time amateur scholarship in Malayan affairs, established an academic reputation through their contributions to the *Journal of the Malayan Branch, Royal Asiatic Society,* in which Civil Servants were encouraged to publish. Sir Richard Winstedt, pioneer Malayan historian; Victor Purcell, one of the few who went into the Chinese Affairs Department; W. L. Blythe, another Chinese affairs officer; and others, such as Sir G. Maxwell, who wrote the classic *In Malay Forests,* gave evidence in print of the pleasure of serving in Malaya. Others, less literary, won the long lasting affection of numerous colleagues, and other associates of all races, by bringing sport to the Malay Peninsula; for if the English tongue is Britain's greatest gift to Malaya, soccer cannot be far behind, and may well be more lasting. E. W. Birch, son of the murdered Resident of Perak, who himself became Resident in 1904, was one of those whose delight it was to see a *padang,* a shady playing field, laid out in every kampong of the State; while a host of other civil servants, by desporting themselves on soccer or hockey fields, or on pony or elephant backs, showed that the 'Heaven Born' had an earthy streak that was of great assistance in maintaining an unobtrusive rule.

Clementi felt that it would be prudent if the peoples of Malaya were associated more closely with this government. In Burma and in India the British relied increasingly on an indigenous administrative staff, and the contrast with the peninsula was glaring. The lack of opportunities to join the Civil Service was criticised by both Chinese, who were barred completely, and by Malays, of whom a few were admitted; and the argument of government, that the Malay States would not welcome Chinese officers, was only partially acceptable.

In 1934 Clementi formed the Straits Settlements Civil Service, which, by restricting itself to the Straits Settlements, helped to divide the peninsula even more, for at least the MCS embraced all territories; but it was a service open at the bottom to non-European British citizens, that is to Chinese or to anyone else born in the British Straits Colony, and even though in practice admittance was at a minimum rate, some of the force of the criticism was diverted.

Criticism of the lack of local officers in the civil service had indeed been largely ineffective. In China the ideal of a scholar had been to serve the Emperor and to secure a mandarin's button, but he had secured that button only after a rigorous examination of an exceptionally high academic standard. In Malaya the original migrants were poor peasants, intent only on making a living, with no desire whatever to serve a foreign state, but by the 1920's many of their descendants were educated scholars again, and the same pull of the centuries was apparent. They wished for nothing better than to secure the social prestige, the security and the salary which service with the government promised. This was denied them, for despite their deep felt hopes, no University was established for them and the mandarin's button was thus effectively reserved for University graduates from Britain.

The desire for a University in Singapore had been expressed as early as 1897 by Dr. Lim Boon Keng, the young leader of the Straits Chinese, and there were several attempts by the English educated Chinese, during the eventful first decade of the twentieth century, to have such an institution founded. All such attempts were ignored by the government, which during the period and after, was concentrating its efforts on Malay education. In 1901 a college was founded by R. J. Wilkinson for the training of Malay school teachers. In 1903 the Malay College, designed to give secondary education to Malays, was established; and during the next decade government-financed Malay schools were introduced all over the peninsula. In 1916 R. Winstedt was appointed to supervise and to enlarge this Malay education. With great zeal he introduced new text books, founded in 1919 the Sultan Idris Malay Teachers College, and ensured that as much government finance as possible went into this primary, kampong level education in Malay.

Pushing against this stream were the Chinese, who could see not one single advantage to them in this Malay education. Almost entirely by public support they managed to establish a King Edward VII Medical College in 1905. They all hoped that it was to be the nucleus of a University, but by 1917, faced by government opposition, they were reduced to encouraging the project of the Methodist Church, which, American supported, planned to establish an American College as the key-stone to its educational endeavours. This stirred the horrified government to action. It was decided that a University would be a fitting memorial to mark, in 1919, the centenary of the founding of Singapore, and amid much enthusiasm $2,000,000 was quickly subscribed. Then came disaster.

The committee appointed by the government to administer Raffles College, as this embryonic University was to be called, was headed by Mr. (later Sir) Richard Winstedt, and in 1921 he was appointed Principal. Under his control the whole project rapidly declined, to be delayed, diverted and diminished into an institution which when it opened at last in 1928 boasted of a fine administrative block but never a library, and which for ten or so years trained a handful of English school teachers to merely diploma status. Winstedt, an administrator, deep in projects for Malay education, gave no support to the idea of a University. He permitted none of his academic staff to have a voice in policy, and he fully endorsed the opinion of the Chief Justice when he told the Teachers Association in 1923 that "there has been some talk here as to the formation of a University. I ask you to disabuse your minds of such hope. There are not in Singapore and the Straits sufficient boys who would be thought proper for university education. . . . It is very much better that a few boys should go home to get a proper education."[10] This complete lack of official interest in a University, expressed by the appointment of Winstedt and the transformation of the project into a small Teachers Training Centre, ended any Chinese support for Raffles College. Lim Boon Keng contributed $10,000 towards it, for example, and then gave $1,000,000 to the new Amoy University, founded to attract the overseas Chinese, becoming its first President. Few Chinese, thanks to Winstedt, ever entered the Anglo-Saxon preserve of the official community or the professional classes, and a great opportunity to win the support of the Chinese in Malaya had been lost.

With English, Malay and Chinese schools all functioning at the same time, and only English education cutting across the racial barriers of the peoples of the peninsula, the administration never tackled the greatest task it could have set itself, the creation of a nation. In this period it never attempted, educationally, to prepare the way by producing a community with a modern outlook, united, as the polyglot population of, say, India or America had become, by one educational system. For a time the diversity in the educational system helped maintain the British in Malaya, but in the long run it has been a political tragedy.[11]

Although in education no unity presided over this diversity, this was achieved in other branches of the administration, and there are great successes to be recorded here. Over the diversity of differing laws and customs for example, the British genius for law and order managed to impose a uniform peace. The administration of justice faced many difficulties, for impartial though it was generally accepted to be, the law which was administered was often at variance with Muslim law, with matriachal custom,

---

[10] *Straits Times*, 9th June 1923.

[11] This pre-war educational diversity has been examined critically by Ho Seng Ong, *Education for Unity in Malaya* (Penang, 1952).

with Hindu beliefs, or with Chinese tradition. The Straits Settlements, being a British Crown Colony, had a law different in many points from that of the Malay States. Land laws, the rights of inheritance, marriage and divorce: all these and much else differed from community to community, yet all disputes were heard with fine patience. The local custom or law was interpreted in the light of British law as fairly as possible, and an acceptable judgement made. The humane justice which resulted from this liberal compromise produced a most valuable base for a peaceful country.

4

Malaya was not merely a stable country during this period but a healthy one as well. Since time immemorial the tropics have been unhealthy, and the few great states in South-East Asia that ever emerged in earlier times, the Khmer empire for example, or Madjapahit, struggled for their greatness against a malevolent nature even more than against envious humans. The most common disease of all was malaria. The mosquito, the really indigenous inhabitant of South-East Asia, has been present in all periods of history, and unfortunately he remains in Malaya even today. It should be a matter of great pride, however, that the successful cure of this disease, if not the actual discovery of its cause, was made largely through applied research here in the Peninsula. Beriberi was another unexplained mystery, while smallpox, cholera, typhus and tuberculosis were all familiar to the Malay kampong and the Chinese hut. The dirt diseases too, dysentery and enteric fever in particular, were unchecked and widespread. To all this and much else the people of the peninsula were resigned. Both by their faith and by their character it was accepted as foreordained. The Europeans, however, unhampered by the traditional attitudes of the Asians, and with a way of thought which demanded a rational answer for every mystery, fought these diseases desperately. In the nineteenth century they were attacked with very little success at all, but in the twentieth century the barrier of medical ignorance was broken at a number of significant places, and a transformation, not merely of the peninsula but of the tropical world, was achieved.

The most dramatic break-through was in malaria itself. In China, in the 1870's, a young medical missionary had discovered through patient investigation that elephantiasis and related afflictions were conveyed by the bite of a mosquito. Never before had it been thought that a mosquito could convey disease, but Patrick Manson, the medical missionary, proved it quite conclusively, and opened up a fresh corridor of thought.

On his return to London he lectured on tropical diseases, and shortly after assuming the post of medical adviser to the Colonial Office in 1897, to which post he was appointed by Joseph Chamberlain, one of his former pupils, Ronald Ross, wrote telling him that he thought that the mosquito might play some part in the transmission of another disease, malaria. Ross, who was in India when he wrote, was laughed to scorn. *Mal-aria* (bad air), the Romans had named it, and everyone knew it came from the miasmas of marsh and swamp. Ross continued with his experiments, and one day, his hand shaking with agitation as he realised the momentous sight he was witnessing, he identified the parasite of malaria in an *anopheles* mosquito. The origin of malaria, the principle cause of death, enfeeblement and social stagnation of a huge part of the world, had been found.

Manson in London publicised his discovery and Chamberlain, immediately aware of the dramatic possibilities thus created, called for the establishment in London of a School of Tropical Medicine. The Seamen's Hospital near the London docks, where people came from all over the world, was due to be enlarged. It was decided to make the proposed School part of this expansion. The Treasury promised half the cost of the building if the tropical dependencies would also contribute. A public appeal in London brought in £12,000; the Federated Malay states and the Straits Settlements each contributed $5,000 (a little over £500), and this with other sums enabled Manson to inaugurate the London School of Tropical Medicine in October 1899.

But this was not all. Chamberlain and Manson had attracted so much attention to the need for a study of tropical diseases, and of the possibilities if they could be cured, that other centres were opened. In Liverpool, with its strong links with West Africa, a School of Tropical Medicine was formed in the same year (1899), with Ross, fresh from India, as its Director. By 1900 Cambridge, Edinburgh, Aberdeen and Belfast were also studying tropical diseases, and by 1910 Paris, Bordeaux, Marseilles, Brussels and Hamburg as well.[12]

Admirable though these institutions were, they studied the problem at second hand. The first hand investigations were carried out at research posts in the tropics themselves, of which perhaps the most outstanding was that established by Swettenham in Kuala Lumpur, where, reacting vigorously to a suggestion made by the first Conference of Government Medical Officers in 1898, he formed in 1900 the Institute for Medical Research.[13]

In 1897 Ross had made his discovery that malaria was transmitted by mosquitoes. The discovery of the cause, however, was not the same as discovering the cure, or of applying a preventative. In Malaya various cures and preventative measures were put forward, but all collapsed, largely because they were inappropriate to an uneducated community. The need to break traditional thought was pressing, for thousands of Chinese and Indians were migrating into malarial Malaya. A major tragedy was at hand.

It was averted by the resolute action of Malcolm Watson. Dr. Watson arrived to take charge of the government hospital at Klang in January 1901. A proud new Federation was endeavouring to build its own port, Port Swettenham, in the nearby marshes and mangroves, and the hospital was overcrowded with malaria cases. No labourer would take quinine, nor use a net, so Watson decided to spend all his money twice over on draining these marshes, and on removing the breeding grounds of the *anopheles* mosquito. In September 1901 Port Swettenham was declared open. After a month's operation, it was almost impossible to secure either a crew to trade with the port, or labourers

---

12 J. Amery, *The Life of Joseph Chamberlain* (London, 1932), vol. 4, pp. 222–233.

13 For a survey of its work see *Fifty Years of Medical Research in Malaya: The Institute for Medical Research, 1900–1950* by various authors (Kuala Lumpur, 1951).

to unload any brave vessel that ventured into the deadly estuary. As Watson's drains were being dug and his swamps filled in at both Klang and Port Swettenham an epidemic raged; but there was a swift change when his work was done, as the following figures of malaria cases show.[14]

	1901	1902	1903
Klang	334	129	28
Port Swettenham	188	70	4

Dramatic though his measures had been, healthy though the area became, he had been very fortunate, for as research continued it was discovered that there was more than one type of *anopheles* mosquito, and these measures of drainage and clearance of shade would have encouraged mosquitoes elsewhere than the marshy lowlands.[15] Watson, who left the government in 1908 to advise the rubber estates, after vigorously introducing his lowland drainage technique whenever he could, showed great mental adaptability in recognising that this was quite inapplicable to the hilly mosquito which had quite different habits; in particular it bred in clear streams, not those that flowed sluggishly through swamps. Watson recommended that all estates should put the water in pipes when it flowed near to the estate habitation, and to leave the dark jungle hanging overhead, a complete reversal of the advice he gave to the estates on the lowlands, yet it worked.

The government however refused to accept his advice, and a serious malaria epidemic occurred in Kuala Lumpur after the lovely Lake Garden area was cleared of jungle in 1906. For over five years (1907-1912), Kuala Lumpur was a very malarious town indeed, as the mosquito thrived in the cleared park lands and swift flowing streams specially created for his death. Finally officialdom faced reality and took the necessary steps.

Sub-soil drainage was very expensive, yet the rubber estates

[14] Dr. M. Watson's work is told in his book *The Prevention of Malaria in the Federated Malay States* (London, 1920).

[15] Some seventy different types of these mosquitoes had been noted by 1960, and it is thought that this list is not complete.

in particular as well as the town corporations adopted it as essential. In 1914 Watson recommended that the mosquito could be prevented from breeding by a much less expensive way, by spraying the streams with oil. This was very successful.

These discoveries of Watson for the prevention of mangrove, flat land and hill mosquitoes are still the basis for the antimalarial work of today. For generations the Institute of Medical Research has continued its investigations into the clinical, parasitological and entomological aspects of the disease, new drugs have been introduced and a wealth of information obtained.[16] Yet if malaria has been tamed to some extent it still attacks among the kampongs of South-East Asia.

Another endemic disease of the nineteenth century which was conquered in the twentieth century was beriberi. Again, Malaya played an important part in this victory. Indeed, it was largely the scourge of beriberi which induced Swettenham to found the IMR, for by the 1890's thousands of Chinese, in particular the tin miners who swarmed into the western States, were suffering and dying from this crippling disease. In 1896 for example, over a quarter of the 45,000 cases admitted to the Federated Malay States hospitals, and 2,000 out of the 6,000 hospital deaths, were directly attributable to beriberi.

What brought this disease? Why did the Chinese tin miners suffer so? No one knew. The cause was discovered by W. L. Braddon, another enquiring government doctor. As early as 1893 he had noticed the Indians and Malays were strangely free from beriberi, and had come to the conclusion that the reason for this lay in their diet. While working in Seremban he gradually narrowed down the difference to rice. The cause of beriberi was in rice he said, and a dramatic experiment in 1907 proved his point. A party of 300 Javanese PWD labourers were separated, and while one group at Kuala Baning was fed boiled white rice, the other group at Durian Tipus was given the unpolished variety. Beriberi broke out eighty-seven days later at Kuala Baning,

---

[16] After 1949 the Institute was assisted in its research by the Department of Parasitology at the University of Malaya. Its head, Professor A. Sandosham, has summarised its work in his *Malariology with Special Reference to Malaya* (Singapore, 1959).

while the other group showed no sign of it at all.

Research continued. In 1910 it was shown that the 'goodness' of rice rested in its outer shell. Remove that and all the nutriment of rice vanished. Beriberi was in fact a vitamin deficiency disease. In 1890 vitamins were unknown substances, but by 1910 these vital ingredients to health had been isolated and listed. Rice, provided its outer husk was not removed, was rich in vitamin B_1. If it was processed to secure a highly polished variety and people ate nothing else their bones weakened, their muscles withered, and they contracted beriberi.

As it remained the ideal of most Malayans to eat this highly polished rice, beriberi was attacked by vigorous efforts to vary the diet. In prisons, schools and public institutions of all kinds the eating of uncured, unpolished rice, together with vegetables and greens was insisted upon. Mine operators, estate managers and others were also made aware of the cause of beriberi, and by the 1920's it had largely vanished, to reappear in the depression and in the years of Japanese occupation when poverty and shortage of other food compelled the uneducated to return to a sparse diet of their beloved white rice.

The elimination of these two endemic diseases permitted the transformation of the Malayan economy. Had they been permitted to exist during the twentieth century, neither the large scale tin nor rubber enterprises possibly could have survived, and the millions of migrants would have suffered an appalling fate.

At the same time other diseases, which had been associated with the tropics for millenia were checked, controlled or occasionally completely eliminated. The plague, a disease from rats, which mankind had suffered long before it was described in the Bible, came to the Malay Peninsula in 1896, an outbreak occurring in Penang. Between 1898 and 1918 ten million people lost their lives in India, but in Malaya constant rat destruction by snakes kept the numbers low.[17]

An efficient Port Health Service played its part too in keeping a watch on the crowded countries nearby: China and India in

---

[17] In Singapore 700 died of the plague between 1900 and 1933, and 300 in the FMS.

particular. Cholera was a constant fear, the last outbreak to date occurring in 1963 in Malacca. Less feared, although more widespread, was smallpox. The first Malayan legislation which made vaccination compulsory was passed in 1891, this method of immunity having been practised since at least 1804. After 1918, when money was released for health developments on a wide front, numerous other diseases were attacked. Yaws, a most prevalent disease in the kampongs, was the subject of a campaign organised by Sir G. Maxwell in 1921. Hookworm, or *ankylostomiasis,* also widespread, was attacked from 1926. In both cases, as with beriberi, malaria and other diseases there was a need for rural and urban education. The methods of modern medicine and the relation of dirt to disease were still hardly appreciated.

A long campaign against leprosy was waged, an uphill struggle that began with a leprosarium in Kuala Lumpur in 1892, leading to a more hopeful attitude in the 1920's, and the building of the Sungei Buloh Leper Settlement in 1930. Here Dr. G. A. Ryrie was in charge for the next thirteen years, his skilled and courageous work gaining him world recognition.

Gradually Malaya became more healthy. In the big cities infantile mortality dropped steadily, and a network of about sixty hospitals and dispensaries spread thinly over the land, assisted the other health measures of the government in controlling or combating the diseases which fifty years before had ravaged the peninsula. But it is a story without an end. Many diseases remain, in particular one major cause of early death and long enfeeblement, an illness which Malays share with the rest of the world: tuberculosis. This and other diseases, now held in check, remind us that the health of Malaya, like its liberty, is a matter of continuing and constant vigilance.

11. THE EAST COAST

Most of the developments in the twentieth century that have gone to make modern Malaya occurred on the west coast. Intensive British administration, Chinese and Indian immigration, the growth of tin mining, the formation of a rubber industry, and a network of roads and railways leading to a major entrepôt port; all this is relevant to the west coast. The east coast is a story of fishermen and padi planters, a narrative not without incident, but one which, despite its relevance to the indigenous peoples, is inclined to be overlooked. Yet an awareness of the east coast is necessary for any understanding of Malaya today, and its problems and prospects should not be ignored.

Kelantan and Trengganu, along with Kedah, came decisively into the British sphere of influence in 1909, when Siam, by the Treaty it signed that year, transferred all its rights of protection and suzerainty. Kelantan already had a British Resident Commissioner employed by the Siamese since 1902, whereas Trengganu was stubbornly independent, and did not accept more than a British consular representative until 1919. Partly as a result of the earlier introduction of modern methods of government then, but partly also as a result of its position on a fan-shaped area of one main river basin which converged on the capital, Kota Bharu, Kelantan by then was well ahead. Until 1919 Trengganu clung to a backward looking independence, its administration being less effective perhaps than that of the Malacca Sultanate centuries before. Its capital city was in much the same condition as Newbold described it in 1838,[1] and the state was divided into a number of more or less equal river basins, virtually independently and most ineffectually administered by high officers of state. Trengganu lagged behind Kelantan then, and it does so still.

However, thanks to the homogeneous composition of their

---

[1] Newbold, *Political and Statistical Account of the British Settlements in the Straits of Malacca* (London, 1839), vol. 2, pp. 62–62.

inhabitants, like Kedah and to a lesser extent Johore, both states were able to play upon the indifference of the British, who were reluctant to expend a lot of money in governing a region which did not pay. We see this reflected again at this time in North Borneo and Sarawak. The east coast states were able to preserve their essential Malay character, to restrict British officers to a minimum, and to restrict the role of the Adviser almost to advising, mainly because of the lack of economic development. Their weakness was therefore their strength.

The governments of Trengganu and Kelantan were shaped only gradually into efficient, forward looking administrations. Development was accepted but slowly as the purpose of the state, displacing only by degrees, in the minds of the Malay leaders, the long ingrained goal of contentment. The Malay peasants however were quick to appreciate that the new administrative machine came much nearer to their idea of contentment than the previous régime. As Graham reported of the earlier period, "There were no written laws, no courts and no police. All manner of crime was rampant, the peasantry were mercilessly downtrodden, but the land was full of holy men, and the cries of the miserable were drowned in the noise of ostentatious prayer."[2] Only the Malay court could have been content with that.

In this shaping however, in the elimination of the *Budak Raja*[3] and *Laboh Batu*[4] for example, in the gradual substitution of efficiency for indifference, neglect and oppression, the British Advisers also secured the steadily increasing support of the more intelligent and progressive Malay leaders. Their part in this, as they accepted and adapted this external influence to suit their own requirements, became appreciably more valuable. Modern Kelantan and Trengganu together with Kedah and Johore are joint achievements, a harmonious working together

[2] Quoted in Emerson, Malaysia, p. 255.

[3] An irregular police force, of youthful, near relatives, which the Sultan of Trengganu used for personal purposes.

[4] A very ancient tax or levy on Chinese junks entering or leaving Kuala Trengganu, the proceeds going to the Sultan and a few relatives. It was abolished in 1912, as was *Krah,* the corvee system.

of the better elements of the two parties involved, with the emphasis slowly shifting, during the decades of experience, from one to the other. For this attempt at indirect rule to be successful, as indeed it was, it could not have been otherwise. The indigenous contribution must neither be overlooked nor underestimated. It was as essential as the external element.

Unlike the Federated States, which had a superstructure of British administrators, very few Europeans participated in this quiet, unspectacular transformation of the east coast between 1910 and 1941. Those who did, the few Advisers and Heads of Technical Departments, and the occasional District Officer, became with their far more numerous Malay colleagues (as in Kedah and Johore), fierce supporters of their states. They became as opposed as the Sultans and their Councils to any suggestion that they might join the Federation. They were determined, decentralisation or not, to preserve the identity, and to maintain the authority of the Malay state. In this they were all successful. Much of this attitude remains still today. From the east coast one can drive easily to the capital in a day, yet it is like moving from one world to another. The capital is not altogether accepted by the coast, and Kuala Lumpur is still suspect in Kuala Trengganu.

The slow adjustment by the Advisers of the existing administration in these states, and the steady acceptance by the Malays of the advantages of change, were complicated in Kelantan for years by the problem of the Duff Development Company. R. W. Duff, a police officer who had accompanied Hugh Clifford in 1895 when he pursued a number of Pahang rebels into Kelantan, secured in 1900 from the Sultan a grant of sovereign rights to 3,000 square miles of the interior. When the British came to Kelantan they endeavoured to secure some revision to this grant, for it established virtually a new sovereign power, even more independent than was Brooke of Sarawak. Expensive purchasing of these concessions and even more expensive litigation saddled Kelantan with a public debt by 1931 of over $5 million. Although this seriously retarded developmental expenditure, Kelantan was able to move steadily forward.[5]

[5] For the Duff dispute, see Emerson, op. cit., pp. 252–262.

Only once, in both Kelantan and Trengganu, was the unobtrusive rule of the British and their Malay allies resisted by arms. In Kelantan in 1915 there was a rising in the Pasir Puteh district, with discontented Malay smallholders led by Ungku Besar and Haji Mat Hassan 'Toh Janggut' rioting against newly introduced land reforms which were misunderstood. It was an area never visited by the Sultan, where the *Toh Kwengs* or local headmen (*Penggawas* as they came to be called after giving up their Siamese designation), were influenced only by the fanatical *Imams,* or prayer leaders, and the peasants had been led to regard the reforms as an anti-Islamic imposition. The disturbance soon died down, and with administration becoming more in touch and more effective it never re-occurred.

A more serious rising occurred in Trengganu in 1928. It arose out of circumstances very similar to the 1930–31 Saya San rising in Burma and to the 1931 Tayung rising in the Philippines. In each case religion was used to arouse the emotions of an ignorant peasantry made discontented by alien interference with their land. In Trengganu the spokesman was Haji Abdul Rahman, an *ulu* or interior leader who disapproved completely of the West, and who opposed, as a fanatical Muslim, the Sultan's acceptance of the British. He looked backwards and encouraged the peasants in his area to oppose the payment of land rent and the recently introduced control of indiscriminate tree felling. He secured the support of a Muslim secret society, and successful in this, he then led a force downstream to restore the old order.

At Kuala Brang, the earliest site, as we have seen, of Islam on the peninsula, and the headquarters of the interior district, the Haji and his men took over the government offices by the river bank without incident. On advancing further downstream, however, and on rebuffing the Sultan himself (which ruined all his chances of success), he and his 1,000 armed and chanting followers were dispersed by the disciplined fire and charge of the Malay police. Toh Janggut, the military leader (no relation to the Kelantan rebel), and ten others were shot dead. The remainder fled back upstream into the interior, where subsequently order was restored and the Sultan's authority re-established. Haji Abdul Rahman was arrested and exiled to Mecca, and several other leaders were sent to Singapore for a number of years.

In both these disturbances, as in the other peasant risings against European administration in South-East Asia during the twentieth century, the religious aspect should not be overlooked. In Burma and in Indonesia it is the religious stirring that first produces the revival of an indigenous life, and it is typical that in Malaya these two isolated riots occurred in Kelantan and Trengganu, for this was, and has remained, the most conservatively religious area of the whole peninsula.

Here Islam is deeply ingrained. In other parts of the country, particularly on the west coast, the mixture of populations, with their various creeds and faith, had led to a weakening of extreme views, and among the Malays there had emerged by the twentieth century two currents of opinion. One, the *Kaum Muda,* consisted for the most part, as we have seen of young western educated Malays, or Malays who had been influenced by the Islamic reformist movement in Cairo. They were a new force in Malay affairs, somewhat in opposition to their Sultans and to the conservative courts. Sayed Shaykh bin Ahmad Al-Haji was one of these, and Shaykh Muhammed bin Salim Al-Kalali, who imparted the drive and much of the finance to the progressive journal *Al-Imam,* was another.

This group however had little support on the east coast. Here no admixture of peoples nor drift of new ideas made Malays doubt or question the traditional leaders of their faith. Here the Sultan and court still exercised a political authority, and maintained in many ways a proud independence and leadership that had long vanished from the Federated States. Their authority still commanded respect, and was little opposed. The constant attacks, by the *Kaum Muda* in *Al-Imam* and then later in the much more popular *Al-Ikhwan* and *Saudara,* on the court and on the religious hierarchy, both of whom obviously had lost ground in the Federated States, carried little weight on the conservative east coast, where the Sultans still reigned and ruled.

The established Malay political and religious hierarchy was known as *Kaum Tua.* Its attitude was conservative, an acceptance of affairs as they were ordered then. Only on the east coast did the *Kaum Tua* outlook go unchallenged. Official Islam here had the solid backing of the people, who, if anything were more conservative, more blindly fanatical and less open to reformist Islam or to modern ideas, than the officials. If the critical *Al-Imam* represents *Kaum Muda,* then *Kaum Tua* is personified by the officially sponsored and extremely conservative *Pengasoh,* a monthly magazine founded in 1918, and published in Kelantan. It was read throughout the peninsula, and it provided a powerful and on the whole successful counterforce to the *Kaum Muda* viewpoint. To the European and Chinese the east coast, because of its lack of opportunities, was a despair, but by many Malays it was envied because of its faith.

This faith was officially nurtured and stimulated during the twentieth century by the *Majlis Ugama dan Ista' adat Melaya,* or Council for Religion and Malay Custom formed in Kelantan in 1916. This Council came to exercise considerable power. It supervised Imams, appointed Muftis, regulated *mukim* boundaries, took charge of Muslim burial grounds, and collected *Zakat* (a compulsory religious tax on padi crops) and *bras fitrah,* a compulsory tax at the end of the fasting month, or *Hari Raya Puasa.* By a general control and encouragement of Islam, particularly by the organisation of religious schools, the Council came to be concerned in nearly all the affairs of the state. So too did its counterpart in Trengganu.

Little attempt was made by the administration to direct this rising religious wave into productive channels. The religious schools, for example, remained quite separate from the government Malay schools; nor was there any suggestion that the former's syllabus might include useful subjects divorced from theology, such as agriculture or hygiene. It was a strange neglect, for whereas the Chinese schools in the Malay States were ignored because they did not come into the official educational system, these religious schools were organised by part of that administration; yet ever since the time of the first intervention in Perak, in 1874, all the Treaties signed by the Malay leaders with the British had stipulated that religious affairs were to remain the concern of the Malays themselves and the British were not to interfere. These *Majlis Ugama* on the east coast merely represented, in an extreme manner, the powers acquired by the State Religious Affairs Departments, which in each state stood divorced and isolated from the other, British administered, Departments of Government. As a result, this increasing devotion and fanaticism was not linked by the government to any effort to improve the lot or to increase the temporal happiness of the east coast people. In a manner quite untypical of Islam, religion was separated from life.

Much of life on the east coast, and indeed Malay life throughout the peninsula, was centred on the cultivation of rice. The subsistence economy of rice and fish is one of the three economies of Malaya. Throughout the twentieth century it has been marked by one outstanding characteristic: a steady drift of disgruntled Malays from the padi field, and an equally steady effort by their overlords to keep them there. As this characteristic still prevails, it warrants investigation. On the one hand Ungku Ubdul Aziz, the noted economist, says "the biggest cause of poverty amongst Malays is because such a large proportion of them (about 1½ million) are dependent upon padi planting as their main source of livelihood,"[6] while for the last sixty or so years administrators have taken the opposite view and have urged the cultivation of more rice. Which attitude is correct?

Rice has been the mainstay of the Malay economy since time immemorial, and one main reason why more of it was not grown before the European began administering the states was the lack of incentive caused by the insecurity of life and the unstable political conditions.[7] Once British rule was effective steps were taken towards this end. But rice growing was, and to a much less extent still is, a way of life as well as an economic undertaking, with ceremonies, rituals and practices which hampered rather than assisted any development. As a result, much of the

---

6 Ungku Abdul Aziz, '*The Causes of Poverty in Malayan Agriculture*' A chapter in *The Problems of the Malayan Economy*. ed. Lim Tay Bo. (Singapore, 1956), p. 13.

7 As W. A. Graham says "the knowledge that any superfluous property of which he might become possessed would speedily be annexed by some members of the local aristocracy or by satellites of the nobility...was usually sufficient to quench all ambition for the amassing of wealth" *Kelantan* (Glasgow, 1908), pp. 70–71.

British drive to produce more padi was nullified.

Nevertheless, as the peninsula was populated by more rice eating Chinese and Indians, and as Malaya's imports of rice steadily increased, it became a cardinal feature of government policy both to make the area self-sufficient, and to keep the Malay (for no-one else would go there) on the land. Malaya has only limited areas where rice can be grown and much has always been imported, so in 1890 a scheme to make irrigated water available over a large area was begun in Perak, on land in the Krian district judged suitable. Completed in 1906 at a cost of $1 million dollars, the Krian scheme opened up 70,000 new acres for padi growing. Smaller schemes were completed near Lenggong in Perak (1,000 acres in 1901), and in Selangor (450 acres in 1900). These schemes settled many Malays on the land. They did not however weaken the country's dependence on outside supplies, as the population kept increasing.

In 1905 a Department of Agriculture was established, and although it gave most of its attention to the highly rewarding new crop, rubber, it did concern itself to some extent with the problems of padi, directing its efforts to finding the most suitable seed for Malayan farmers. The Department's influence in the padi fields was negligible, for it was not until 1938 that experiments produced the high yielding seed for which it had been searching, and it was more through legislative rather than agricultural effort, that the government assisted rice growing.

Throughout this period two tasks were confused in the bureaucrat's mind. Many felt that by supporting padi cultivation the Malay farmer was being helped. He was regarded not as a farmer who could be encouraged to grow other, more rewarding crops, but as a peasant smallholder who grew rice. To many the Malay was a peasant who could grow rice and nothing else. This image persists. Legislature after legislature agreed with the Resident of Negri Sembilan, who said "no form of agriculture is more essential to the people of this country and more deserving of the encouragement of the government than the cultivation of rice."[8] It condemned Malays who "left their padi for new

[8] *Annual Report,* Negri Sembilan, 1897.

crops which they cannot themselves utilise and the market for which depends on outside world conditions beyond their orbit,"[9] and for thirty years the government legislated to keep the Malay growing rice.

In 1913 was passed the first FMS Malay Reservation Enactment. Land was reserved for Malays only, on which rice had to be grown. Similar Acts were passed in all the Unfederated States between 1930 and 1941. Long before this, however, beginning in Malacca in 1886, the Government had alienated land where only rice could be cultivated. Whether land was reserved for Malays only, or for rice only, it was the same thing. Malays had to grow rice. A number of other legislative measures were taken, such as the Straits Settlements Rice Cultivation Ordinance of 1934 and the Irrigation Areas Ordinance of 1922 and others designed to break the Chinese rice mill monopoly and to prevent uneconomic fragmentation. And for a time events disguised the failure of the policy.

The desire of most Malays was, and is, to own land. Only in Malay Reservation areas was it made easy for them to achieve this social goal. With this understood, it can be seen why in Kelantan padi holdings increased from 100,000 acres in 1909 to 175,000 acres in 1921, equalling the granary (and Malay only area) of Kedah. Most other states recorded some increase, and the government felt that the Malay was showing due appreciation of the government's efforts of the administration. But in fact the government was not helping the Malay to a better, more contented life at all. By endeavouring to equate rice to Malays it was acting in the face of giant socio-economic forces it could not withstand. Two developments in particular should have made it clear by 1941 that padi growing was a depressed industry in Malaya, and that the Malay was basically a farmer, able and willing to grow more remunerative crops than padi.

In the first place there was the growth overseas, in Burma, Thailand and Indo-China, of a vast export production of good, cheap rice. In these three countries over 25 million square acres had been cleared and were growing padi by 1920, and some 3

---

[9] *Proceedings, Legislative Council*, FMS, 1933, p. C293.

million tons were being exported. Malaya had only a few thousand square acres of land where rice could be grown, and the country needed perhaps 300,000 tons. The country had only a million farmers, themselves interested in other crops, as compared to the twenty or so million Burmese, Thai and Vietnamese who were devoted solely to the cultivation of rice. With these huge surpluses easily available and offered at a low price, government policy became more and more out of touch with reality. It was not possible for Malaya, without the land and the people, to compete. And why should it?

The second development was internal, a steady drift of the Malay from the padi field. Nothing that the government could do could stop his (and more particularly her) determination to seek a better life. Custom took second place to comfort. The back-breaking life of padi planting was abandoned without regrets for the past. The dire results forecast from this change were not realised. The Malay remained a farmer, but where he had abandoned rice growing, he became a happier and wealthier farmer. In 1933, for example, even though it was near the bottom of the depression, every acre of rubber gave him over three times more income than an acre of rice.[10] Is it so very surprising that the Malay farmer planted rubber in preference to padi? And yet even today, when the conservative less well educated east coast, with its emphasis on padi, is the most backward area, there are people who forget the outside world, who condemn the Malay farmer for growing rubber, and who lament unrealistically that Malaya does not grow more rice. It is as absurd as lamenting that Britain does not grow more wheat.

The interest shown by the government in rice production was not equalled by any similar interest in the fishing industry. It was almost completely neglected in this period, although it remained the second mainstay of the Malay economy. Along with rice growing it was a depressed occupation, keeping down the Malay, and thus Malaya. No enquiry and little legislation were effected to assist it. It was divided into a predominantly Malay occupation on the east coast, and a Malay-Chinese enterprise on

[10] P. T. Bauer, *The Rubber Industry* (London, 1948), Table II, p. 62.

the west. Before 1941 there was hardly any mechanisation (except by Chinese on Pangkor Island), and the fishing was a daily venture close offshore. The picturesque fishing fleets would depart from the river mouth at dawn, and sail over a blue sea to return before sunset, their sails spread to catch the afternoon breeze. The beauty of the surroundings concealed the hard, dangerous work and the poor return. The possibility of help occurred to few, and the poverty and the problems of the fisherman occupied the attention of no one but themselves.[11]

Slightly more attention was given, though for strategic reasons, not economic, to the fishing activities of the Japanese.[12] Japanese interests and Japanese citizens in Malaya had been sufficiently numerous to justify the appointment of a Consul in 1890, and Japanese fishermen were based in Malaya from early in the twentieth century. Whereas the Malay rarely left his home overnight, and fished comparatively close offshore, the Japanese was largely a deep-sea fisherman working for a company, and he was often absent from his home for six months or more. The Taichong Fishing Company, for example, which established itself in Singapore in 1922, had a field of operations stretching from the Redang Islands off Trengganu down to Batavia (Djakarta). Its fishermen would be left in an area for a month or more, usually basing themselves on an island, but living in their fishing trawlers most of the time, and meeting at regular intervals with a motor carrier, which would speed their catch to Singapore. Other Japanese fishermen and pearlers from Singapore operated as far afield as the coast of Burma and the Andaman Islands, the north-west coast of Australia and the Celebes.[13]

By the 1930's the deep-sea mechanised techniques of these

[11] There was one outstanding exception. R. Firth, Professor of Anthropology at the University of London, studied their life in 1938 with rare skill and sympathy, to produce a masterpiece, *Malay Fishermen: Their Peasant Economy* (London, 1946).

[12] For an outline of them, see M. Nomura, *Fifty Years of Nanyang* (Singapore, 1937).

[13] This wide ranging oceanic enterprise of the Japanese has been renewed and extended since the war. In 1961, for example, a whaling fleet on its way to the Antarctic and a mother fishing boat back from the east coast of Africa called at Singapore.

Japanese fishing companies were supplying Singapore with over half, nearly 5,000 tons, of its annual supply of fresh fish. In addition large quantities were being frozen for trans-shipment to Japan by the numerous Japanese liners that called at Singapore.

Japanese activities on the east coast were not confined to deep-sea fishing however, and it is fortunate for Kelantan and Trengganu that they were not. A railway, built by 1931 at great cost diagonally across the peninsula to Kelantan from the western railway network, quite failed to open up the country. It was unable to initiate any worthwhile development in a region without providing an exit. Japanese enterprise, in discovering, working and exporting iron ore, provided these subsistence economy states with a working revenue as no other industry did.

Before embarking on mining investment the Japanese had been in Malaya as planters, particularly in south-eastern Johore. By 1921 over 1,000 of them were clustered around the Johore River, growing rubber on 80,000 acres. But the rubber slump together with government policy, in restricting sales of land to Japanese to a maximum of 50 acres, combined with the rapid industrialisation of Japan and its insatiable demand for iron ore, which it lacked, led to the search for iron ore, and an investment of capital in iron mines.

This search began in Johore in 1920, when a small but rich iron area was discovered by a Japanese named Ishihara in the Batu Pahat district. Encouraged by this success the Japanese Company that the pioneer had formed, Ishihara Sangyo Koshi Ltd., began searching for other deposits. They were soon found, and in 1922 mining began near Kemaman, in Trengganu. In 1928 another Japanese firm acquired a 50 year lease on the large deposits at Bukit Besi near Dungun in Trengganu. It built a 25 mile railway, endeavoured to develop the open roadstead at Dungun, and steadily increased production. By 1938 the Nippon Mining Company had a labour force, mainly of Indians and Chinese, of nearly 3,000, and in that year it exported to Japan nearly 1 million tons of ore.

Another valuable deposit was discovered by the Japanese in 1934 in Kelantan, some 50 miles inland from Kota Bharu. After a favourable lease had been secured, mining began in 1938. Over

200,000 tons were exported the following year, on which, as in Trengganu and Johore (where another iron hill was discovered in 1935), a 10% tax was paid. By 1938 iron ore exports to Japan from the east coast of Malaya totalled over 1½ million tons. They supplied over a third of the Japanese requirements and contributed substantially to the revenue of the east coast. The link between the two had become very close. It was to become even closer.

12. SINGAPORE

Throughout most of the nineteenth century the role of the government in Singapore had been similar to that of a policeman; in which role, as the measures taken against the secret societies have shown, it became increasingly efficient. But in matters of public health the government was ignorant, indifferent and inactive. As the influence of the British humanitarian movement began to make itself felt in Singapore however, to be dissipated but not quite dispersed by the commercial attitude which reigned there, and which exalted private business as the only motive for human action, a few timid steps were taken to add to this solitary responsibility.

In 1856 a Municipality was established with powers to clean and maintain the streets, to drain the town, to demolish unsafe houses, and to effect such other measures as would assist in urban health and development. Unfortunately it was a weak body, restricted initially by the East India Company and subsequently by the India Office, in many ways. For instance the municipality was not even permitted to pass by-laws, and in 1872 the Colonial Governor felt that it should be merged with the recently created (in 1867) Legislative Council. He failed in this, and partly because the municipality was overshadowed by the central government and, partly because of the lack of civic consciousness amongst the sojourners in Singapore, the government of the town did not develop.

In an attempt to instil more drive into it, Weld appointed a full time President of the Municipality. The post had been held previously as a part-time appointment by a senior government officer more concerned with other matters. It is from this date (1888), that a real municipal government began to operate. Nearly all the increased responsibilities that it accepted had a bearing on the health of the community. In these health measures the outstanding pioneer was Dr. W.R.C. Middleton. Appointed Municipal Health Officer in 1893, he retired in 1920, having been instrumental in countless ways in the improvement of health in what had become a hopelessly overcrowded, insanitary and disease-ridden town. He was the right man in the right place at the right time. Tropical diseases were becoming understood, and their successful prevention was being widely practised. The need for effective sanitation and the necessity for food regulations and housing restrictions were increasingly recognized as being part of the responsibility of government. Matters improved still more after 1913, when a further re-organisation of the municipality was undertaken. Elections, ineffective since they were introduced in 1856, were abandoned, and responsible bodies nominated commissioners in their place. Middleton and others were able to go ahead with important health projects which steadily reduced the death rate. In 1911 this stood at 51 per thousand. By 1936 it had been halved, to 24 per thousand.

In addition, from the beginning of the century large scale water-retention works were undertaken,[1] and gas and electric power was generated and distributed. In 1917 a Commission headed by G. Maxwell was appointed to enquire into the housing conditions of Singapore.[2] Middleton showed its members, less familiar than he with the terrible cubicle life of the emigrant Chinese, shop house jammed against shop house, where rooms and passage-ways were divided and sub-divided into minute cubicles, which all too often became the coffins of family after family. One of the results of this Commission was the formation in 1927 of the Singapore Improvement Trust, an autonomous body charged with abolishing these slums and with building adequate homes at low rental. Nevertheless, the cubicles remain.[3]

Middleton and the municipality in general were assisted to some extent by the charity of the Chinese. It is traditional to establish an alms house, to give gifts, or to build a hospital as an act of piety or thankfulness, and one of Singapore's biggest

---

[1] To become the Achilles heel of Singapore, as they were extended to Johore.

[2] Its findings are recorded in its *Report of the Singapore Housing Commission*, 2 vols. (Singapore, 1918)

[3] *Upper Nankin Street*, by B. Kaye (UMP, 1960) illustrates this all too vividly.

hospitals, the Tan Tock Seng Hospital, was initiated in this way. In other respects however, nearly all efforts at improving the town suffered through a widespread reluctance on the part of the population to participate in the administration, or in any way to assist, even by the paying of rates and taxes. To many Chinese charity was traditional, but to the labouring class (which constituted the overwhelming mass of the migrants) it was traditional to avoid government at all costs; and when this government was alien, and the sojourner intended in any case to return to Canton in five or ten years, the difficulties that faced the administration can perhaps be seen. It is only in recent years that this traditional way of thought, this apathy and indifference to some extent has been broken, and that more and more Chinese have come to think of themselves as belonging to Singapore, and have taken a full part in the life of the city.

This change of outlook has come in stages, and although it is nowhere near complete it is possible to see that the pioneers were the Straits-born Chinese who were English educated. The leaders of their movement (the Straits Chinese British Association), were undoubtedly the most socially conscious. Far more prepared to accept non-Chinese ideas which were applicable to life in South-East Asia, in one extremely important respect they led their Chinese educated brethren against the European administrators and towards a vital health reform: the control and elimination of opium.

Active though the municipal councillors were in other health measures, they took no steps against the smoking of opium, for the government of the Straits Settlements, and to a lesser extent, the Federated Malay States, were directly maintained by the sale of opium, in a manner only comparable to that of the East India Company a century before. The opium farmer was protected by the government as a prize asset. With its three ports insistent upon a maintenance of their free port status, import and export dues were denied it. Another customary form of government revenue, income tax, was tried briefly in 1920–1922 and found to be an impossibility. The sale of opium then provided the government with the major part of its income. British policy throughout the century was to protect this opium revenue, and various Ordinances and Acts, which in practice were commercial regulations guarding a branch of commerce, rather than laws protecting the people, assisted the farmer. The following shows how effectively this was done.

	SS Opium Revenue	*Total SS Revenue*
1880	$1,500,000	2,500,000
1890	2,200,000	4,300,000
1900	2,300,000	5,400,000
1904	6,400,000	11,000,000
1910	3,400,000	9,300,000

Although, as Miss Cheng states: "before the twentieth century there was no anti-opium movement in the Straits Settlements, there was only anti-opium sentiment,"[4] the need for such a movement had already been expressed by leading Straits Chinese, by Dr. Lim Boom Keng in particular. He and others felt that opium smoking was demoralising, and they knew that its mass consumption, rather than being an integral part of Chinese culture, was a sign of its nineteenth century decadence. In this they reflected the attitude of the reformers and revolutionaries in China itself. In 1906 Dr. Suat Chuan Yin established, in the face of government indifference to the grave social problem in its midst, the first refuge in Singapore for opium addicts, and in the same year an Anti-Opium Society was formed, with Tan Boon Liat as its first president. Antipathy to opium then spread among the Straits Chinese and although they faced the resentment of the many with vested interests in opium and the opposition of the government, together with a large section of the business community, who feared for the revenue of the Colony, the steadily growing international reaction to the opium traffic came to their aid.[5]

In 1907, after a number of questions had been asked in Parlia-

---

[4] L. Cheng, 'British Opium Policy in the Straits Settlements' *Journal, South-East Asian History*, vol. 2, no. 1. (March 1961).

[5] A prominent leader in this movement was Dr. Wu Lien Teh, another Chinese who received his medical training in England. His *Plague Fighter* (Cambridge, 1959) tells of his long and courageous campaign. Another was Dr. Chen Su Lan.

ment, the British Colonial Secretary wrote to Sir John Anderson, the Governor, saying, "I do not see how the introduction of apparently ever increasing quantities of opium into a British Colony and Protectorate can any longer be defended". He recommended steps "for minimising and eventually eradicating the evil."[6]

Anderson, therefore, to the disapproval of many, including the *Straits Times,* formed an Opium Commission. Tan Jiak Kim, head of one of the oldest Straits Chinese families, (the man whose energy had led to the formation of the King Edward VII Medical College), with Dr. Middleton and four other Europeans, was charged with investigating this Chinese social problem. The Commission reported in 1908, recommending that the government should slightly restrict its sale, for example opium should not be consumed by women in brothels, and that the commission itself should take over the government monopoly.[7] In this recommendation, it is possible that the Commission may have been influenced more by the falling payments from the farmer (they dropped from $4,250,000 in 1904 to $3,000,000 by 1908), than by the interest in opium being displayed in London and elsewhere. These recommendations were adopted in 1910, and the effectiveness of direct government control and the elimination of the farmer was soon shown. By 1920, revenue from opium was nearly $20 million, since for a decade it had increased steadily.

But during this decade world opinion hardened considerably against the drug. Conferences in Shanghai (1909) and at the Hague (1912), were followed, once the League of Nations was formed, by attempts at international control. In China too the nationalists regarded opium as a sign of decadence, and this, together with the expression of world moral opinion through the League of Nations, was of paramount importance.

After securing complete control over the importation, the preparation and sale of opium, the government at last, from 1929 onwards, felt that it was necessary to take restrictive steps, and

---

[6] Colonial Office to Governor, 25th April, 1907. Quoted by L. Cheng, op. cit.

[7] *Report of the Opium Commission* (Singapore, 1908), Cmd. 4321, 4322 (1909).

it was made compulsory for all addicts to register. During the previous ten years the consumption of opium had decreased, less through government policy than through the slackening of what had been a widespread Chinese habit, from 1,700,000 tahils in 1919 to 1,300,000 tahils in 1929. From then on, as the government tightened up the registration system, and particularly after a League of Nations Conference had met in Bangkok, the South-East Asian centre of the opium industry, and new international measures for combating the drug traffic were agreed to, in 1931 the consumption of opium at last decreased.

At the end of December 1934 the register of smokers was closed. No additions of new smokers were allowed. None of the migrants could legally buy opium, and by 1938 only 500,000 tahils of expensive opium were being sold to perhaps 27,000 middle-aged and elderly people, out of an estimated total Chinese population in the Straits of 862,000. At the same time the swift activities of the Preventive Service kept smuggled opium to a minimum. However even as late as 1927, when the service was founded, the measures it took to suppress smuggling "were designed primarily for the protection of the opium revenue," (but) "they became gradually the spearhead of the opium smoking suppression policy of the Colonial Government".[8] These measures must have been effective on both counts, for while the number of smokers decreased each year, the opium revenue increased, rising from $5 million in 1931 to $8½ million in 1938.

Much of this revenue had been put year by year into an Opium Revenue Replacement Fund, which, standing at $57 million by 1938, had been invested abroad. The interests from these investments were to become very useful after the war, for in 1943 the British Government decided that the time had come to adopt a policy of total prohibition of opium smoking, and upon its return to the peninsula this was introduced.[9]

Addicts made intense efforts to secure opium from Yunnan,

---

[8] *Annual Report of the S. S. Customs and Preventive Service*, 1938, p. 299.

[9] This war-time decision is reminiscent of the act, morally commendable but economically injudicious, to abolish the slave trade, taken during the Napoleonic Wars.

Persia and elsewhere, but although a hard core of perhaps 12,000 remained, opium smoking after the war was never permitted to become again a major social characteristic of the Chinese in Malaya. In the elimination of this, of what came to be generally accepted by the Chinese and Europeans in Malaya as an evil, we must give credit to the pioneers, the Straits Chinese.

While they did not themselves take the initiative, for they were, after all, very much the governed, and not the governors, the Straits Chinese also supported the steps taken by the administration in its efforts to ameliorate the condition of Chinese women and children in Singapore and Malaya in general. Most migrants were men, and until 1927 brothels had existed for their use, and women could be brought from China to work in them. After 1927 the government forbade such female migration, and after 1930 the brothels were closed. Not surprisingly, cabarets and dance hostesses then became a feature of Singapore life, and the Chinese Protectorate was active in combating this. But was prostitution immoral, as distinct from illegal? Only slowly did the full weight of Chinese opinion in Malaya agree to this; certainly not before 1940.

Another Chinese social characteristic was the *mui tsai* problem. The *mui tsai* were young girls sold to other families as domestic servants. In China it was an old custom that saved many unwanted daughters from a childhood death. The girl would be taken into another family, with obligations on the new parent to see that the little girl was clothed, fed, and eventually married. These ameliorating conditions often did not prevail in Malaya, and the poor child was virtually a slave.

This institution had never been recognised by the British in Malaya, nor was it practised by the Straits Chinese. Nevertheless this form of servitude existed quite clearly amongst others, and in 1925 an Act was passed in an effort to control it. This had the support of the Chinese unofficial member on the Legislative Council, as did the much more effective *Mui Tsai* Bill of 1932.

The custom died hard amongst the conservative Chinese, and Tan Cheng Lock, the great Straits Chinese leader, was one of those with the courage to say that its practice in China did not necessarily endorse its applicability in Malaya, where conditions were different. Slowly opinion among the Chinese veered to his side, that it was immoral to purchase small children to become domestic chattels. In 1937 a Commission appointed to consider the problem of *mui tsai* submitted a Minority Report which recommended its complete abolition, and firm protective steps to safeguard the particular class of child concerned. Legislation followed in 1938–1940, and was generally acceptable to the Chinese community.[10]

The Straits Chinese, in their attempts to obtain various political, educational and social concessions from the government, in many cases led the new Chinese into an acceptance of the changed order, an acceptance on the part of the new Chinese however based more on approval from China than on agreement with the Straits Chinese themselves. In other respects they secured a privileged position in comparison to the new Chinese, for their relationship with the government, even when they opposed opium smoking, was generally one of support. Loyalty to the Crown was one of their proud maxims.

It was a maxim they did not share with the organisation which truly captured the between-war loyalty of the new Chinese migrants, the Kuomintang. Through this nationalist party organisation, which became in effect the government, China endeavoured to secure and strengthen its hold over the minds and the pockets of the overseas Chinese. It was not interested in Malaya territorially, it is doubtful if it ever seriously regarded the peninsula as terra irredenta, but saw it merely as the home of those whose wealth was very useful for China. China wanted its people overseas to remain Chinese in every way, always to look back in unquestioning filial obedience to their country of origin; and thus the work of the KMT in Malaya was China-centred. In pursuing this aim it put the Straits Chinese into a serious dilemma, victims of two loyalties; and it ran up increasingly against the British administration, whose role, quite clearly, was Malaya-centred.

In 1922 Sun Yat Sen established the Overseas Affairs Bureau,

---

[10] These social problems are brought out very clearly in V. Purcell, *The Chinese in Malaya* (London, 1948), pp. 174–193.

whose task was to look after the migrants, but conditions in China itself (which must always be borne in mind when considering any aspect of the history of the Chinese in Malaya), made this organisation ineffectual for some time. As war lord struggled with war lord, as disorders and division in China persisted, only a minimum contact was maintained. In 1923 however, the KMT in the south were reconciled to the communists, and there was a quick growth of overseas agencies, particularly in the Chinese schools.

Following the initial step in 1920 of establishing a tenuous control over these schools, the government began offering financial grants to aid them in 1923. Both act and grant were resented by the schools, which wanted no foreign, non-Chinese control, and wished merely to be left alone. In 1925, alarmed at the growth of KMT or communist inspired anti-British actions and belligerent attitudes, which included strikes and other disturbances, all branches of the KMT in Malaya were suppressed, and the following year the surveillance over the schools in the Federation and in the Straits Settlements was increased by the establishment of Assistant Directors of Education charged with these Chinese responsibilities.

The reaction of the KMT was to go underground. It established a number of adult night schools, and at both these and the day schools the new national Kuo Yu language was taught, eliminating in the schools the old literary language and the South Chinese dialects. At both day and night schools the extremists, communist or KMT, aroused passions with their China-centred teachings. They were attacked by the government, many Hainanese night schools being raided and suppressed, but in 1927, on the second anniversary of the death of Sun Yat Sen, certain Chinese schools of Singapore, inflamed by their teachers, broke out in the Kreta Ayer riot. Seven deaths and much disorder resulted before law and order were re-established.

In that same year Chiang Kai Shek broke with the communists, and in 1928, leading his southern men northwards, he established himself and the KMT as rulers of a united China. The nationalists had triumphed, and a new China had emerged. Nine Singapore Chinese schools were closed that year, having used their premises for political purposes, and although the extreme communists were eliminated from the KMT, its new base of strength in China stimulated anew its strong pro-China attitude.

In 1930 Sir Cecil Clementi arrived in Singapore fresh from Hong Kong. On the day of his arrival some forty delegates attended a KMT conference in Singapore. The organisation had become brazenly open during the regime of Clifford, but Clementi viewed the party as dangerously anti-Malayan and he acted swiftly to stamp it out. The KMT leaders were summoned to Government House, and were told that their organisation was a threat to the preservation of law and order, and was to be dissolved forthwith.

Immediate protests by Chinese organisations in Malaya carried little weight, suspect as they were, but representations by China itself were more effective. With large trading interests in China, and with Japan growing steadily stronger, Britain desired the goodwill of the new China, and a compromise was reached, whereby Chinese in Malaya could join the party as long as no branches were formed in Malaya itself. Ignoring this restriction by the formation of secret branches, the KMT existed until the Japanese arrived, the fierce supporter and chief instrument for the maintenance, stimulation and growth of a 'China in Malaya'.[11]

The KMT effected this mission largely through the Chinese schools. In 1929 the Chinese Government held a large conference to discuss overseas education, and followed this with another in 1930. Instructions were then transmitted overseas, and in late 1930 the Chinese Consul-General in Singapore called together the headmasters of all the Chinese schools to make sure that they acted upon the regulations drawn up for them by the KMT in China. These regulations for overseas Chinese schools dealt with finance, establishments, curriculum, textbooks, discipline, management committees, teaching staff, students, holidays and study societies. Scarcely a single aspect of the schools' affairs was

---

[11] There were 12,346 members in ninety-six branches and sub-branches all over Malaya by 1933. See the *KMT Year Book* (1934), as quoted by Png Poh Seng, Journal, South-East Asian History, vol. 2, no. 1 (March 1961), p. 12.

omitted from the calculations of the Chinese Government, and hardly a single aspect of the schools' affairs associated the student with his Malayan environment, for he struggled constantly against it.

From 1934 onwards the hold of the KMT over these schools, already strong by reason of these regulations, and particularly by the constant arrival of KMT staff and textbooks, was strengthened by financial grants to the schools from the Chinese government. Although Dr. Purcell, who was involved in Chinese education at this time, says that this "could not be viewed by the Malayan Governments with complacency",[12] on retrospect it seems almost a disaster that the full resources of the governments were not thrown more effectively behind a policy which would have effectively combated this KMT control, and which in addition might have grouped into one the divided educational streams of Singapore and the peninsula.

From 1931 onwards the scrutiny and banning of the most virulent anti-British text books began, but few if any local Malayan-centred Chinese textbooks were ever produced, and the student was fed on material devoted exclusively to China. The banishment of extreme teachers was also initiated, but again this negative step was not followed by positive action in establishing a Chinese teachers' training college. Some encouragement was given to these schools by the introduction of inter-school examinations and sport from 1935 onwards, and the government's control was slightly increased by amendments to the 1920 Act in 1937, both indicative of a less passive attitude on the part of the government, but it was too little a change and too late. In the 1930's, the schools were the centres of incident after incident in which the authority of the state was questioned, checked or thwarted, and it was only because inside those schools there was a constant struggle for the student mind between the KMT and the MCP (the Malayan Communist Party) that these incidents were not more violent. The old nineteenth century secret societies had been suppressed by the 1890 Dangerous Societies Ordinance and were kept innocuous. The danger lay in the

[12] V. Purcell, *The Chinese in Malaya*, p. 233.

KMT. As it was, by 1938 there were close on 1,000 Chinese schools in Malaya where nearly 90,000 students received an education, and loyalties which set them apart from the rest of a divided Malaya.[13]

The very great majority of the people of Singapore, as with the rest of Malaya, were not unduly concerned with this. Most people felt that they were getting what they wanted. If they wanted an English education, there was a school for them. If they preferred a Chinese education, as many did, there was one for them too. There were Malay and even Tamil schools for those who wished for an Indian education. There was a service for all, and if it was not something of which one could be particularly proud, for no one pretended that the standards were high, at least it catered in a manner for everyone. Very few felt that it was a tragedy, and hardly anyone worried about it at all.

The attention of Singapore was focused far more intently on commerce. In this Singapore is not unlike medieval Venice, except that it has a large proletariat, or working class. It is an island port whose life-blood is international trade, and the heart of Singapore's story in the twentieth as in the nineteenth century, is to be found in the developments there. In the final outcome commerce, not politics, rules Singapore.

This commerce was dominated by the European Houses of Agency. As the twentieth century unfolded these firms came to link together the agricultural and mining activities of the peninsula with the commerce of Singapore and the technical ability and investment potential of Great Britain. They became distinguished, after a nineteenth century career as plain merchants, for the diversity of their effort in the twentieth century. They accepted the wholesale selling responsibility for the ever increasing products of the industrial West which they brought out to Singapore, while at the same time undertaking managerial and supervisory roles over mainland estates and mines. In addition these companies retained their buying interest

---

[13] There were 1,015 Chinese schools in Malaya in 1939, but this included 34 Mission schools without KMT staff, where 4,006 students out of a total of 91,534 were educated. V. Purcell, op. cit., Appendix VI.

in Asian raw materials, and promoted or controlled shipping and air lines, and insurance firms.

Many of these firms had been founded in the nineteenth century by individual merchants. There had been no mainland investment, no mines nor estates when Alexander Guthrie began in 1821, and he had built his business buying and selling Straits produce. His nephew, James, had expanded this merchant house, but it was largely the work of Sir John Anderson, who joined it in 1876, that prepared it for the twentieth century. In 1903, after it became a public company, its prestige and power enabled it to secure capital in London for various rubber companies which it formed, while the success of these mainland estates, over which it retained supervisory control, made its venture in the 1920's, when it formed a number of oil palm companies, less problematical. It became associated with tin as well, while in Singapore it continued to expand its commercial side buying goods from all over South-East Asia. The first firm in Singapore, it is still nearly the biggest, although overshadowed now by Sime Darby and Company, and the Borneo Company.

Boustead and Company was another agency house that grew out of a private merchant's enterprise in the nineteenth century and it too adapted itself skilfully to the possibilities of diversification presented by the twentieth century. In 1903 the importation of frozen Australian meat had been initiated and Boustead's participated in the formation of the Singapore Cold Storage Company. Ice, and refrigerator facilities for the preservation of foods of all kinds, have done much to make the lives of all who live in the tropics more pleasant. One then can hardly begrudge Boustead's the profit it necessarily earned from these services.

Harrisons and Crosfield began life in 1844 not in Singapore but in Liverpool, as the enterprise of a tea merchant, the East India Company monopoly having gone, and only came east at the end of the century, there to be another to adapt itself successfully to the agency system. During the twentieth century the Company acquired varied fields of interest in South India and North Borneo, as well as Malaya, with engineering and shipping agencies, together with managerial responsibilities over tea, rubber and other estates which it had initiated.

However, not all of the enterprising Singapore firms had such diverse activities as these three. McAlister's founded in 1857, still concentrates on commerce, while Mansfield's merely broadened, by airlines and tourist work, its transport business of the nineteenth century, when under G. Bogaardt in the 1870's it was concerned with almost every small steamer which came into Singapore roads.

It was on its shipping above all, despite its powerful road and rail links (a causeway connecting it to Johore having been built in 1924) that Singapore always depended. Throughout its history, this characteristic has remained unchanged. Singapore has been "essentially a great shipping junction where the ocean-going traffic from all over the world met the local shipping of the Archipelago."[14] In studying the growth of Singapore one must remember that it is not merely part of Malaya, but that also through its waterfront it is linked with most of South-East Asia as well.

The commercial growth of Singapore therefore belongs almost as much to a study of South-East Asia as to a more limited account such as we are giving here, of Malaya only, where regional developments can be treated merely briefly at best, or regretfully omitted altogether. With Singapore as the centre of our studies, however, we must remember that to understand the whole story of commerce in Singapore it is necessary to study the history of South-East Asia. This will not be attempted here.

The European agency houses which dominated the trade of Singapore were competing with firms in which European and Asian capital mingled, and with others whose capital and enterprise was entirely Asian: Middle Eastern, Indian or Chinese in particular. Characteristic of the former was the Straits Steamship Company, established in 1890. It was financed jointly by Straits Chinese and Westerners, to ply the shallow waters of the Malayan peninsula. Then, when the more liberally minded Dutch unlocked a large number of their previously restricted

---

[14] Allen & Donnithorne, *Western Enterprise in Indonesia and Malaya* (London, 1957), p. 210.

small river ports in Sumatra and elsewhere (150 by 1912), the company's activities extended to the archipelago and also, on the outbreak of the First World War to British Borneo, where the Germans had acquired a shipping monopoly. The small vessels of the Straits Steamship Company, with their distinctive black, blue and white funnels, became a common sight in Singapore waters, as they carried their cargoes to and from Borneo, Sumatra, Trengganu or beyond. They still sail today, contributing to the commercial wealth of Singapore.

There are a thousand firms characteristic of the latter, firms with Asian capital and enterprise, Jewish firms such as Sadka's, which has been importing foods from all over the world to feed Malaya's millions throughout this century; Indian firms such as Barkath's or Mottiwallah's, the modern counterpart of the ancient Indian traders who came to Kalah and Tumasik a thousand years ago; and of course Chinese family-controlled firms, ranging from the small shopkeeper who pays a good price to a few modest coffee producers in south Sumatra to great establishments such as the Overseas Chinese Bank, which in its way rivals the great western banks, such as the Chartered and the Hongkong and Shanghai Bank, that grew with Singapore in the years between the wars.[15]

Singapore's growth was not uneventful: it suffered its setbacks as well. In Indonesia the development of Dutch control over the islands during the early decades of the century introduced orderly government which fostered the economic growth of the archipelago. This in its turn often assisted Singapore, particularly as a more liberal policy towards foreign trade was adopted, but also unfortunately, Singapore was by-passed as when harbour facilities were improved in Macassar and Beluran, or when the big Dutch shipping lines introduced direct trading. Furthermore the extension of Dutch control often permitted the indigenous people on the islands to gain access to credit facilities, and this helped to undermine the Chinese middleman. Singapore

---

[15] For a most interesting survey of Chinese banks in Singapore, see Tan Ee-Leong *The Chinese Banks incorporated in Singapore and the Federation of Malaya* (JMBRAS, vol. 26, pt. 1, July 1953).

Chinese newspapers with their pages of South-East Asia news, reflect the intense interest of the Singapore traders in this area, and it is obvious, as Allen and Donnithorne state, that "a lessening of Chinese control was often synonymous with a decay of the Singapore interest."[16] As Indonesia in these inter-war years accounted for from a quarter to over a third of all of Singapore's imports, and was by far the greatest single supplier of goods, as well as being an important purchaser from Singapore, this could have been very damaging. By and large however, as the trade figures indicate, Indonesia maintained and strengthened its percentage of a trade that was itself developing and so it appears that the Singapore Chinese adapted themselves in a satisfactory manner to the Dutch-Indonesian developments.[17]

Singapore was less able to combat the economic nationalism of the Siamese, the British in Burma or the French in Indo-China; nor, and this is more relevant, was it able to expand upon the waters of international trade made sluggish by the effect of the great world-wide economic depression. Nothing like the buoyant conditions of the post Second World War period were seen in Europe or Asia, yet with peace and order widespread over South East Asia, each decade witnessed a growth of the trade of Singapore.[18] By 1938 it had reached $689.9 million.

There are two characteristics about this trade that may usefully be noted. Firstly there is the steady shrinkage of the trade area. The long, thin trade routes of the 1830's to Manila, China, the distant islands of the archipelago and to Indo-China, are replaced by the short, broad connections of the 1930's with south Sumatra, British Borneo and the nearby islands and Malaya. From Malaya the raw commodities, which epitomise Singapore's export trade, reached the docks, by the 1930's, in innumerable trucks driven and owned by Chinese, for they completely captured the road transport of the peninsula, whilst on the seas British shipping held its own.

---

[16] Allen & Donnithorne, op. cit., p. 218.

[17] In 1921 Indonesia's exports to Singapore were 20% of Singapore's total imports. They were 27% in 1938.

[18] This trade is examined, almost item by item, in L. A. Mills, *British Rule in Eastern Asia* (London, 1942), pp. 110–173.

It is still too early to ascertain whether this shrinkage of area is continuing, although the feeling is that it is a development that has not been arrested. Neither, since the war, is there any indication that Britain's prominent position in this trade (which was the second but less easily observable characteristic of it) has not been maintained, despite fierce and unrelenting competition.

Before the First World War its chief competitor (a most successful one), was Germany. Its ships and companies, prominent among them being Behn Meyer & Company, secured a steadily increasing proportion of business. It was partly this commercial activity that aroused the political apprehensions of Malaya mentioned earlier. In a day, on the outbreak of the First World War, all this was lost, never to be recovered.

In the inter-war years Britain's chief competitor as the supplier of manufactured goods was Japan, particularly in the depression years of the early 1930's when its low textile prices, for example, considerably lower than those of England or India, swept the market. Britain, largely by reason of its political control, was able to re-establish its trade after it had effected a ban on Japanese goods, and the percentage of British trade with the Malayan market was maintained, as the following figures show.

MALAYA

	Imports from			Exports to	
	U.K.	Indonesia*	Japan	U.S.A.	U.K.
1923	14.0%	33.4%	3.0%	40.5%	13.8%
1931	13.7%	38.1%	3.9%	32.9%	11.3%
1938	18.6%	17.0%	2.3%	30.0%	14.2%

(* largely rubber and other raw materials for re-export when processed)

This commercial rivalry of Japan was only part of a greater menace to Malaya which became increasingly dangerous during this period. Many, however regarded the commercial activities of the Japanese not as a menace to them but as an opportunity to buy goods at prices they could afford. Japanese businesses in Malaya, particularly their almost complete monopoly of iron ore workings, which they had secured along the east coast of Malaya, were regarded from the imperial viewpoint, with disfavour; but Malayans generally did not consider this commercial infiltration as being undesirable and they found it difficult, if not impossible, to view Japan as a dangerous enemy. Even the animosity of the most patriotic KMT Chinese, who instituted periodic boycotts of Japanese goods, was not sufficient to drive them away. It is difficult, however, to secure a balanced picture of the Japanese by confining ourselves to the internal Singapore scene. It is necessary to look at the developments during this period outside, in Asia and Europe, and to see how they came to affect Malaya. This is considered in the following chapter.

13. WAR

In the first forty years of the twentieth century the Malayan Peninsula was in many ways a peaceful, placid country, but it was enjoying a calm before a great storm. Elsewhere in Asia great changes were sweeping through ancient countries, and Japan, in particular, had become the dynamic heart of an Asian cyclone. This cyclone was to affect Malaya, with most momentous results.

Japan, brought into contact with the outside world in the 1850's, had embarked on an industrialisation programme that produced, along with its need for markets, a belligerent outlook and a rapidly expanding population. Vigorous and aggressive, Japan had defeated China in 1894–95 and then Russia in 1904–5. This second victory had been preceded in 1902 by a naval treaty with Great Britain, which gave Japan a free hand in the waters off East Asia, and which permitted it without fear of complications, to destroy the Russian Fleet as it came up to Korea.

The Anglo-Japanese Alliance of 1902 marks the beginning of the British ebb from East Asia, an ebb that was not clearly apparent until 1941. By that agreement, which enabled Britain to withdraw the greater part of its East Asian fleet to meet the menace at home of the new Germany, it began to surrender the power that it had established in the South China Sea during the previous century.

With British naval power on the wane, Japan was able, during the First World War, to seize the Pacific island empire of Germany, having acquired Formosa in 1895 and Korea in 1910. So dominant did Japan become in East Asian waters during the war that when a third class South Indian garrison battalion mutinied in Singapore in 1915, to terrify the select residential area of Tanglin, Japanese naval units were amongst the first in helping to quell it.[1]

[1] The Japanese liberated the interned crew of the German raider *Emden*, sunk off the Cocos Islands earlier in the war.

The 1914–1918 war was a most tragic trial of blood, a long drawn out draining of European strength and enterprise. It marks the end of the expansive period of European territorial imperialism, as a dreadful weariness fell over the countries which had participated in it; with two exceptions. Neither the U.S.A., which entered the fray in 1917, nor Japan shared this war weariness. It was the continued belligerency of Japan in north-eastern Asia, where its generals felt there was room for an empire, joined with the fears of the U.S.A. anxious for its protégé, China, as well as for its position in the Pacific, which brought about the Washington Conference of 1922.

At this Conference, called to discuss naval disarmament in the Pacific, it was agreed that no new naval bases were to be built in the Pacific east of 110° East longitude,[2] while in addition a balance of naval power was obtained by a battleship ratio of 5:5:3 between the U.S.A., Great Britain and Japan. This Conference alienated the Japanese, whose extremists regarded it as publically humiliating. They conveniently forgot that Britain's five ships had world-wide responsibilities, and that America had a two-fleet navy to maintain, so that Japan's three battleships could be concentrated; nevertheless it "had neutralised an area of the Pacific, leaving the potential antagonists virtually beyond each others reach".[3]

The longitude limitation stipulated by the Conference laid upon Great Britain the necessity of abandoning Hong Kong as a naval base, which was in any case recognised as strategically unsuitable, and of retreating from the South China Sea. But if the Indian Ocean was to be maintained as a 'British lake,' and if there was to be any protection at all for the large numbers of merchant ships that plied to China, then there had to be a defensive base as close to the 110° East longitude as possible, and one which would accommodate a fleet. This was particularly necessary owing to the great failure of British East Asian diplomacy in the inter-war years, for although the 1902 Treaty with Japan had lapsed, Britain had not secured any similar alliance with the

---

2 This parallel runs between Malaya and Japan.

3 C. N. Parkinson, *The Pre-1942 Singapore Naval Base* (U.S. Naval Institute Proceedings, September 1956), p. 947.

U.S.A. After the Washington Conference the U.S.A. withdrew into its isolationist position, and took comparatively little notice of Far Eastern events.

The decision which was taken in 1923 to build a base at Singapore, 1500 miles from Hong Kong, was criticised by politicians and press in Britain, until after its completion, as an aggressive move likely to antagonise the Japanese. They failed to appreciate that it marked a retreat from East Asia, and that it was a defensive bastion, not a sally port. Retarded however by these critics, even stopped by them when they were in power, as with the Labour Government of 1924, the base was slowly built on the marshy, mangrove coast of Singapore on the Straits of Johore.

After the Washington Conference Japan concentrated its attention for nearly two decades on acquiring an empire in north-eastern Asia, moving from Korea into Manchuria in 1931. Then with Manchuria as a most useful base, its army began penetrating North China (Jehol) from 1933 onwards, and then, from 1935, into Inner Mongolia. In 1937 Japan attacked China proper, and after widespread and deep penetrations it became more and more locked in a paralysing struggle, unable to bring about a victory.

In this war the Japanese army had exercised a virtually independent authority. It was one of the defects of its constitution that the armed services were very largely free of democratic or political control, and were able to act with little consideration of any public opinion. During the 1930's this freedom was exercised in particular by the army. The navy waited, watching through its Japanese businessmen, barbers and photographers in Malaya the snail-like progress of the base in Singapore, and noting also the British decision, announced at the Imperial Conference in London in 1937, to adhere to its policy of retaining its fleet in European waters, sending units eastwards only when necessary. Thus, the Japanese noted, there was to be a base, but no ships.

The tragedy is that events in Europe, which warranted the retention of the fleet, made it increasingly unlikely that any units could ever be sent to Singapore. In 1939, when Europe's slide from collective security had led to war with Germany, the base, which had been opened officially in February 1938, was nearly complete. A graving dock, quays, cranes, workshops, barracks, hospitals, large quantities of fuel, oil, water and ammunition in underground stores, equipment of all kinds, and a skilled labour force, all defended by guns, nets and search-lights, with an airfield nearby: all this had been assembled on the Straits of Johore, and the work costing millions of pounds (£18 million by 1937) had found employment for thousands. Indeed, as the base was without ships, its contribution to Singapore's economy was (and always has been), far greater than to its defence.

The collapse of Holland and France in June 1940 in the face of German invasion was perhaps the decisive factor in hardening the Japanese attitude towards South-East Asia.

The moderates in Japan, who had been able to restrain the extremists until then, weakened, as they felt that Britain's collapse would surely follow. The Army, trained on German lines, had for some time favoured a policy of close alliance with Hitler. An aggressive new government was formed, determined to establish control over South-East Asia. Japan's military economy had one very dangerous weakness: oil. Japan produced only 10% of its annual requirements of this commodity, the rest coming from the U.S.A. (50%), the Dutch Islands (10%), and elsewhere. If Japan controlled South-East Asia, so it was reasoned, it would have an empire which could sustain it indefinitely, not merely in oil, but in other raw products, such as rubber, tin and iron ore. On 27th September four days after moving into northern Indo-China, Japan signed the Tripartite Pact with Germany and Italy.

For Japan September 1940 was perhaps the opportunity of a thousand years. Holland and France were defeated, Britain was alone, America was indifferent. An invasion of South-East Asia launched then would have carried her into India and over Australia. With Indian and Australian troops absent from Egypt, that country too might well have collapsed. The Axis powers would thus triumph. Japan, however, held back, partly through fear of Russia, and all through 1941, although it moved closer and closer to war, it did not attack.

During that year, however, preparations were made for striking. In March 1941 Japan secured the consent of the colonial French to move into south Indo-China, in particular to the fine harbour at Camranh Bay. In April Japan signed a neutrality pact with Russia, which permitted Japan to ignore its own northern fields of interest. In June Germany invaded Russia, and Japan felt free to turn its full attention to the south; particularly as, two days before the invasion on the 20th June the U.S.A., placed an embargo on the export of oil. A month later, as Japanese moves into Indo-China became imminent, all Japanese assets in the U.S.A. were frozen, thus ending all trade between the two countries. Britain followed suit; so too did the Netherlands. It meant the virtual cessation of all trade between Japan and the rest of the world; and yet the 'tiger', faced by these deadly thrusts, still did not spring.

In Japan there were still those who sought to obtain by negotiation what others wanted by war. The Prime Minister, Konoye, was one of these, and in late August he sought a personal meeting with the American President, F.D.R. Roosevelt. He was rebuffed, and in September, with diplomacy discredited, it was decided that if the embargoes could not be lifted by October, then to avert national collapse, war must follow. Konoye resigned, and General Tojo, the Army man, took over.

Meanwhile, Malaya slumbered on. Its defence against attack, as the months of 1941 went by, were deplorably weak, but it became steadily stronger than in 1940, when the country had been almost completely defenceless. By December 1941 there were three weak divisions of trops in Malaya (the 8th Australian, and the 9th and 11th Indian), together with a considerable number of base and administrative troops. Air defence consisted of several hundred aircraft, while into the hitherto empty naval base there moved, on the 3rd December the *Prince of Wales* and *Repulse,* two of Britains battleships, to form the nucleus of the Eastern Fleet. They came to Singapore at the insistence of Mr. (later Sir) Winston Churchill, Britain's leader, who felt that their presence would intimidate the Japanese from moving south. It was a bluff, and the bluff was called.[4]

---

[4] For an excellent historical survey of the events that led to the building of the Singapore naval base, and of the sending and sinking of these two battleships see the official British war history, *The War At Sea,* by S.W. Roskill. vol. 1, 'The Defensive' (HMSO, 1954), pp. 553–570.

Mahan, the naval historian, has said that "in places which justify fortification both the works and the garrison must be adequate to all probable exigencies".[5] In Malaya, neither the works nor the garrison were adequate, and thus the collapse of Singapore was inevitable.

The war in South-East Asia, of which the Malayan campaign was but a part, began on the 7th December 1941, when the Japanese, in a wide arc of carefully planned aggression, attacked the U.S. naval base of Pearl Harbour, on the island of Hawaii, there to put out of action all eight battleships of the U.S. Pacific fleet; over half of the heavy bombers of the U.S. Far Eastern Air Force were destroyed by raids that self-same day on the Philippines; while both Hong Kong and Malaya were invaded.

The invasion of Malaya by the Japanese had been anticipated as early as 1937 by General W.G.S.Dobbie, General Officer Commanding, Malaya, who forecast exactly what in fact did happen: a landing in north-east Malaya and south-east Thailand during the monsoon period. Nevertheless, despite this, and despite the steady drift to war, Malaya was caught unprepared, and while militarily the shortages could be explained away, bearing in mind the world-wide crisis and the needs of the African and European battlefront for trained men and machines, the greatest deficiency was the mental unpreparedness for the onslaught. The Malaya-wide inability to comprehend the danger or to grasp it when it arrived reminds one of the mental blindness of the Europeans in India before the Mutiny.

The campaign, from beginning to end, was a disaster. From the first landings of the 18th Japanese Division near Kota Bharu, in Kelantan, and of the 18th Division at Singora, in Thailand, the Japanese never suffered a major reverse, and within seventy days, thirty less than they had allowed for, their three divisions (the Imperial Guards Division being the third) had conquered Malaya and captured Singapore.

In the first twenty-four hours they virtually destroyed the air force, while within three days they had sunk the *Prince of Wales* and *Repulse*, bombing them on the 10th December near

---

[5] Mahan, *Naval Strategy* (London, 1911), p. 194.

Tioman Island. On land the soldiers staggered back from defeat after defeat. Jitra, north of Alor Star, was the first major set-back, where the British and Indian troops were out-fought and out-manoeuvred on the 11th and 12th December, forcing the abandonment of north Malaya. This was followed on the 7th January by a swift, determined attack by the Japanese on the 11th Division defending the Slim River which almost destroyed it as a coherent force, and led to the withdrawal from Central Malaya. Then in northern Johore the Australians were outmanoeuvred, and they too, after heavy fighting, were forced to withdraw. By the 31st January all the Malay Peninsula was in the hands of the Japanese. Singapore was invaded on the 8th February, and after fierce fighting, where the bravery of the troops (in which the locally raised Malay Regiment figured as conspiciously as the rest) was far above the skill of the leaders, the general commanding, Lt. General A. E. Percival, surrendered the island on the 15th January.

It has been recorded that the total loss to the British Commonwealth, of men killed or captured by the Japanese, was approximately 166,600. Of the three Japanese divisions, led by General Yamashita, that effected this victory over the British in Malaya, their casualties were approximately 15,000.[6]

Elsewhere it was the same. Indifference on the part of the ruled; and incompetence, lack of preparedness, inefficiency, bungling and heroic bravery on the part of the colonial powers; are the characteristics of the story, civilian and military, in Hong Kong, the Philippines, the Pacific Islands, Indonesia and Burma, until the fury of fighting ends, and Japan emerges triumphant: master, within three short months, of all South-East Asia.[7]

However, this conquest should be seen as a brilliantly executed

---

[6] The figures are taken from the official British war history *The War Against Japan* (vol. 1, 'The Loss of Singapore'), by Woodburn Kirby. (HMSO, 1957), p. 473. The book gives a sober, critical and detailed account of this campaign.

[7] An excellent survey of this war against the European in Asia is given by S. E. Morrison, '*The Rising Sun in the Pacific*', being vol. 3 of the *History of the US Naval operations in World War II* (Boston, 1950).

and skilfully planned campaign, not as a war, and the Japanese weakness in mistaking the former for the latter was soon apparent. After this campaign was over, its lack of plans, except a defensive determination to hold on to what it had secured, was clear. Japan had gone swiftly to war, but it had little appreciation of what that war would entail beyond this first campaign. For Japan to be successful, it had to defeat its enemies by achieving a total victory; but this it did not do, nor set out to accomplish. In 1941 Japan had no plan for the invasion of India, nor for the conquest of Australia. The Japanese had no strategic thought at all beyond the occupation of South-East Asia, and while their tactics in the South-East Asian campaign were brilliant, their lack of thinking on a global basis led inevitably to their defeat. Had Japan concerted its strategy with Germany as Britain did with the U.S.A., it might in 1942, have snatched victory from the Allies. Its navy could range then from Africa to western U.S.A.; its divisions, blooded in battle, were supreme; while its airpower could not have been checked. Yet this fatal flaw emerged, and by the time new plans were prepared for the invasion of India and an attack on Australia, the Allies had revived. They had swiftly learnt the lessons to be learned from the collapse of South-East Asia, and in late 1942 were able to check decisively, the next Japanese onslaught. From then on the British in Burma under the command of Lord Mountbatten, and the U.S.A., led by Admiral Nimitz and General MacArthur on the wide expanse of the Pacific passed over to the offensive. They were to push back the Japanese, in jungle and naval battle, until in 1945, shortly before a victorious British Army in Burma was to land in Malaya, and as a vast U.S. force was assembling to invade Japan itself, two atomic bombs were dropped by American airmen on Hiroshima and Nagasaki in Japan. This hastened the collapse of the Japanese war spirit at home, and precipitated a surrender on the August 14th.[8]

This surrender came a bare few weeks before the British were to land again in Malaya, and the re-occupation, although bloodless,

[8] The formal surrender agreements were signed in Tokyo Bay on the 2nd September.

followed the accelerated pattern of that plan, troops landing at Penang on the 3rd September, at Singapore on the 5th, while the main landing parties went ashore on the invasion beaches between Port Dickson and Port Swettenham on the 9th. It was not until the end of the month, however, that the peninsula was fully reoccupied: a fateful interregnum, as it appeared later.

It has been said, that the Japanese, during their period as masters of the peninsula, "had behaved with great brutality, and the period of their occupation had been one of shortages and hardship."[9] In Malaya the people who suffered most, once the British soldiers and civilians had been marched off to prisoner of war and internment camps, were the Chinese. Japan referred to its area of conquest as the Greater East Asia Co-prosperity Sphere, and although in other parts of South-East Asia, such as Burma, the Philippines and Indonesia, a semblance of power was in due course handed over to the locals, and the independence of their countries proclaimed, from the first Malaya was governed as a direct Colony of Japan.[10] Singapore (or Syonan as it was renamed) was administered separately, but by the military. Its rule was harsh.

A large scale massacre of Chinese in Singapore was organised a few days after the surrender, and throughout the years of occupation the *Tekkikan* (Japanese secret service), the *Kempeitai* (the army espionage service), the police and the garrison army were interrogating, torturing and killing Chinese suspected of anti-Japanese acts or opinions.[11] They won little support either by this, or by the reverse of the medal, when they dragged out of retirement the aged Lim Boon Keng, ordered him to form a committee of prominent Chinese, and instructed it to raise 50 million dollars with which to pledge the support and co-operation of the Chinese throughout Malaya in the war aims of the Japanese. After this had been achieved, by June 1942, and presented to

---

[9] F. S. V. Donnithorne, *British Military Administration in the Far East* (HMSO, 1956), p. 156.

[10] Excluding Kedah, Perlis, Kelantan and Trengganu, which were ceded to complacent Thailand by a treaty of the 20th August, 1943.

[11] For a graphic account of this, see *Malaya Upside Down*, by Chin Kee Onn (Singapore, 1946).

General Yamashita, the Japanese used the Overseas Chinese Association (the organisation which had been established to raise the money), as a useful channel of contact. It played a most difficult role with considerable success.

Quickly the effect of being shut off from the outside world was felt in the Malayan Peninsula, and particularly in Singapore. Food of any kind became extremely scarce, and the Japanese attempted to establish colonies of Singapore people in various parts of the peninsula. A Chinese colony was established at Endau, in north-east Johore; at Bahau in Negri Sembilan for Eurasians and Catholics; and on Bintang Island for Malays and Indians. All were unsuccessful. Hundreds died, and no one who survived remembers his days there without a shudder. But whether in the colonies or in the towns, the two characteristics of the occupation remained: economic hardship and Japanese brutality, and their attempts at indoctrination, through the primary schools, were not successful.

Japan and China had been at war since 1937, and its brutality can be explained (although never justified), by the hostility shown by the Chinese in Malaya towards the Japanese from long before that date, and by the fact that Chinese communist guerilla forces were operating in the jungles of the peninsula. Similarly, its harsh treatment of European internees, and its use of prisoners-of-war on the infamous Siam railway, where thousands died, showed quite clearly that it was a power that fought to hold South-East Asia by standards unacceptable to the West. Nevertheless it was war, man's greatest blunder, and the European in Malaya, who had fought that war, suffered with the Chinese and Eurasians.

The Indians and Malays in Malaya however received different treatment, for the Japanese looked on the former as possible allies in the government of India, and on the latter as probable allies in the government of Malaya, and they were cultivated as friends, rather than whipped as enemies.

As tension in East Asia mounted during 1941, and as units of the Indian Army began arriving in Malaya, the Japanese had sought to establish contact with them through Indian agents. Among the more notable of Indian political refugees who had sought asylum in Japan was Rash Behari Bose, who as a youth had attempted in 1912 to assassinate the Viceroy, and who was protected in Tokyo by the powerful hand of the Black Dragon Society. During 1941 he secured the agreement of the Japanese that Indians in territories occupied by the Japanese would not be treated as enemy subjects, and that an Indian National Army would be formed from surrendered soldiers who would be organised to liberate their country.

In Thailand a number of agents, led by Swami Satyananda Puri and Pritam Singh, were infiltrating into the advanced units of the Indian Divisions in Malaya, and when the Japanese smashed into them, on 12th December, a number quickly surrendered and co-operated with the Japanese in forming the nucleus of the INA. Chief of these was Captain Mohan Singh, and while Pritam Singh formed branch after branch of the civilian Indian Independence League, Captain Mohan Singh (or General as he became), had established the 1st Brigade of the Indian National Army even before Singapore had fallen, and some units actually participated in its capture.[12]

Within a few months of the surrender, almost half of the Indian prisoners-of-war, 20,000 Sikhs and Hindus out of 45,000, had joined the INA, many merely to enjoy the better food and the liberty denied to the Ghurka and Muslim Indians who refused to volunteer, others out of a desire to participate in what they felt then would be the liberation of India. Under Japanese encouragement a Conference was held in Bangkok in June 1942, presided over by Rash Behari Bose, at which it was decided to raise an Army from Indians all over South-East Asia. In the attempts by Mohan Singh to keep this INA free of Japanese control, however, in order to prevent it from becoming a puppet force, a thorough disillusionment of Japanese intentions spread throughout the movement, and upon Mohan Singh's arrest in December the INA was disbanded. Rash Behari Bose proved quite unequal to the task of maintaining enthusiasm in the Independence League and fell from favour. The Japanese then

---

[12] D. H. James, *The Rise and Fall of the Japanese Empire* (London, 1951), p. 212.

secured from Germany the erstwhile rival of Nehru and ex-President of Congress, the fiery Subhas Chandra Bose.[13] In July 1943 he arrived in Singapore to revitalise the Indian Independence League, forming it, in fact, into a Provisional Government of Free India, and to have the INA built up to the strength of two divisions, with a third division in the making.

These divisions, recruited very largely in Malaya, were moved to Burma. The 1st Division went in 1943, and Subhas Chandra Bose went with it to follow it, so he thought, into India. Units of the 1st Division assisted in the February offensive of the Japanese in Arakan, and some advance troops entered India; but only momentarily, for the reverses inflicted on the Japanese necessitated a general retreat, and the INA Division was virtually eliminated by infuriated Indian troops. This same fate did not befall the 2nd INA Division, for it came to Burma later, and after it was attacked in January and March 1945 it surrendered *en masse*. Bose flew back to Malaya to inspect the 3rd Division, and then in June 1945 he died in an air crash on Formosa, while flying to Japan.

Was Bose a patriot, or a traitor; i.e. statesman or a quisling? He had tried as far as possible to keep an independent status in his relations with the Japanese. He warned his men, as did Aung Sang, the Burmese Army leader, whom Lord Mountbatten, the Allied Commander, recognised after the war, to beware of Japanese treachery, and it seems clear that he was for Japan only to the extent that Japan was for India. Today, as a man who fought, however misguidedly, for his country's independence, his picture hangs in Hindu temples throughout India; and in Malaya he is remembered as the man who swayed mass rallies on the Singapore *padang*, as the leader who formed these divisions of Indians, and who kept the Japanese from insulting Indian women, and saw that their homes were not violated. Nehru himself came to Malaya, in March 1946, probably just a little thankful that Bose was a martyr, and not a rival, and his reception was overwhelming. Even if they had a nationalist spirit for India, and not for

---

13 For an outline of the career of this remarkable man, see Hugh Toye, *The Springing Tiger* (London, 1959).

Malaya, for that was yet to come, the Indians in the rubber estates and elsewhere in the peninsula had been woken up by Bose, and they were never to be the same again.

The Japanese adopted a policy somewhat similar, of encouragement and control, towards the Malays. Before the war Malay political attitudes had been divided. Firstly, there had been the rather conservative view of the Malay unofficial members on the Federated Legislative Council, which was shared by the Singapore Malay Union *(Kesatuan Melayu Singapura)*, the organisation formed in 1926 by Inche Mohammed Eunos, the first Malay unofficial on the Legislative Council of the Straits Settlements. This viewpoint was that of the educated Malay, anxious not to destroy the Malay social hierarchy which the British, by their intervention and occupation had recognised and preserved, but merely to secure more power for it. The educated Malays offered no firm opposition to British rule, but merely agitated gently for a share in that rule. On the other hand there was a socialist left-wing group of poor Malays and disgruntled Malay school teachers, who attacked the Malay upper classes for their support of the British, and who urged for immediate independence. This group, led by Ibrahim bin Yaakob, and Ishak bin Haji Mohammed, formed in 1937 the *Kesatuan Melayu Muda* (The Union of Malay Youths) in Kuala Lumpur. In 1940 the revolutionary activities of this small group led to the internment of their leaders, to be released immediately by the Japanese, well aware of their attitudes, with whom they then worked, in the manner of Aung Sang in Burma and his Thakin party, during the occupation.[14]

As with the Indians, however, the Malay KMM group became too pro-Malay and not sufficiently pro-Japanese to suit the interests of the new occupying force, and although an armed unit, the *Pembela Tanah Ayer* (PETA), was formed, with Ibrahim Yaakob at its head, KMM was dissolved. It was not until 1945 that under the new encouragement of the Japanese another civilian left-wing party, the *Kesatuan Raayat Indonesia Semenanjong* (KRIS) was formed, led by Dr. Burhanuddin and

[14] For this Malay pre-war political activity, see Radin Soenarno, *Journal, South-East Asian History,* vol. 1, no. 1, (Singapore, March 1960).

others. In August 1945 it discussed with the Indonesian leaders Sukarno and Hatta the possibility of the Malay Peninsula being incorporated into Indonesia. Sukarno had discussed independence with the Japanese and an independence declaration was due, but the collapse of Japan on the 10th August ruined left-wing hopes. On the return of the British all the leaders were arrested, and Malay leftish sentiment was suppressed for a decade.

This nationalist movement had never captured, during the war or before, the support of the mass of Malay peasantry, who accepted in most things the guidance of their aristocratic leaders, or the British District Officers. These Malay aristocrats were preserved in office during the occupation, and Japanese state governors even wore Malay dress to win their favour.[15] The Malay social structure and framework of life was generally supported, while the status of the Malay, if anything, was raised. As a result, no strong anti-Japanese action occurred, no Japanese Birch was murdered, while Malay co-operation with the Japanese, particularly at the beginning of the occupation, was marked.

For these two sections of the community then, although both became disillusioned by the Japanese, it was more the economic hardship of the occupation rather than any brutality, that explains their relief at the ending of the war, for if anything they had been more encouraged in those years than before. Their relief was shared by the mass of Chinese too, who had suffered brutality, and who had shared their economic hardships and shortages. All felt that the prison door was opening, and the world outside could be seen again.

One large group however did not share this simple, unalloyed happiness, and that was the so-called Malayan People's Anti-Japanese Army, the force that had been assembled in the jungles during the war by the Malayan Communist Party. Formed from the nucleus of a few small groups that had been armed and

---

[15] Japan administered the Malay States through a number of governors, civilians who took their orders from the Army Commander in Singapore. They were able to utilise the very great majority of the pre-war administrative staff, while special military forces, sponsored by the Japanese, also found little difficulty in securing Malay volunteers.

trained by the British in 1941–42, kept under control and steadily enlarged thereafter by the MCP and kept clear of any but the most trifling of clashes with the Japanese, the MPAJA attracted to itself all the rebellious and discontented elements of the country. By the nature of the Japanese rule these elements were almost invariably Chinese. They were methodically and continually indoctrinated with communist philosophy, a philosophy which included a belief, a determination, that Malaya was destined by their efforts to become a communist state. The MPAJA came out of the jungle 7,000 strong, determined to replace the colonial regime, and to translate its belief into action.[16]

The war indeed had effected here a transformation, as it had in many other aspects of Malayan life. However, there are no indications whatever to suggest that if the war had not occurred, the communist movement would even have created a major threat to the state. Yet by 1948 it felt strong enough, thanks very largely to the war, to challenge that state by an armed attempt to seize power. How had this movement been established? What were the reasons for its strength?

The history of communism in Malaya, so it is thought, does not precede the 1917 revolution in Russia, but followed the success of the communists there. After the formation in 1919 by Lenin of the Comintern—the organization charged with establishing communist parties and then states outside Russia—a few agents drifted into Singapore during the following few years. In 1923 the Comintern established its Far Eastern Bureau in Shanghai and deputed to it the cause of communism in East Asia. This Bureau was able to assist, during the 1920's in the formation of communist parties in Indo-China and Indonesia, while from 1923 until 1926 it was able to participate, with the Chinese Communist Party (formed in 1921) in the penetration of the Kuomintang, both in China and throughout South-East Asia as well.

In Malaya, however, the communists found that their message

---

[16] For a detailed account of the MPAJA from 1941 to 1945 see G. Z. Hanrahan, *The Communist Struggle in Malaya* (New York, 1954), pp. 31–45, and J. H. Brimmell, Communism in South-East Asia (London, 1959).

from Marx, and their anti-colonial programme, fell very largely on deaf ears. The Malays, who had found great personal contentment with their simple way of life, and who regarded the British not as oppressors but rather as teachers and advisers, were quite unmoved by a doctrine that seemed alien to their faith and their life. So too the Indians, who although they were attracted to the anti-colonial message which the Comintern deemed suitable for the basis of the Asian communist parties, nevertheless were well aware that their best interests in Malaya, where they enjoyed a standard of living higher than in India, were best safeguarded by two paternalistic governments, and not by any other. Even amongst the Chinese, strongly individualistic inside their clan, family or society framework, animated by a fierce determination to climb the economic ladder of success, the doctrine of Marx that everyone should stay at the bottom, was little appreciated except amongst the Hakka and Hailams. Both these South Chinese races were regarded by the great majority of Chinese as uncouth and inferior, and, as races fully aware of their inferior status, they were resentful and secretive. In China this had offered possibilities to the missionary, but in Malaya, with few wealthy men or valuable contacts to help them, these two races stayed at the bottom of the swaying, jostling ladder that led up to economic independence: a fertile ground for communism.[17]

In 1926 the communist agents in the KMT, working mainly in Hailam night schools, were able to form a Communist Youth League. After Chiang Kai Shek broke with the communists, and they were expelled from the KMT in 1927, the Nanyang Communist Party was formed, responsible, as its name implies, for Indonesia as well as Malaya. It languished. The communists in China had their hands full there, and the party did not concern itself particularly with this sluggish area full of inferior people as the Chinese considered, so in 1930 the NCP was dissolved. In its place in the same year the Malayan Communist Party was formed, and placed under the guidance not of the Chinese but

---

17 This is well brought out in L. W. Pye, *Guerilla Communism in Malaya* (Princeton, 1956), pp. 47–62.

of the Comintern, which opened a branch in Hong Kong, the Southern Bureau, to organise a Union of Soviet Republics in South-East Asia.

Although communist infiltration had been severely disrupted by the break with the Chinese Nationalists in 1927, and was for a time almost completely severed by swift and effective police swoops in Indo-China, Hong Kong and Singapore in 1931, two factors assisted in the slow growth of the Malayan Communist Party during the 1930's.

The party was able to exploit the anguish and misery caused by the world wide depression of the early thirties, and as tin mining was curtailed and controlled by and for Europeans, as rubber restriction was enforced by and for Europeans, and as many other avenues of economic advance narrowed or closed completely, the anti-colonial, anti-capitalist stand of the communists, and their promise of a better world for the workers under a different system, led to the formation of many new cells, with particular headway being made through the schools and the minute unions of Hakka and Hailam workers. As a result, industrial unrest, inevitable in any case in the circumstances, was intensified and made militant and bitter; although it is doubtful if communist leadership improved the lot of the Singapore worker in any way. It is even doubtful if the communists intended that it should. They were revolutionaries, not reformers of the capitalist system, and there are signs that as the world recovered from the depression, support for the communists began to wane. The high water mark was reached in 1935. Labour agitation amongst rubber tappers, tin miners and others reached serious proportions. It culminated in the Batu Arang strike in Selangor, when the communists closed down the coal mine and established a Soviet commune. Malay military units were used to smash this, and to retake the mine, and thereafter communist influence began to wane as conditions improved throughout Malaya.

In 1937 the Japanese attacked China, and the communists in Malaya were able to recover from their setbacks by enlisting to their aid that most powerful of emotions, patriotism. A movement based on love of China was safer than industrial work, for there was far less chance of deportation to China as a result (a terrible fate for communists, for it meant summary execution), and it was more effective, for the anti-Japanese, pro-China organisations which were formed attracted many thousands who otherwise would never have come near a communist meeting.

For some time the Party continued its anti-colonial activities as well, particularly in the Chinese schools, but from mid 1940, with a unified anti-Japanese attitude agreed upon between Nationalists and Communists in China, this was abandoned. In December 1941, when Japan invaded Malaya, the Secretary-General of the Party, Lai Teck, pledged to the Colonial Government the assistance of the Party (which perhaps numbered 5,000), and in Singapore seven groups of guerrillas were hurriedly trained, a total of 165 men, to operate behind the Japanese lines.

This nucleus, based originally in Perak, Selangor and North Johore, fought during 1942 for bare survival, it established during 1943–1944 a strong civilian feeder system, trained during 1944–1945 in ever increasing numbers on makeshift parade grounds, indoctrinated the flow of recruits, stored the equipment dropped from Ceylon based bombers, and grew to become the 7,000 determined, fanatical, ignorant young men and women that in early September 1945 marched out of the jungle.

In that month, in the hiatus between the Japanese collapse and the arrival of the British military administration, the Communist Party took over the government in large areas of the peninsula, and savagely settled some old scores amongst the Malay police and others who had worked under the Japanese. The assumption of political authority by the Chinese, and their lack of respect for the Malays, produced an immediate and severe deterioration of race relations. Throughout the twentieth century the two races had lived side by side, scarcely touching each other; complementary, not competitive. The political power exercised in September 1945 however, and the brutal manner of the communist vengeance was the last straw to people mentally and physically sick after four years of war, and Malay armed reaction was vicious.

In Batu Pahat in Johore, for example, the Malay kampongs, led by Penghulu Salleh, carried out a series of massacres of Chinese villagers. Salleh, a Sufi saint, acted in complete opposition to the non-militant, pacifist teachings of his faith, yet he was able, so strong was the religious-political feeling of his followers, to lead hysterical raids throughout the Batu Pahat area. Similarly on Pangkor Island, and in various parts of Perak, in Trengganu and elsewhere, the seizure of political power by the Chinese was followed by savage Malay retribution, which the communists were quite unable to combat.

The swift action of the British Military Administration, reinforced by the responsible attitude of community leaders, such as Onn bin Jaafar, saved Malaya from the edge of the pit of communal anarchy.[18] The riots and massacres ceased. The BMA then rapidly attempted in every way possible to return the country to normal. The MPAJA was disbanded, and its members returned to civilian life. The prisoners-of-war and Japanese were repatriated, the schools re-opened, and the public services revived. All this and much more the 'banana colonels' of the BMA set in motion; yet when the military administration ended in 1946, all Malaya heaved a sigh of relief, for although it had helped Malaya up to its feet again, it had been the end of a long war, the morale and the morals of the army had deteriorated considerably, and as the *Straits Times* noted of the official history of it, "the word 'corruption' is not in Mr. Donnison's index. It should be." And again, "That the BMA was generally felt to come out badly in comparison with the Japanese in their respect for private property is a sorrowful and true indictment."[19]

With its passing, Malaya stopped looking backwards and prepared for peace ahead; instead, within two years there was to be another war.

---

[18] Dato Onn bin Jaafar, who became a national figure a year later with the formation of the United Malay National Organization, was the District Officer of Batu Pahat at this time. He played a dramatic part in stopping the rampage of Penghulu Salleh.

[19] *Straits Times*, 26th November 1956.

14. MERDEKA

The war over, it took some time for the world to become stable again. It needed several years for the changes created by the war to become clearly recognisable and acceptable as the new order of things. The changes that had been initiated in South-East Asia, for example, were not readily or immediately discernible to many. The most significant change, in the mental attitude of the people, brought a new universal demand for national independence. This was ignored by the imperial powers, as typifying (as before the war), merely the viewpoint of a minority. India and Burma however led the re-assessment, and by 1948 their independence was a fact. In Indonesia and Indo-China it was denied, and in each country began a war for independence.

In Malaya too it took several years to clarify beyond a shadow of a doubt the feeling of the people, particularly of the Malays, for independence, although the first strong evidence of this came shortly after the Japanese surrender. During the war a Malayan Planning Unit of the Colonial Office, formed in July 1943, had recommended that the pre-war mess of initials (SS, FMS, UFMS) should be abolished, and that excluding only Singapore, a single Malayan administrative unit should be constructed; that it should be made a colony, with the legal independence of the Protected States replaced by a new allegiance to the British crown; and that all who lived in this country should be the citizens of it. These recommendations had been accepted by the British Government and in October 1945 Sir Harold MacMichael was sent out to secure the signatures of the Sultans to treaties whereby they relinquished their sovereignty.

He acted as swiftly as Swettenham in 1895. In a few weeks every Sultan had agreed without demur to his state becoming a British Colony. In view of the later uproar over this from their followers, one must remember that the war had just ended, that the Sultans had sat out that war with their position maintained by the Japanese, and that with war trials under way in Singapore the continuation of the Sultanate in many cases was uncertain and debatable. It seemed scarcely the time to argue or even to discuss. They signed.

No such inhibitions restrained their followers. They had been offered no time to consider the implications of the changes before MacMichael came, as the announcement of the decision to form a Malayan Union, as it was called, was not made in London until shortly before he arrived in Malaya. But by the time he left, in January 1946, the Malays had realised that by the formation of the Malayan Union, and by the introduction of the liberal citizenship proposals, there would be a basic change in the peninsula, a change moreover highly detrimental to them.

To them the Protected Malay State was more than a name: it was where the Malay was protected. The Malayan Union meant the removal of that protection. The citizenship proposals and the cession to Britain both implied the end of the pre-war Malay State, and the creation of a Colony where the Malay was merely another inhabitant, alongside the Chinese and Indian. There was a swift surge of protest, aimed in particular not at the sultans' surrender of sovereignty but at the proposals which gave Malayan citizenship to all who had been born in the peninsula, or who had lived there for at least the previous ten years.

This sudden outburst of emotion caught the British by surprise. It was difficult for them to believe that the Malays, who for so long had regarded the British as kindly teachers or policemen, and had rarely questioned their actions, were violently opposed to the changes that they had introduced. This opposition was made very clear, however, by Onn bin Jaafar.

The Malayan Union proposals had been made in October 1945. Scarcely a month later, Onn, the fifty year old District Officer of Batu Pahat in Johore, and son of a famous Mentri Besar, had formed the Malay League of Johore, and it was this Unfederated State of Johore that was to spearhead the opposition. By January Onn had formed the Peninsula Malay Movement of Johore, a swelling voice against the granting of citizenship to non-Malays and the cession of the States to Britain. In March Onn presided over a pan-Malayan meeting of Malay organizations, and in May 1946 he was elected president of the United Malay National

Organization (UMNO).[1] Here for the first time had been created a mass pan-Malayan political party; and from that date until Merdeka in 1957, and beyond, the major theme in Malayan affairs has been this broad, powerful thrust by the Malays organized in UMNO for Malay national power.

Faced by this unprecedented opposition, which was reported very accurately by a two-man Parliamentary delegation that came out in mid 1946, the British began realistic negotiations with UMNO. A successful compromise was achieved, whereby the British aims of creating one state and of establishing a strong central government, as well as the Malay objectives of maintaining the legal independence of the States and of restricting citizenship very largely to Malays, were achieved. The Malayan Union, which had been introduced on the 1st April 1946 (and whose citizenship proposals had never been operative), was dissolved, and after the signing of fresh treaties with the Sultans, returning them their sovereignty, a new Federation of Malaya was established on the 1st February 1948.

This was a Federation in name only. It included all the prewar States and Settlements, except Singapore, but to none of those States was any real administrative power given. The central government, built up in Kuala Lumpur after the BMA ended in March 1946, was continued. Malayan Union or Federation of Malaya; only the titles were different, for in essence it remained administratively the same, the British government of Malaya, even if, in the Federation, the Malay States remained Malay States, and did not become a British colony.

This British government, and indeed the whole country, was soon plunged into an even graver crisis than that precipitated by the Malayan Union proposals. In that same year and within a few months of the formation of the Federation, the Malayan Communist Party, in June 1948, rose in armed revolt. The Emergency had begun.

The Communists had benefited considerably from the confusion of the immediate post-war years. In Malaya, even more

[1] For a detailed study of this, see Ishak bin Tadin, *Dato Onn, 1946–1951*, (JSEAH, vol. 1, no. 1, Singapore, March 1960).

than in most other parts of the world, the grave dislocations caused by the war had been redressed but slowly. The shortages of nearly everything, the blackmarkets, the high costs or inaccessibility of new equipment and necessities of all kinds, had only slowly diminished. A new Labour Government in Britain, opposed to much of what it considered in general terms imperial, was relinquishing all claims to power in India and Burma, and hastening considerably the administrative hand-over in Africa and elsewhere. In Malaya it encouraged the formation of hitherto scarcely tolerated trade unions, and attempted a clean sweep of the colonial administration. The communists profited both from the internal difficulties and the external encouragement to indigenous development, and as the only organised body in being, quickly seized power in the trade union movement.

As the most vigorous and militant section of the working class, the immediate effect of their power, by organising a large number of strikes, was to raise rapidly the wage structure of many people; but as the immediate post-war unbalance was redressed, the communist leadership then became increasingly at variance with the best interests of the workers. The communists aimed at overthrowing the capitalist régime, not at making the workers more contented partners in the régime, and as 1947 gave way to 1948 their hold over the unions began to slacken. Government action, in insisting that all office bearers (except the secretary) should have at least three years experience in the industry they represented, and in breaking up the Pan Malayan Federation of Trade Unions (which the MCP dominated), gave strength to the genuine labour movement that was emerging. The Singapore Harbour Board strike in January 1948, in which the communists struck in clear opposition to the workers' advantage, was perhaps the turning point.

Nevertheless, this was the moment taken for revolt. No major decision such as this of course can be taken by any local communist party, then or now, for all are controlled from abroad, and probably it was at a Conference of South Asian Communists in Calcutta in February 1948 where the instructions were given, not merely to the Malayans but to all the other communist parties in South-East Asia: to resort to arms. These instructions were based more on an appreciation of Russia's needs than on any local assessment of the situation. However they were obeyed blindly and fanatically, and Malaya was plunged into war again.

Chin Peng, who in early 1948 had replaced Lai Teck, the discredited war time leader, as head of the MCP, vanished into the jungle with an estimated 6,000–8,000 soldiers, assisted by double that number of more or less willing civilian informers and food suppliers. He immediately introduced a wave of terror which could not be suppressed. From large concealed camps groups of well armed communists attacked mines, estates and villages without mercy, and, for some time, without fear. Yet these platoons of soldiers, concealed in every State in Malaya, never advanced beyond this. At the outset, in June 1948, the regular armed forces of the communists consisted of fifteen regiments, each of approximately 400 men. No regiment ever seized and held any sizeable settled area. It hit hard and disappeared, depending on terror to overthrow the state. By terrorism alone, by perpetuating atrocities mainly against civilians, it hoped to achieve victory, and while it came to grips if necessary with the police, it did its utmost to avoid attacking the Army. From the writings of its own leaders such as Mao Tse Tung and Lenin, it should have known that no rebellion has ever succeeded by the sole use of these means. Terrorism can assist guerilla warfare, but if success is to be won, the guerillas in their turn must in the end play merely a minor role to a main revolutionary army. This remained far beyond the reach of the communists.

Nevertheless, the suppression of these trained and disciplined platoons and regiments, with their civilian organisation feeding and recruiting for them, was a most difficult task. Even though it was clear by the end of 1948 that the rising had failed in its principal aims, the steady flow of discontented Chinese into the jungle continued, to remain the most perturbing feature of the whole Emergency. Twelve years of ceaseless action were necessary to break the revolt, and to bring peace again to Malaya.

At the beginning, much of this action was inadequate and inept. There were very few troops in Malaya—two newly formed Malay regiments, three British and six Gurkha—and the Federation Police, on whom fell the full brunt of this military rising, had been non-existent two years before, and it was still in the early stages of assembly and organisation. Suddenly it was faced with life and death problems of a military nature quite beyond its experience. It had to enlarge immediately, and to undertake, with new men, undreamt of responsibilities. The military likewise had to devise new methods of attack and defence, and both had to seek the co-operation of a civilian administration barely recovering from the previous war, and attempting to recapture the attitude of the pre-war days; and all this in the midst of a plural society of Malays newly arisen and discontented, Indians celebrating the independence of India, and Chinese watching China turn communist.

For several years the war against the communists was fought only by the armed forces of the administration, led by the British. As with the war against Japan (although not to the same extent), the rest of Malaya watched. It disapproved of the communists, but at the outset it did very little to help, and the struggle was left very largely to the British. The British fought the war as they have fought the opening stages of nearly all their wars, by muddle, defeat, and improvisation; as atrocity followed atrocity, and as no end to the darkness ever seemed possible.

The turning point in this horror of the jungle came with the appointment of General Sir Gerald Templer in January 1952 to replace the murdered Sir Henry Gurney as High Commissioner of a despondent Malaya. With Gurney's murder Malayan morale, low after four years of an apparently unsuccessful struggle to eliminate the communists, had sunk to new depths. With the arrival of Templer in Malaya however, as with the arrival of Montgomery in Africa, there was no looking back. But as with the arrival of Montgomery, neither could have done much had not the ground-work already been prepared.

In particular the 500,000 Chinese squatters who had eked out an independent existence scattered along the jungle edge, and who, one and all, had fed or otherwise assisted the communists, had been brought together and placed in 'New Villages' behind wire.[2] At one stroke the communists had lost their greatest food

[2] For a study of life in these 'New Villages', see Han Suyin *And The Rain My Drink* (London, 1956).

supply as a result of the implementation between 1949–1952 of the Briggs Plan, as this resettlement was known after its originator, Lt. Gen. Briggs, Director General of Operations in 1950. An entirely new character had been given to Malaya by the formation of nearly 600 Chinese villages, offering a tremendous opportunity to create Malayans out of the hitherto solitary and indifferent Chinese.[3]

In addition 10,000 discontented Chinese had been repatriated to China, removing a cankerous sore from the body politic. The army had been strengthened, to number, by 1952, 42,500 men, four times more than in 1948. Home Guard and Kampong Guard units had been raised, and Federation Police had been greatly, almost dangerously, expanded. What was lacking however was the will to win. Without this, all else was in vain. Templer, the first High Commissioner to be vested both with supreme military and civilian power, was given all possible authority. He used it with energy and brilliance, and in two years he brought about a transformed Malaya.

Templer's appointment had been made by a new Conservative Government in London headed by Winston Churchill, and Templer was able to utilise his support to great effect. Equipment of all kinds, such as helicopters for quick attacks in the deep jungle, more efficient radio sets, and automatic rifles, poured in. But it was Templer who gave a new spirit to the troops, a new direction to their planning and a new vigour to their leadership. Militarily his two years (1952–1954), were marked by a series of highly successful operations, and by the time he left large areas of jungle were cleared of all communists.

Brilliant though his military activities proved to be, Templer was far more than a professional soldier, and it is perhaps in his civilian campaign, in his political, economic and social measures (to which his second year of office was increasingly devoted), that he succeeded in establishing beyond doubt, in the minds of nearly all Malaya, not merely that the communist revolt had

---

[3] These 'New Villages' also offer many serious problems, and if mistakes made in the nineteenth century in the Chinese settlements are to be avoided, they need to be studied intensively.

failed, but also that it had been a revolt against Malayans and not merely against the British in Malaya. As he himself said, "the answer lies not in pouring more soldiers into the jungle, but rests in the hearts and minds of the Malayan people."[4]

Of all his measures, it may be that his willingness to replace the wholly nominated Legislative Assembly by the introduction of Federal-wide elections, perhaps the boldest step he could take, was the most successful, for by so doing he accepted completely the feeling of the great mass of non-communists in the peninsula, and kept within constitutional bounds their desire for *merdeka*. To have kept an iron restraining hand on the political advance of the country until the communist revolt was over would have been to encourage apathy towards the struggle, indifference as to who won, and an odious comparison between colonialism and communism. By perceiving that the movement for independence was genuine, by recognising that anti-colonialism was not necessarily pro-communist, Templer was far wiser than many of his advisers; but that, no doubt, was why they had remained mere advisers.

Among the influential groups pressing Templer for elections had been not merely UMNO (which had remained in being, after securing the abandonment of the Malayan Union, largely in order to prosecute its new objective of *merdeka* or independence), but also the body of Chinese formed in February 1949, the Malayan Chinese Association. Previous to this the Chinese had never been able to come together in any mass Malayan-centred organisation, for their divisions had been too deep to permit it. Divided between locally born and immigrants, divided educationally, economically and linguistically, the Chinese in Malaya, as in South-East Asia as a whole, had never become a community able to sponsor and sustain a mass organisation. Even the KMT before the war, with all the attraction it generated amongst the immigrants with its patriotism for China, and thus able to break many barriers, never became a mass party. Yet at last these divisions were bridged, and the Chinese ignorance of, and in-

---

[4] Quoted by L. A. Mills, *Malaya: A Political and Economic Appraisal* (Minnesota, 1958), p. 63.

difference to parliamentary politics was overcome by the MCA.

The MCA had come into being largely through the work of Tan Cheng Lock, the distinguished Straits Chinese leader. Born in 1883 into a long established Malacca family, and beginning life as a school teacher, he participated in the establishment of the rubber industry, eventually becoming the wealthy director of a large number of rubber and industrial companies. Unlike many of his associates however, he devoted his interests not merely to economic gain, but also to public service. Assisted no doubt by his English education, Tan Cheng Lock became an outstanding leader of the Straits Chinese, taking over the mantle from Lim Boon Keng. He was appointed to the Straits Settlements Legislative Council in 1923, and became a persistent agitator for liberal reform. He urged the Malayanisation of the Civil Service, the abolition of the official majority in the Council, the use of Malayan Asians on the Executive Council, and made the first call, in 1926, for the creation of a united, self-governing, Malayan nation. In this he moved above his championship merely of the Straits Chinese and assumed the role of a Malayan statesman; and although he retired in 1935, to spend four years in Europe, his prestige maintained him, and when he returned to Malacca after the war, he assumed without serious challenge, the leadership of the awakening Chinese. Tan Cheng Lock lamented that political organisations had of necessity to be communal, at that stage of Malaya's development but he felt that in the face of the strong post-war Malay *merdeka* movement there had to be one organisation to protect the interests of the Chinese. He spoke repeatedly on this theme, urging the Chinese to sink their differences.

Tan however was a philosopher-statesman, and although accepted by the Chinese as a sage, in direct keeping with Chinese tradition, and able, to some extent, to bridge the cultural divide of his people (and in this he is reminiscent of Smuts of South Africa), he was not a good political organiser. Here the ability of such men as Leong Yew Koh and Lee Hau-Shik proved useful. Determined to create an anti-Communist Chinese Party, a determination made more impelling by the outbreak of the Emergency and the suspicion it thrust on the Chinese, the MCA was formed in February 1949, and Tan Cheng Lock was elected first president of an organisation which rose, within three years to over 300,000 members. Before it dissipated itself, to reveal again the still remaining apathy and the lack of political cohesion amongst many of the Chinese in Malaya, the MCA had assisted considerably in the movement towards *merdeka,* particularly by its association and collaboration with UMNO.

Tan Cheng Lock found that he had much in common both with Templer and with Tengku Abdul Rahman, the Kedah Malay who replaced Onn in 1951 as the leader of UMNO. At that stage Abdul Rahman was little known; but within ten years he was to become one of the oustanding characters in South-East Asia. Born in 1903, one of the sons of the Sultan of Kedah, he went to school firstly in Bangkok (in conformity with Kedah tradition), and then to the Penang Free School, joining it on its centenary in 1916. Between 1920 and 1930 he was in England, where after graduating from Cambridge he tried unsuccessfully to secure a London law degree. For the next fifteen years (1930–1945) he was one of the most popular District Officers ever to work in Kedah. He was popular with the people, but not with his relatives, the ruler, the court and the administration generally, for he was too much opposed to feudalism and colonialism to be their favourite.

After the war he went back to London, and in 1948, while Dato Onn was leading a thoroughly alarmed Malay community, he at last secured his law degree. Working with him was Abdul Razak, twenty years younger, destined to be his right hand man. Both returned to Malaya, to follow with intense interest the political developments. The Tengku moved to the Federal Attorney-General's Office, but he found that his legal training had forced him into an impossible position, for he increasingly felt that he should be an active participant in politics, a role which as a government magistrate was denied him. He made his attitude very clear however, and his air of authority and leadership, and his honesty and experience suggested him as the successor to Onn when he resigned to form his ill-fated all races, non-communal Independence of Malaya Party.

"The Tengku", as he soon became known, rallied the Malays who in late 1951 were demoralised at the loss of the mercurial Onn.

He led them at a pace they could follow, and in a manner they appreciated. His speeches echoed their sentiments; his actions and way of life, in public and in private, portrayed a leader who sought the happiness of his people, and of a man who, despite the strong mindedness necessary in a political leader, could unashamedly but modestly enjoy the simple pleasures of life appreciated also by his followers. With Tengku Abdul Rahman, Abdul Razak and Khir bin Jahari, UMNO became much more mature and sure of itself as it pressed for more Malay education, for elections, and for independence.

The possibility of this latter goal being achieved was first realised, perhaps, in 1952, when the local branches of UMNO and MCA came together under the guidance of Lee Hau Shik to arrange an electoral truce for the first Kuala Lumpur Municipal Elections. Lee's proposal, that an alliance be formed, at first met with opposition from other MCA leaders, but he persisted, and the UMNO-MCA Alliance won by such a clear majority that the device was extended throughout the country. With the two major parties collaborating throughout 1952, the fears of communal strife, of a country divided between Malays and Chinese, died down, and the pressure on Templer and the British Government increased accordingly.

Templer rose to the occasion. A committee of the Legislative Council was appointed in June 1953 to draw up plans for Federal election in 1955. Offered a spate of suggestions by hurriedly formed parties, its report, submitted in February 1954, reflected the conservative attitude of many of the Legislative Councillors who compiled it: a cautious introduction of forty-four elected members into a chamber of ninety-two, with the date for the elections left vague, to be held presumably when the jungle war was over.

To Abdul Rahman and Tang Cheng Lock this was inadequate. Templer, with rare courage, agreed. The practice of permitting Colonial Legislatures to find their feet first with an elected minority, and then advancing by slow stages to a majority and then to a fully elected House had been an axiom of British colonial administration for over one hundred years. This Templer ignored. He rejected the recommendations of the Report, and, with the consent of the rulers, announced in April 1954 shortly before his departure that there would be fifty-two elected seats (that is, an immediate majority), and that elections would take place the following year, 1955, communist insurrection or not.

Throughout 1954 Malaya began to come alive. The promise of elections, the prospect of an independent life awakened everyone. There was a stirring, far deeper than politics, and innumerable facets of a cultural life, long dulled under a colonial régime, began to shine. There was a somewhat self-conscious scrutiny taken of Malayan architecture, and attempts were made, through Rural and Industrial Authority (RIDA) formed in 1950, to develop arts and crafts, particularly along the east coast. Malay literature, stimulated by Indonesia, began to flourish, while it became gradually the custom for support to be given to Malayan painters. The works of such artists as Teng, Hussein and Soo Pieng became well known and an ever increasing number of successful exhibitions showed that here was the beginning of a renaissance. Two years later the dominant Malay element in this was gathered together in a highly successful three day *Pesta* or Festival. In education too the government began to meet the people's wishes. The University in Singapore (established in 1950) rapidly expanded, while new schools were built all over Malaya.

This new independent life was resisted by some, but encouraged by others; none however were able to ignore it, for everyone felt the stirring and beginning of a belief in Malaya. The year 1955 was entered with a determination that swept away nearly all support from the communists and, except in the dominated sections of Johore, they were pushed to one side, as an almost extraneous element in Malayan life. Nevertheless, it took until 1960 to eliminate them.

Economically it was a bad year, and 1955 was only a little better, with the price of rubber, increasingly threatened by the American synthetic product, recovering but little from its collapse which followed the Korean War boom. The rubber trees of Malaya had become very old. The various restriction agreements, government ban on new planting and the war had stopped expansion for several decades, and there was a national need for both new trees and re-planting of the better stock developed by the Rubber Research Institute. Tin, still the other great revenue earner, also experienced a depressed market, while the long term anxiety of a complete exhaustion of tin land, had come appreciably closer.

Nevertheless, by general world standards of the mid twentieth century, Malaya lived well. There were very many poor people, but there was no starvation. The working community and the growing middle class were appreciably better off economically than ten years before and very much better off than fifty years before; there were doubts as to whether they were as well off politically and educationally as they could hope to be. Educationally there were moves aimed at producing national schools, which whether their bias was English, Malay or Chinese, nevertheless would produce young graduates with interests, languages and loyalties not markedly dissimilar from each other. The ultimate aim, of a single educational system which would break down the plural society, and by which multi-racial Malaya would be united by a knowledge of Malay, came increasingly to the fore.

Templer had been supported in his determination to keep abreast of the Malay *merdeka* movement by Oliver Lyttleton, Conservative Colonial Minister, and it was Lyttleton who persisted in moving the Colony of Singapore along the same road. Singapore had been excluded both from the Malayan Union in 1946, and from the Federation of Malaya in 1948, partly because its Chinese population when combined with the Chinese on the peninsula would have made the Chinese numerically the largest race, and this was displeasing to the Malays, partly because it would have imperilled its free port status, and partly because it was a British base of great importance. These reasons for exclusion could have been countered and quite probably Singapore could have become part of the Union or the Federation had there been strong pressure by Singapore leaders then; but there was none whatsoever, and both the British and the people of Singapore lost an opportunity of redressing Swettenham's blunder.

The Straits Settlements Legislative Council shrank to become the Singapore Legislative Council, to jostle uncomfortably with the City Council, and a timid attempt was made to introduce democracy into its hallowed chamber. Six seats were given away for election in 1948, with another three in 1951. Over half of the few who voted were the politically conscious English-educated Indians. The Chinese did not bother. It made no difference: they were still governed by the British.

But the experiment had to continue. Faced by the growth of radical attitudes, the British policy of concession and retreat, rather than of resistance and denial (as with the Dutch and the French), was continued. Its policy was to protect its investment in Singapore as in Malaya. This had been its underlying motivating force throughout its régime. By 1953 there were many who thought that this policy could be gained by following the stand of Hong Kong, where the Union Jack was nailed to the mast and all apparently was flourishing. There were many others however, who pointed to the difference of location, and of social temper, between the two. Lyttleton was flexible enough to appreciate the difference, and to grasp the feeling of Singapore, and in July 1953 he had a committee appointed, under the chairmanship of Sir G. Rendal, to investigate the question of constitutional change in Singapore. As with its Federal counterpart, it too reported in February 1954. Its recommendations entailed almost full home rule. A thirty-two man chamber was to have twenty-five seats elected, with almost full powers passing to the leader of the majority party. As in the Federation elections were listed for the following year, 1955.

These elections followed very different courses. In the Federation of Malaya the UMNO-MCA Alliance swept all before it. Very largely due to the Malay vote (1,100,000 out of 1,280,000 actual voters), it captured 51 out of the 52 seats. UMNO had become, within a few years, almost as powerful and almost as monolithic as the Indian Congress Party, and Abdul Rahman had become a beloved father symbol to his people. He pressed for complete independence. After interviewing, and rejecting Chin Peng (in November 1955), he flew to London early the following year. Here he found he was beating his fist on an open door. The British agreed to hand over power as quickly as practicable. August 1957, just two years after the first elections, was fixed as the date for *merdeka*.

In Singapore however, events did not run so smoothly. The 1955 elections saw the success of a moderate left-wing body, the Labour Front, led by the lawyer David Marshall. However, he had won only ten seats, and to secure a majority he formed a coalition with the three seats of the Malay Union Alliance. These, together with the five nominated seats that automatically supported the government, gave him eighteen out of thirty-two; a bare minimum.

The precarious position of the government was made no stronger by the action of the militantly inclined Chinese schoolboys who rioted that year; by the growing support for a better disciplined People's Action Party led by Lee Kuan Yew; and by the failure of Marshall, at talks in London in 1956, to secure a promise similar to that given to Abdul Rahman for further constitutional advance. Marshall however then resigned the leadership, and was replaced by the trade unionist Lim Yew Hock, who managed to remove some of the difficulties, and to secure in 1957 the promise of complete internal self-government for Singapore in 1959, with the abolition of all nominated seats and of the vestiges of control by the Governor. The Legislative Chamber of 51 seats was to be fully elected, and apart from defence and foreign affairs, which were to be in the hands of an Internal Security Council, where Britain and the Federation were also represented, it was to have full sovereign powers. Lim Yew Hock however was not able to enjoy the fruits of his negotiations, for when the 1959 elections were held, the victors were the PAP which became the first government of the State of Singapore. It immediately faced with vigour the problems created by a rapidly increasing population and an economy still largely commercial and non-industrial in character; while it proclaimed that its major political objective was independence to be secured by merger with Malaya.

Meanwhile in the Federation of Malaya, the agreement secured by Tengku Abdul Rahman for independence had led to the formation in 1956 of a Commonwealth Constitutional Commission.[5]

---

[5] Its members were Lord Reith and Sir Ivor Jennings (Great Britain), Sir W. McKell (Australia), Mr. B. Malik (India) and Mr. Abdul Hamid (Pakistan).

Although composed entirely of non-Malayans, the constitution it produced shortly before independence, was evolved after intimate consultations with the British, with UMNO, and with other Malayan bodies, and in several respects it incorporated uniquely Malayan features. This absorption and quiet adaptation of external influences is of course characteristic of the peninsula throughout its history. It created a royal Head of State, for example, a *Yang di-Pertuan Agong,* to be elected by and from the nine Sultans. This was an obvious adaption of the procedure in Negri Sembilan, which elected its *Yang di-Pertuan Besar*. It preserved a nominated upper house, it safeguarded Malay privileges and it wrote into the constitution many of the restrictions that the Emergency had imposed on what both non-communist Asia and Europe now regard as traditional individual liberties.[6] Power rested with the fully elected Lower House of 104 members.

Merdeka came to a sober Malaya on 31st August 1957. Little of the wild excitement that witnessed India's independence in 1948 was evident, for too much had happened in Asia since then for that to be possible. In particular, a decade of democracy had shown a clear decline in competency and value, and Malaya, divided racially and educationally, was inexperienced in many ways. Nevertheless, a particularly powerful tide of Malay nationalism was running strongly. *Merdeka* was a proud moment for an historic land, in which much of the past which had shaped the present was remembered with affection. No malice accompanied the phased British withdrawal; little time was lost in lamenting past omissions or mistakes. As an independent country of six million people, a democratic member of the Commonwealth by choice, Islamic by faith, and tolerant by nature, Malaya looked not back but to the future.

[6] After 12 years, the Emergency ended on the 21st July 1960. In the fighting 113,509 communists were killed or had surrendered; 4,425 members of the Security Forces and 4,668 civilians were killed or wounded.

15. MALAYSIA

The early years of independence in Malaya were characterized by a steady economic development, exceptional among the countries of South-East Asia. Quietly but steadily the standard of living was improved. While the political movement towards Malaysia came increasingly to the fore in the later stages of this period (1957–1963), it is the economic life of the country then, that first warrants our attention.

It was most fortunate that Malaya entered upon its independence with little bitterness and even less bloodshed. Had its path to freedom from colonialism been marked by the savagery experienced in Indonesia or Indo-China, its efforts to develop would have been most difficult. As it was there was no violent wrenching away, but a civilized parting which permitted the transfer of power to be effected in a co-operative manner that reflected credit on both sides, and which enabled much that was good to be retained.

Although power passed clearly and fully to the Malayan people, this power was not exercised in a negative anticolonial way, but rather in a positive pro-Malayan way; so the stability of the country was maintained and its basic assets were unimpaired. Among the tangible assets were numerous sources of income, such as rubber estates and tin mines that continued to produce, 7,000 miles of roads competently maintained, and a 1,000 miles of railway. The State was a "going concern". Another asset was its multi-racial citizenry, viewed by some, because of its diversity, as a major element of weakness, but which gave strength just because of its varied contributions, all necessary and complimentary, both to the structure of the state and to the working of its economy.

Perhaps its major asset was intangible, in that it began its independent life with a feeling of confidence, due to the precious inheritance of law and order, stability and an efficient administration. It was this above all which provided the country with the environment so necessary for a purposive and continuous economic development. Even before *merdeka,* Malaya had embarked upon its first Five Year Plan with a public investment of $1,150 million, and in 1961 it launched its second Plan. This had the ambitious target of increasing the national product by 4% per year. To assist this growth a proposed public investment of $5,050 million was budgetted, much of it to be spent in rural development.

The spearhead of the drive for rural development in Malaya was (and is) a government body which was created shortly before *merdeka:* the Malayan Federal Land Development Authority. It faced a critical position of under-development in the rural areas. The long period of rubber restriction pre-war, the 1941–1945 war, and the Emergency which followed, had almost eliminated agricultural growth. There was a fierce desire to expand, and with the Emergency, if not over, at least very much under control, the Land Development Authority launched a large, imaginative and well-planned drive to develop production on the land as the basis of the country's wealth.[1]

There were many factors favourable to this. Vast areas of crown land were available near to existing road systems; there was a universal wish for individual land-ownership; and there were proven crops of high value, well known to prospective farmers.

These assets, together with other factors favouring it, enabled the Authority by mid-1962 to have organized and executed thirty-five detailed development schemes all over Malaya, involving the agricultural settlement of 4,500 families on 120,000 acres of land cleared of jungle and planted; each area with new roads, houses, schools, hospitals and shops built nearby. This outstanding land development continues.

One of the major reasons for the effectiveness of Malaya's agricultural expansion had been Tun Abdul Razak, the dynamic leader at the head of the government department formed for this purpose after Independence: the Ministry of Rural Develop-

[1] This is well described by D.E.M. Fiennes, *The Malayan Federal Land Development Authority* (*Journal of Local Administration Overseas.* vol. 1, no. 3, July 1962, pp. 156–163).

ment, which itself is an indication of how democracy can bring development into previously neglected areas. He introduced a new idea into central planning for agriculture: instead of planning what he thought they wanted, as bureaucrats elsewhere were doing, he asked the people themselves what they wanted. The answers were simple but sensible requests from the poor peasants, increasing in complexity with the sophistication of the person involved. All the answers were tabulated and co-ordinated, and at the monthly meetings of the Ministry Tun Razak brought to this programme (which included the Land Development Authority's work), the technique of the Emergency. The problems were urgent; decisions and action were demanded and responsibilities had then to be accepted; telephones rang, and the Minister likely as not was demanding that "bottlenecks" be removed in some remote district. This approach, which to many officers was an ordeal, caught the imagination of the people. Without doubt, Malaya has had one of the most effective rural development programmes in all of South-East Asia.

Rural development was only one, although a major, activity of the new Malayan government. It set out also to stimulate industrial development. Again it has been successful. By the 1950's, encouraging new industries to establish themselves in the tropics was not easy. Sixty years ago the British were able to secure large sums for investment in Malayan rubber, partly because the savings of the British middle class were considerable and partly because the profits from this new crop were large. Neither of these two factors were relevant by the 1950's. We may never again see large-scale, overseas investment in South-East Asian agriculture; but agricultural development as well as industrialization, based very largely on the savings of Malayans themselves, is still a possibility. Indeed, it is a necessity. The stability of the country, and the standard of living, has attracted many firms, some already located in Singapore. At Petaling Jaya, a new town created out of old jungle near Kuala Lumpur, 6,000 acres were cleared and prepared for industry and were fully occupied by the end of 1962. Just on $30 million of new capital from Malayans and others was attracted. To make more power available, a large hydro-electricity complex, involving large dams and hydro-turbine works, and costing $150 million, was constructed in the Cameron Highlands, beginning in 1959.

A third major activity was in education. At the same time as Petaling Jaya was filling with new industries, a new University was rising between it and Kuala Lumpur. Education indeed received a priority only inferior to the rural development programmes in the Five Year Plans. Indicative of the intelligent way in which power was secured from the British, and the manner in which local feelings secured paramount consideration in episode after episode in the 1950's, were the ways in which the educational system had been scrutinized at official level by the Malayan political alliance, even prior to independence, and the Razak Report of 1956 had made recommendations towards a national system. The latter had been incorporated in the 1957 Education Ordinance which was amended in 1961.

The Razak Report and subsequent actions were all in favour of a system whereby the four main cultures of the country were maintained for the enrichment of all, while at the same time the national language, Malay, gradually became the main medium of instruction in all schools. It was hoped that in this way the young people of Malaya would not be cut off from the relevant learnings and skills of the outside world and that the country's development would not be retarded by knowing only one language of regional utility; but that at the same time, by the sharing of the national language, much else would be shared, and the plural society of Malaya would come to have common loyalties. Education was seen at last as an essential factor in the creation of a united nation. All were agreed that education was the answer to many of the problems of the country; all vigorously supported the construction of new schools and the emphasis on science and technology; all saw in education the main hope for the future.

These activities of the government were put to the test in the elections of 1959. The country had been administered by the UMNO-MCA Alliance elected in 1955. Faced in Parliament with only one opposition member, the four years of power had been to some demoralizing, and the Alliance had grown weak. Shortly before the elections the Tengku resigned his post as Prime Minister and became a full time re-organizer of UMNO. In this he was very successful. In a well conducted election, the Alliance was returned to power (although with an increased opposition). The moderate attitude of the Malay UMNO voters (who constituted the majority), found full accord with a strong element among the Chinese, and the Alliance government with Tengku Abdul Rahman Prime Minister again, continued on its purposive way.

There were elections that year in Singapore as well, and as has been stated earlier, they resulted in a victory for the People's Action Party. Led by Mr. Lee Kuan Yew, it turned immediately to the implementation of its two major aims: industrialization, and independence through merging with Malaya.

While Mr. Lee attended personally to the political objective, the economic development of the island was entrusted to his colleague, Dr. Goh Keng Swee, Minister for Finance.

As with the rural development of the peninsula, Singapore moved into its industrialization with a number of assets inherited from its history. By the 1950's Singapore had become a large, wealthy and well-developed city. Although still largely dependent upon trade and commerce (in which it held a pre-eminent position in South-East Asia), nevertheless it possessed nearly two and a half thousand manufacturing firms employing over 50,000 people. Its chief asset undoubtedly lay in its urban population.

Here was an economic asset unrivalled in South-East Asia: a skilled, educated and versatile community, 1.7 million people with the group ideal of hard work. These people had changed in many ways from the early pioneers of Singapore, in fact their social change is the essence of Singapore's history, but they still possessed the dynamism and the will to succeed, the vitality that has been evident since 1819. This is the dominant note of Singapore today. Increasingly through the nineteenth and twentieth centuries, as more and more women migrants joined their men folk, and as migrants elected to live and die in Singapore, rather than return to their former home-lands (two very important social developments), the vitality has been combined with stability.

The government then was able to count on a community that, almost alone among the peoples of South-East Asia, had achieved the psychological and sociological conditions necessary for economic development. There were other factors as well, particularly in the complex business infra-structure of the port. Singapore by this time possessed thirty-four banks, most of them over fifty years old, with a long experience of international trade. There were over eighty insurance companies, together with a highly efficient stock exchange, as well as the world's leading rubber market and other financial institutions.[2]

The port of Singapore itself was another outstanding asset. It had grown to become the fifth largest port in the world. Major capital investments and generations of skilled employees had built up all the services and facilities, not merely those that go with a deep water port, but also those which are necessary for the specialized techniques of entrepôt trade. These had resulted in Singapore becoming the most efficient major economic unit in South-East Asia. Unlike its only rival, Hong Kong, it was, like New York, not cut off from its mainland, and its trade per head of population was the highest in Asia. (In terms of total trade handled annually, Singapore is third in Asia, after Japan and India; it handles nearly twice as much trade as all of Indonesia).

Nevertheless, despite these advantages, Singapore was faced with difficulties. A major new factor in world history over the last 200 years has been the steady growth in population. This has been particularly marked in Asia. Singapore's population has been increasing at an annual rate of 3.9%, nearly double that of Western countries; and because Singapore is a stimulating place, because it is still a wealthy city and there are greater prospects for employment in this developed area than in the peninsula, there is also an annual migration into Singapore of 0.6%. This annual increase moved increasingly into unemployment. Big steps were necessary to halt this. The answer lay in a merger and industrialization.

The major step taken by Goh Keng Swee towards industrialization was the formation of the Economic Development Board and the implementation of the Jurong plan. "Jurong in Malaysia"

[2] For a brief study of this, see K. G. Tregonning, *Singapore In Malaysia* (Singapore, 1963).

will be the most exciting catch-word in South-East Asia in the 1960's, for here, some ten miles outside Singapore city, a new city, equal in size to the old, is being built essentially for industry. Here will be the industrial heart of Malaysia.

The Economic Development Board can be regarded as the launching pad for industrialization, modelled on the statutary bodies that have been effective elsewhere, for example in Israel. The Jurong industrial plan, being ably executed by R. A. Sandford, has been its outstanding contribution. Here a new, deep water harbour, four times the size of Port Swettenham, is being built, together with, over an area of 9,000 acres, new steel mills, ship-building yards, textile factories, a large oil refinery, and numerous other industries, as well as all the facilities and services necessary, such as roads, railways, and housing for the hundreds of thousands of necessary workers. Sandford in creating a new city has had an 800 million gallon reservoir built by damming a river, has had vast quantities of earth moved to fill in swamps and to level hills at an average speed of 50,000 tons a day, and has driven ahead in a dynamic way, backed by a determined government.

From the beginning, the able use by the government of the inherent assets possessed by Singapore made the goal of industrialization seem reasonable and realizable; a merger seemed far more difficult. As an off-shore island that had become the 'New York' to a developing Malaya, providing shipping, banking, commercial, trading and other major services for its natural hinterland, Singapore was playing an ever increasing role in Malayan affairs. For it to be incorporated again directly in the peninsula (it had of course once been part of Johore) would not appear to be against the flow of history. Indeed, to possess a vigorous port of nearly 2 million people would materially benefit Malaya in many ways. But the post-war political motivation of Malaya was primarily a strong Malay movement; and at *merdeka,* and for some time after, the general feeling in Malaya was similar to that felt in the pre-war days, that Singapore was a separate State with separate interests. Many in Singapore shared this feeling. Malaya to them was a foreign land. Prospects for a merger then seemed slight.

Slowly the attitude changed. The absorption of the other two Straits Settlements had been uneventful. It was difficult by 1960 to imagine that Penang and Malacca had ever not been integral parts of a Malaya. The example of these large urban communities, was a useful precedent. Singapore however was still something different. Was the precedent valid?

As the Emergency came to an end, and a few hundred remnants of a vicious army sought refuge in the jungles of South Thailand, the thankful people of Malaya came to regard Singapore as the main communist threat to the democratic and peaceful life of independent progress they were enjoying. In this attitude they found an ally in Mr. Lee Kuan Yew and his government, who, believers in democracy and freedom of choice themselves, and dedicated to their Malayan environment, did little to encourage Chinese chauvinism or communist activities on their island.

Without doubt however there were many in Singapore who had not accepted the regional conditions of life, and who did not believe that parliamentary government or democratic principles were applicable to the affairs of their society. There were significant signs of communism in Chinese language schools and elsewhere, and to the Malayan leaders it seemed possible that democratic forces in Singapore, divided as they were between the PAP and other parties, might not be strong enough to contain them.

Under the 1959 Constitution of Singapore, the island government had full internal powers. However, a Security Council, of three British, three Singapore and one Malayan representative, controlled security. Was this sufficient? By 1961 Tengku Abdul Rahman had come to believe that it was not. Influenced by his desire to keep Malaya safe, as well as by the major historical factors that indicated Singapore as an integral part of Malaya, he decided that a merger was the answer. On 27th May 1961, he made an historic speech suggesting that it be considered as a practical and worthwhile measure. He went further than a mere merger between Malaya and Singapore, however; he called for a political association covering the Borneo territories of North Borneo (Sabah as it was once called previously), Sarawak and

Brunei as well. He thus initiated the movement towards Malaysia, and gave another reason why he can be considered one of the really outstanding leaders of South-East Asia.

The Borneo territories during the twentieth century had led a life separate from, but strangely similar to, the history of say Kelantan or Kedah; one of the more active of the Unfederated Malay States. Both Sarawak and North Borneo (and Brunei) had become British Protectorates in 1888 and from that time on (although no tin was ever discovered and so no development comparable to Perak or Selangor occurred), there was a close parallel between the development of Borneo and that of the Malay States.

The first similarity to be noted was in administration. Although in Sarawak the personal rule of Rajah Brooke, in North Borneo rule by a Chartered Company, and in Brunei rule by a British Resident, implied diversity, this diversity was more apparent than real. These three governments in fact administered their territories in very much the same manner as the Advisers were doing in Kedah or Kelantan, where a few Europeans were working with the established indigenous institutions.

The basis of their control, in the Borneo territories as in the Malay States, was an acceptance of their presence at that time, by the bulk of the population. Had there been widespread and sustained opposition they could not have stayed there for any length of time at all. In all of Sabah for example, there were only fifty-odd European officials and about the same number in Sarawak, so they (of necessity and choice) worked with whatever local leaders and local institutions they could find. This was very much the same as in, say, Kelantan and Trengganu.

The core of this government was the administration of British justice. In Sarawak, the Treaty of 1888 gave the British Government no rights of interference in internal matters at all (unlike North Borneo) and the justice of the Brookes' came to cause considerable disquiet. I should imagine it was one of the reasons that influenced Britain in placing Sarawak directly under its control in 1946. Even here however, and in North Borneo, the routine of courts, the treasured procedures and implementation of Codes of Law were much the same as in Malaya.

North Borneo constantly secured as its governors, administrators who came over from Malaya with their Malayan experience, with Malayan laws and directives, and they adapted them to suit Borneo conditions. This continued post-war, and several MCS men, 'Malayanized' due to *merdeka,* continued their service in Borneo. Before them there had been such men as Lord Milverton, W. H. Treacher, W. W. Birch (whose father was killed in Perak in 1874) and many others. So it is no coincidence that Borneo regulations became very similar to Malaya's.

The Borneo territories have also shared a twentieth century social and economic history similar to the Malay Peninsula in many respects. The major social characteristic has been the migration and settlement of Chinese, a steady trickle moving into both States. Those migrating to North Borneo came mainly from Hong Kong, while Sarawak received many of its Chinese from Singapore. Sibu in Sarawak, and Jesselton and Sandakan in Sabah, grew during the twentieth century as urban centres of Chinese, in a manner very similar to Kuantan, Kota Bharu, or Johore Bahru. With them they brought their schools, as elsewhere in Malaysia.

The history of Malaya's major agricultural crop, rubber, is echoed in Borneo. All that happened in the Malay States—boom, depression, restriction, estates and smallholders, export tax and international control—happened too in the Borneo States. But the economy differed to some extent. Timber grew to become a major export, while pepper, a crop of some antiquity, maintained a hold in Sarawak it never secured elsewhere. Copra, padi, buffalo grazing and sago cultivation were aspects of its economy it shared to only some extent with Malaya, while the large oil deposits of Brunei had no counterpart whatever. Unlike tin in Malaya, those oil deposits played no appreciable part in developing more than a minute section of the region however, as the revenue was never spent.

Educationally too the Borneo States had a pattern similar to west Malaysia. Although it was much less sophisticated and far more primitive (indeed educational inactivity is one of the most criticized aspects of the pre-war régime in these territories), nevertheless the English mission schools had laboured diligently amongst the pagan, indigenous peoples—the Dusuns or Kadazans in North Borneo, the Ibans and Land Dayaks in Sarawak—and had spread the use of English thinly throughout the area; and the government schools had reinforced this. The Chinese schools added to the literate community, while Malay-language schools also existed.

As a result of this shared history, although east Malaysia presented differences to west Malaysia—many aspects of its traditional culture were quite unique and very much at variance with the customs and culture of the different peoples on the peninsula—at the same time there were many similarities. The pattern of life was very much the same. The rubber tapper, the fisherman, the padi planter, these were recognizable types, with similar problems and prospects, on both sides of the South China Sea. The institutions were much the same too. The district office, the government school, the coffee shop, the court house, all these were shared, derived from a common experience inside the same regional environment.

East and west Malaysia shared also the Japanese Occupation, but while the rest of Malaysia endured it, to North Borneo goes the credit for alone trying to end it. In Albert Kwok Fen Nam it found a leader in the grim days of 1943. He led a rising near Jesselton which for a few days usurped the Japanese control of the west coast. It was savagely crushed and a brutal retribution was exacted. North Borneo was perhaps the most completely destroyed part of the British Empire in 1945.[3]

When the war ended the two odd and impoverished survivals from the nineteenth century, the British North Borneo Chartered Company and the personal rule of the Brooke dynasty, ended, and the Protectorates became in mid-1946 British colonies. This change in administration presented an opportunity (as had 1888, and as had been suggested during the depression years) of integrating, or federating the territories with Malaya. The opportunity was not realized, and from 1946 until 1961 the pace of development was so different, with west Malaysia surging ahead

[3] K. G. Tregonning, *Under Chartered Company Rule—North Borneo 1881–1946* (U.M.P. 1959).

to *merdeka*, that the idea grew less and less a possibility.

Then in 1961 came the Tengku's speech and immediately it came within the orbit of practical politics. The Borneo States, or east Malaysia, had benefited considerably from their new post-war status. More money was invested in them, and a far more liberal attitude encouraged schools, hospitals and other material benefits. This was most marked in Sabah which had benefited by being almost completely destroyed during the war. At the time, and for years after, this had seemed a terrible blow. Everything had to be rebuilt, everything had to start from the beginning, while Sarawak could continue almost as before. But as it rebuilt, new ideas moved in with the new buildings, and development and growth brought a lively attitude and vigour in marked contrast to Sarawak, where people in pre-war buildings continued with pre-war habits and ideas, unmindful in their backwater of the tremendous tide of nationalism that had swept South-East Asia. Britain itself however had been yielding to this tide, not merely in Asia but in Africa as well, and it was slowly initiating steps to prepare the Borneo territories for self-government too.

The Tengku's suggestion of Malaysia was seized on with alacrity by nearly all concerned, in west and east Malaysia. It was welcomed immediately by the Government of Singapore and in August 1961, less than three months later, broad agreement was reached in principle between the two Prime Ministers for a merger of the territories.

The British Government also welcomed the idea and invited the Tengku to London to discuss it. He flew there in November 1961 when it was agreed to appoint a British-Malayan commission to ascertain the views of the Borneo people. Politically in 1961 these States were in a position similar to Malaya pre-1955. There were unofficial members of the legislatures but they were nominated, selected by the Governor after consultation with the communities concerned, and therefore there were no elected representatives who could claim they spoke for the country. At the local government level perhaps North Borneo was more developed than Sarawak, but neither had advanced very far. Economic growth had out-distanced political evolution, as it had in Malaya.

The Commission was headed by Lord Cobbold. It toured east

Malaysia for two months (19th February to 18th April, 1962), receiving over 2,000 letters and memoranda and holding over 50 public hearings at which nearly 700 groups made representations. In Sarawak all the newly formed political parties were interviewed. These included the Sarawak United People's Party, which from its inception in 1959 had been a left wing party of Chinese; the Party Negara, a more conservative party of Malays and Ibans; the Sarawak National Party; and the Barisan Ra'ayat Jati Sarawak, a small mixed party. All these, apart from the SUPP, which was becoming strongly communist in its membership, were in favour of Malaysia, but with reservations. Six of these pro-Malaysia parties formed an Alliance to contest the 1963 elections, whereby considerable power was given to Sarawak, and this Alliance secured a majority. Its leader was Stephen Kalong Ningkan.

In North Borneo Donald Stephens, the leader of the Kadazans, or Dusuns, the largest ethnic group, spoke for almost the entire State when he supported Malaysia. However the various parties, while agreeing in principle to the idea of independence through Malaysia, felt that safeguards were necessary if Borneo was not to be subjected to other forms of imperialism. This view received endorsement in the December 1962 elections which made Stephens the Chief Minister.

The Cobbold Report was published on 1st August 1962. It affirmed that 70% of the 1.3 million people of the Borneo territories were in favour of Malaysia. However it also reported on the reservations held by Borneo, in particular on the language and immigration issues, and on the Head of State. With all the goodwill in the world, the Borneo territories were not prepared to become merely part of a greater Malaya. They did not want Malay as their language as English was well established as the link between them (and they had historic fears of Brunei Malay domination), nor did they want immigration to pass out of their control. They feared a flood of Chinese. As a result, it was recommended that education and immigration remain with the States. The proud Borneo territories also wanted, when independent, for their heads of state to be eligible to be elected as Head of the new Federation. As this was basically a Muslim religious ceremony, the Commission could not see how a non-Muslim could participate; and merely recorded the feeling.

The British and Malayan Governments accepted the report. At the same time they agreed to the formation of a joint committee, to devise the constitutional arrangements necessary to ensure the safeguards requested by the Borneo States. This, the Lord Landsdowne Committee, reported in early 1963 and its recommendations were embodied in subsequent legislation introduced in London and Kuala Lumpur to give constitutional effect to the Malaysia agreement.

These constitutional arrangements reflected a weakness, an internal sore, which may prejudice the working of the new Malaysia. The economic disparity too, with west Malaysia developing agriculture and moving ahead into industrialization, while east Malaysia is far less advanced, may also produce tensions similar to those that affected the northern and southern States of the USA in the 1860's. Fortunately the recommendations of a World Bank Mission in 1963 (The Rueff Report) that a common market be created, has produced a viable economic unit; yet the contrast between east and west Malaysia may still encourage separatism. The disparity in education too, with universities, technical colleges, agricultural colleges and other research centres all based in west Malaysia, and only the beginnings of secondary education appearing in east Malaysia, is another possible unbalance that could cause internal friction.

These internal problems, while possibly more long lasting and deep rooted, received scant attention in the final year preceding Malaysia. The external problems occupied all minds. These were Brunei, the Philippines, Indonesia.

Brunei had stayed on the fringe of the Malaysia movement. After the Tengku's initial suggestion, Donald Stephens had formed, in June 1961, the Malaysia Solidarity Consultative Committee with representatives from the parliaments of Malaya, Singapore, North Borneo and Sarawak. This had four useful meetings, but Brunei sent only observers. Similarly the Cobbold Commission paid only a courtesy call at Brunei, and did not include it in its considerations, for although the Sultan of Brunei and the British Government would have welcomed the opportunity for it to join, yet the one political party in the State, Party Ra'ayat, holding all the elected seats in the Brunei Legislature (one less than the official, nominated posts), was completely opposed to it. In the face of this opposition, led by Ahmad Azahari, the Sultan had to restrain his own feelings of support.

On 7th December 1962, on the anniversary of Pearl Harbour, the followers of Azahari rose in armed revolt. Azahari himself was in Manila, and later moved to Djakarta. The revolt, aimed only partly at Malaysia, partly at the imperfections in the internal structure of the state, was suppressed, and gradually Brunei's problems of great wealth and poor people with different tribal backgrounds became again something to occupy the minds of only a few; perhaps too few. The Sultan, still regarded as the ruler of his people, stayed clear of Malaysia.

The Philippine problem was caused by the official acceptance in Manila of representations which held that it had a legitimate claim to North Borneo. This claim, based on the agreements signed by the Sultan of Sulu in 1878 which permitted British occupation of the east coast of North Borneo, was initially ignored by the British, but subsequently in 1963 was refuted in talks in London. Manila also expressed opposition to Malaysia as permitting a possible infiltration of communists to territories close to its own shores. As it had not voiced these fears until near to the withdrawal of the British, it indicated a pro-colonial attitude surprising to many.

In its opposition to Malaysia, it turned to Indonesia. Here the vehemence of Sukarno, its chief of state, had led to the disruption of its relations with Malaya in early 1963. The Tengku conferred with Sukarno in Tokyo, and then in August in Manila conferred with both Sukarno and Macapagal, the Philippine President. At the latter conference agreement was reached to seek the view of an impartial arbitrator, such as the United Nations Organization, as to whether the Borneo people were in favour of Malaysia or not. In addition, the three statesmen pro-

---

[4] Previously, Malayan initiative had led to the formation in 1961 of ASA (Association of South-East Asia), to produce greater economic and cultural co-operation between Malaya, the Philippines and Thailand. Thailand was not consulted over the formation of Maphilindo.

posed a loosely knit regional body, Maphilindo.[4]

Indonesian opposition to Malaysia was only partially assuaged by the Manila Agreement. The Brunei revolt had been supported by it, and there was clear evidence to show that armed disturbances in Sarawak, which followed the revolt, were encouraged by it. Armed raids into Sarawak from Indonesian Borneo (Kalimantan) by men in Indonesian army uniform became commonplace throughout 1963.

These raids, and the external opposition generally, took the place of the opposition by imperialists in other colonial movements towards independence, in that they acted as a national unifying force. Indonesian opposition should assist considerably in the development of Malaysia, particularly in the creation of a national spirit.

A United Nations team, accompanied by Philippine, Indonesian and Malayan observers, toured the Borneo territories in late August 1963. In effect its task was to check that the elections of December 1962 (in North Borneo) and June 1963 (in Sarawak) which had produced pro-Malaysia majorities, were valid elections.

The formation of Malaysia was postponed from 31st August until 16th September in order that the UN team could undertake its work. There were signs however that the Indonesian attitude to this new State would not be altered by any UN decision. Sukarno, the Indonesian army, and the Indonesian Communist Party, the three most powerful bodies, were united in opposition.

This, far more than any other single international incident since *merdeka* in 1957, focussed the attentions of Malayans on external events. Although Malaya had played an interesting role at the UN, the prospects of internal development inside Malaya had been the pre-occupation of most, and the country by and large had an attitude of non-alignment, almost of indifference, to most of the events that occurred outside it. The Emergency had given it a distaste for communism, but foreign affairs had been, for over a century, the concern of foreigners; the international relations of Malaya had not involved Malayans. Now with Indonesian 'confrontation', as its policy was called, there was a rapidly growing appreciation of foreign policy, and a realization that a small country was not entire unto itself.

The UN team reported in favour of Malaysia, and with most towns bedecked with bunting, flags, triumphant banners and arches, and with celebrations, but also with a few misgivings and doubts (and with Indonesian hostility sustained), Malaysia duly came into being on 16th September 1963. With scarcely a backward glance at the British, who in many ways had prepared them well for it, Malaysian leaders, after the celebrations, turned to face the problems and the prospects of independence.

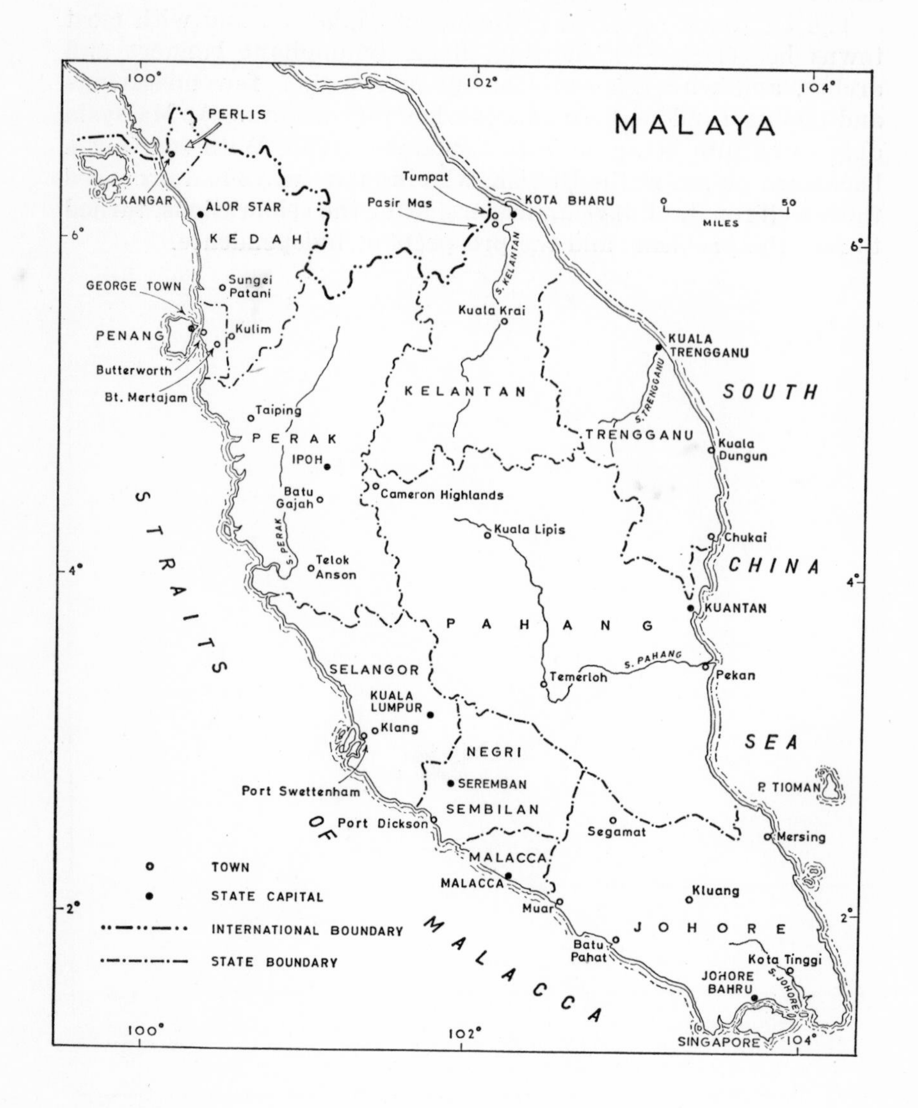
MALAYA
100°
102°
104°
6°
4°
2°
0
50
MILES
PERLIS
KANGAR
ALOR STAR
KEDAH
GEORGE TOWN
Sungei Patani
PENANG
Kulim
Butterworth
Bt. Mertajam
Tumpat
Pasir Mas
KOTA BHARU
S. KELANTAN
Kuala Krai
KELANTAN
KUALA TRENGGANU
S. TRENGGANU
TRENGGANU
Kuala Dungun
SOUTH
CHINA
SEA
Taiping
PERAK
IPOH
Batu Gajah
Cameron Highlands
S. PERAK
Telok Anson
Kuala Lipis
Chukai
KUANTAN
PAHANG
S. PAHANG
Temerloh
Pekan
STRAITS
OF
MALACCA
SELANGOR
KUALA LUMPUR
Klang
Port Swettenham
NEGRI
SEREMBAN
SEMBILAN
Port Dickson
Segamat
P. TIOMAN
Mersing
MALACCA
Muar
Kluang
JOHORE
Batu Pahat
Kota Tinggi
S. JOHORE
JOHORE BAHRU
SINGAPORE
TOWN
STATE CAPITAL
INTERNATIONAL BOUNDARY
STATE BOUNDARY

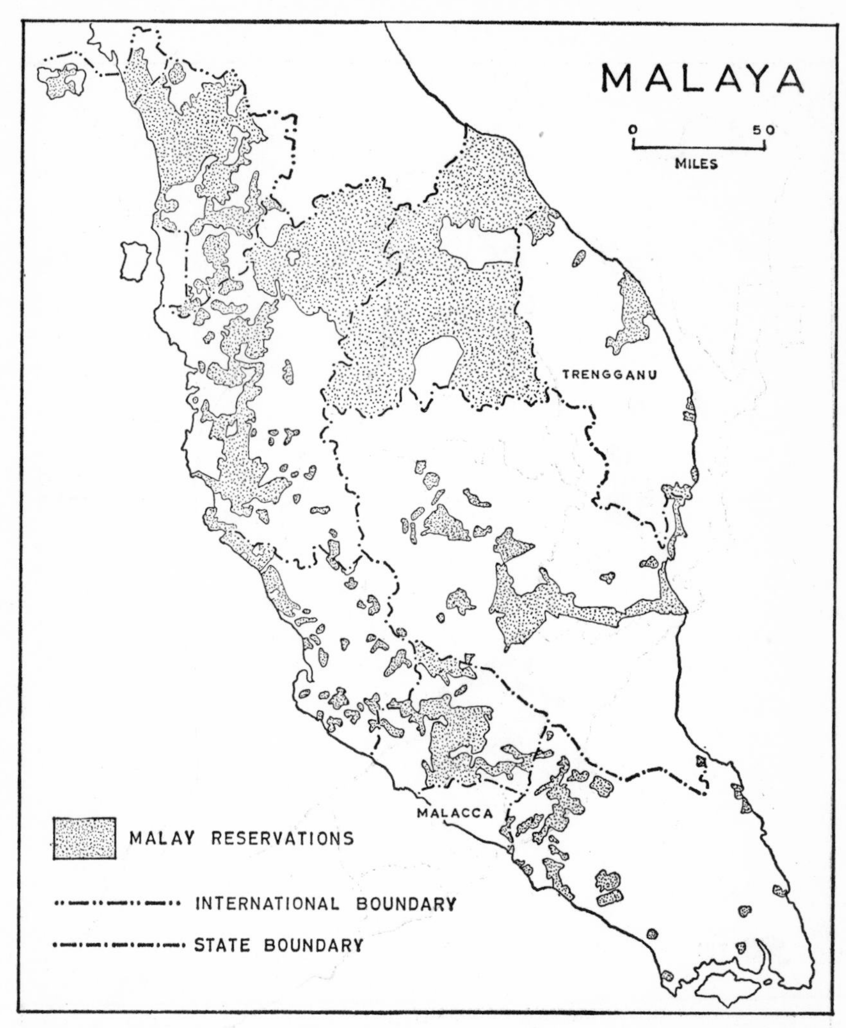

Note: In Trengganu no Malay Reservations have been declared, but Malays have special privileges under the Trengganu Malay Reservations Enactment No. 17 of 1360 A.H. which affected principally the areas indicated.

Note: In Malacca there are no Malay Reservations, but persons of Malacca domicile have special privileges under the customary lands ordinance.

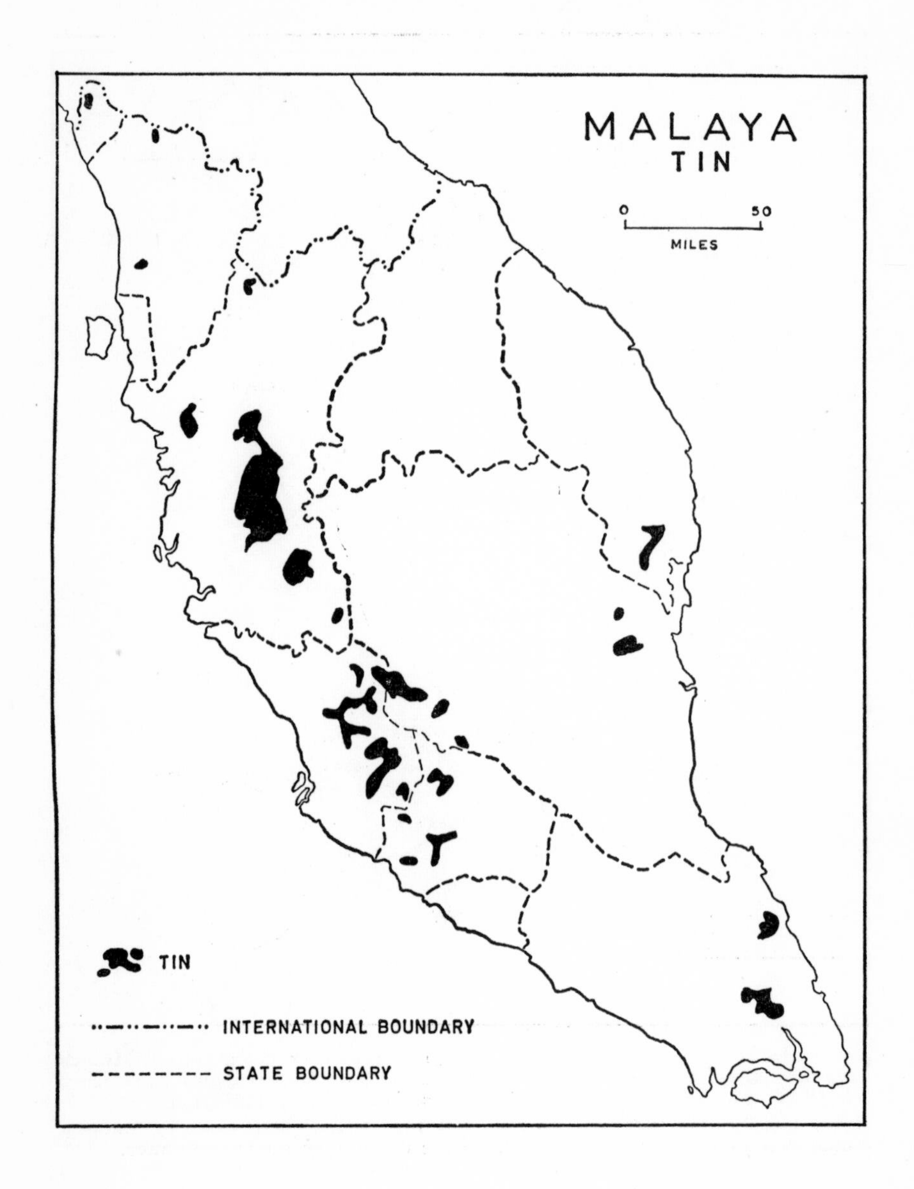
MALAYA
TIN
0
50
MILES
TIN
INTERNATIONAL BOUNDARY
STATE BOUNDARY

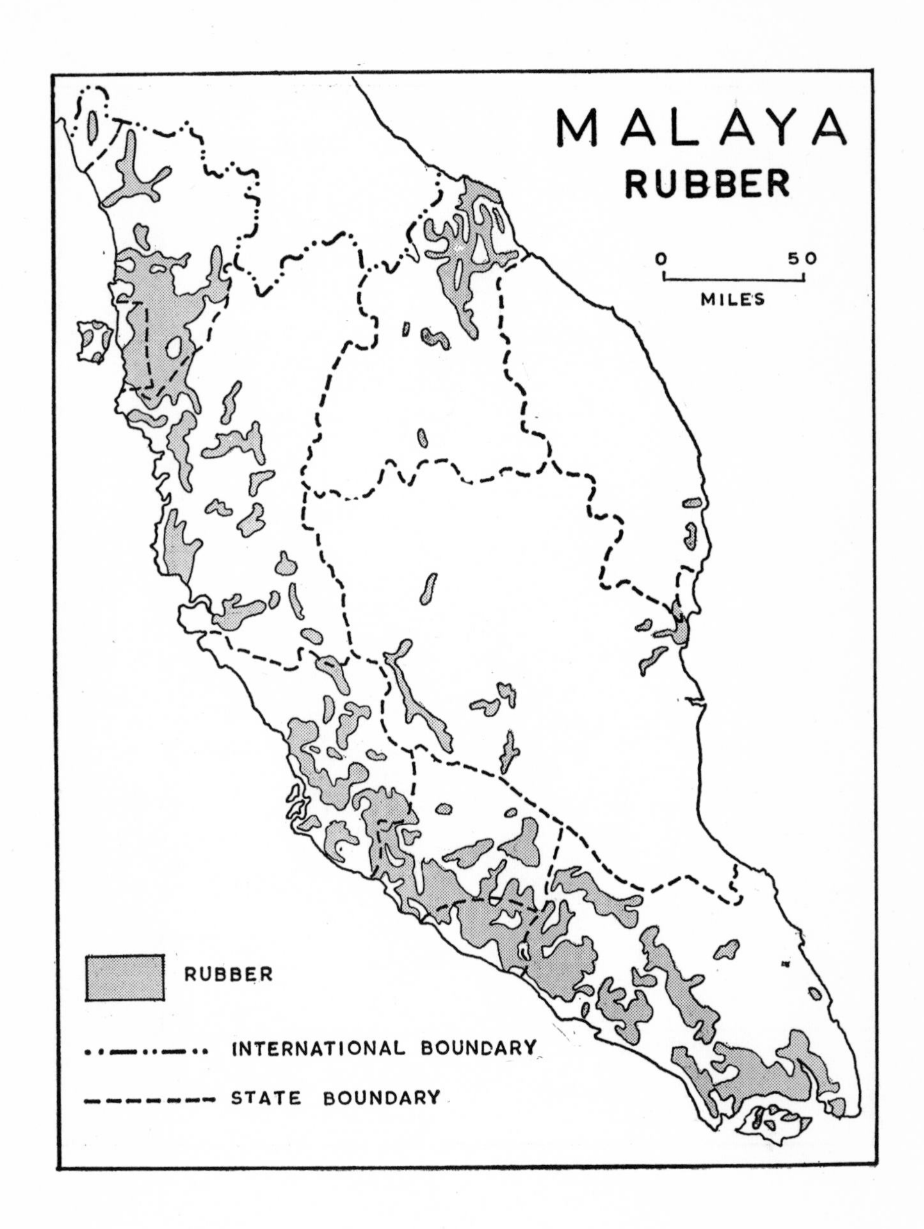
MALAYA
RUBBER
0
50
MILES
RUBBER
INTERNATIONAL BOUNDARY
STATE BOUNDARY

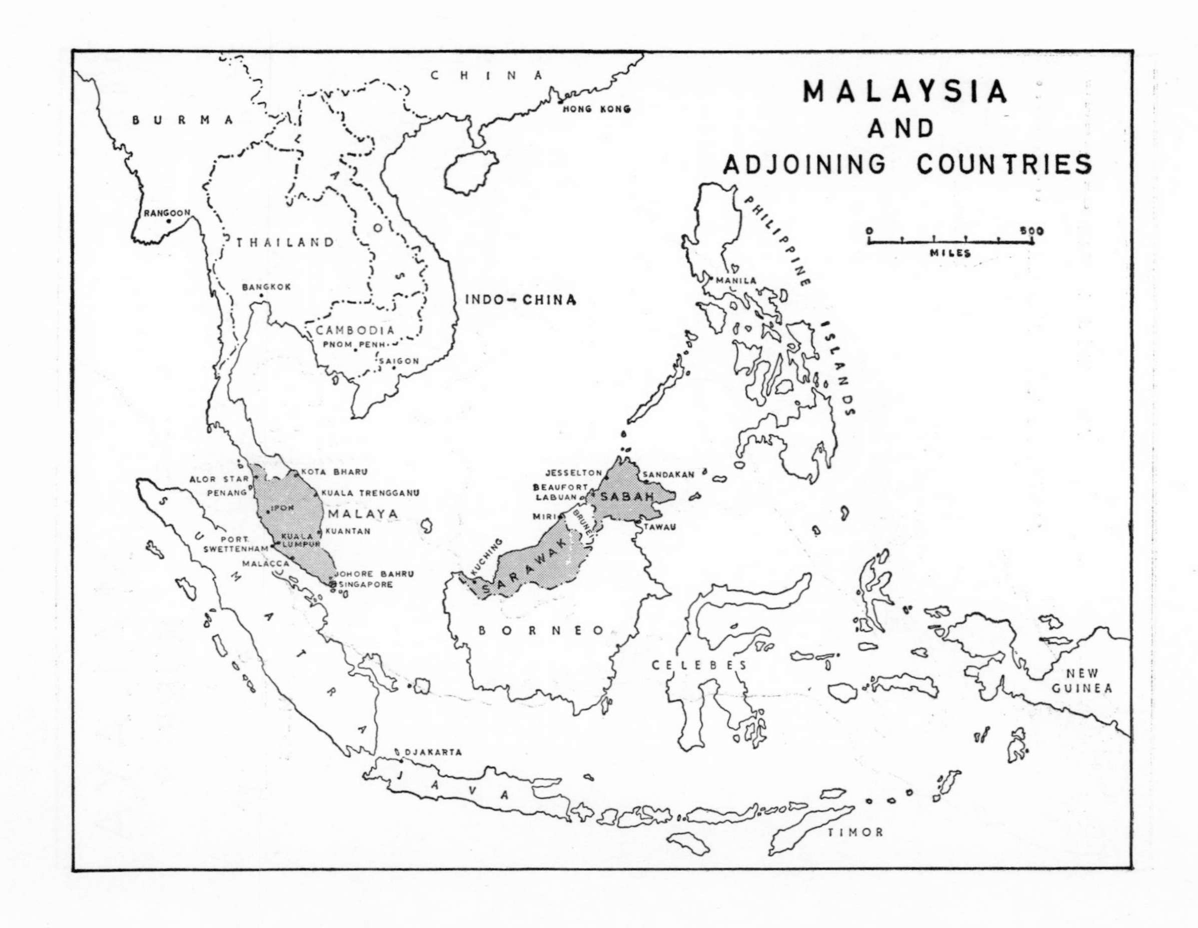
MALAYSIA
AND
ADJOINING COUNTRIES
0
500
MILES
BURMA
RANGOON
CHINA
HONG KONG
THAILAND
BANGKOK
LAOS
CAMBODIA
PNOM PENH
SAIGON
INDO-CHINA
PHILIPPINE ISLANDS
MANILA
ALOR STAR
PENANG
KOTA BHARU
KUALA TRENGGANU
IPOH
MALAYA
KUANTAN
KUALA LUMPUR
PORT SWETTENHAM
MALACCA
JOHORE BAHRU
SINGAPORE
SUMATRA
JESSELTON
SANDAKAN
BEAUFORT
LABUAN
SABAH
MIRI
BRUNEI
TAWAU
KUCHING
SARAWAK
BORNEO
CELEBES
NEW GUINEA
DJAKARTA
JAVA
TIMOR

SELECT BIBLIOGRAPHY

A great number of books have been written on Malaya's long history. No attempt to list them here has been made, for a comprehensive bibliography of Malaya would require another book. I have compiled merely a select list of books and articles which for the most part are readily available, possess excellent bibliographies themselves and which are useful for further reading.

This list of twenty or so books, together with the references made throughout this History to the various authorities consulted, may be of some use to individuals and institutions wishing either to build up a basic Malaysian collection, or merely to seek information on a doubtful point.

Two Malayan *bibliographies* that are available are:

H. R. Cheeseman — *Bibliography of Malaya,* (London, 1959).

Beda Lim — *Malaya. A Background Bibliography.* (JMBRAS, vol. 35, 1962).

Two basic *Journals* for all interested in Malaysia are:

Journal, Malayan Branch, Royal Asiatic Society

Journal, South-East Asian History

G. C. Allen & A. G. Donnithorne — *Western Enterprise in Indonesia and Malaya* (London, 1957).

J. H. Brimmell — *Communism In South-East Asia* (London, 1959).

H. P. Clodd — *Malaya's First British Pioneer* (London, 1948).

C. D. Cowan — *Nineteenth Century Malaya: The Origins of British Political Control* (London, 1961).

R. Emerson — *Malaysia* (New York, 1937).

J. M. Gullick — *Indigenous Political Systems of Western Malaya* (London, 1958).

Norton Ginsburg & C. F. Roberts	*Malaya* (Seattle, 1958).
D. G. E. Hall	*A History of South-East Asia* (London, 1964).
G. Irwin	*Nineteenth Century Borneo* (The Hague, 1955).
H. J. Marks	*The First Contest For Singapore 1819–1824* ('Gravenhage, 1959).
L. A. Mills	*British Malaya, 1824–1867* (JMBRAS, vol. 33, pt. 3, 1960).
	British Rule In Eastern Asia (London, 1942).
	Malaya: A Political And Economic Appraisal (London, 1958).
J. Norman Parmer	*Colonial Labor Policy and Administration* (New York, 1960).
C. N. Parkinson	*British Intervention In Malaya, 1867–1877* (Singapore, 1960).
V. Purcell	*The Chinese In Malaya* (London, 1948).
	The Chinese In South-East Asia (London, 1951).
Lucian W. Pye	*Guerrilla Communism In Malaya* (Princeton, 1956).
S. Runciman	*The White Rajahs* (Cambridge, 1960).
F. Swettenham	*British Malaya* (London, 1955).
K. G. Tregonning	*Under Chartered Company Rule: North Borneo 1881–1946* (London, 1959).
P. Wheatley	*The Golden Khersonese* (Kuala Lumpur, 1961).
R. Winstedt	*The Malays. A Cultural History* (London, 1953).
	A History of Malaya (Singapore, 1962).
C. E. Wurtzburg	*Raffles Of The Eastern Isles* (London, 1954).

INDEX

The numbers in italics refer to references in footnotes.

DATE DUE